# MOTHER'S DAY IS OVER

# MOTHER'S DAY IS OVER

## REVISED EDITION

*by Shirley Rogers Radl*

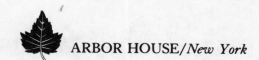 ARBOR HOUSE/*New York*

Copyright © 1987 by Shirley Rogers Radl and Steve Davis Publishing
All rights reserved, including the right of reproduction in whole or in part in any
form. Published in the United States of America by Arbor House Publishing
Company and in Canada by Fitzhenry & Whiteside Ltd.

Manufactured in the United States of America

10  9  8  7  6  5  4  3  2  1

Library of Congress Cataloging in Publication Data

Radl, Shirley L.
    Mother's Day is over.

    Bibliography: p.
    1. Mothers.   2. Parent and child.   3. Child rearing.
I. Title.
HQ759.R25   1987      306.8'743      86-20570
ISBN:0-87795-864-5

*To Lisa and Adam,*
*for teaching me the meaning of*
*truth, beauty, and love.*

# Contents

# *Preface*

I decided to write about my feelings on motherhood when I had been a mother for six years. For several months, I had brooded over what seemed to be a real contradiction: How was it possible for me to genuinely love my children, Lisa and Adam, and yet to dislike nearly everything associated with the role of motherhood? At first, I was reluctant to publish my views, fearing that my words, born out of concern for my children's, my husband's, and my own future, might be attributed to supposedly negative feelings about my children. But, at the time, the pressures put on young women to have children were so overwhelming and without balance that I decided to "go public."

The mass media was portraying an image of motherhood that I, as a mother myself, saw as so unreal that it was laughable. Indeed, I did sometimes laugh when I contrasted Madison Avenue's and Hollywood's views with the scene that was being played out daily in my own home. What wasn't funny to me was that millions of young women (and men) were presumably buying these images right along with the sponsors' products. In the interest of fairness, honesty, and the welfare of future generations of children and their mothers, I felt it was time to set the record straight. Thus, in 1973, I attempted to do just that in the first edition of *Mother's Day Is Over*.

As I had expected, my explosion of the myths of motherhood was not met with universal approval. After all, I had taken on America's sacred cow. I did not then, however, nor will I ever, attack mothers themselves or children—just the role. But I received threats, religious tracts, crank telephone calls, and a few negative book reviews. I had, in the eyes of some, committed the unspeakable sin of telling the truth.

A Catholic mother of eight took me to task in one review, and a mother of five stormed out of a meeting during a speech I was making. Because they themselves were up to their ears in the responsibility of child rearing, I can only imagine that they could not tolerate the idea of other women hearing the facts of life after birth and perhaps choosing not to have children.

But not all of my critics were from that camp. As I have long believed in Margaret Sanger's view that no woman shall be free until she can choose whether or not to become a mother, I did not expect to be criticized by liberationists. But I was. One young feminist reviewer whacked me up the side of my head for using the word "guilt" too frequently. (However, in confirmation of my feeling that guilt and motherhood are inseparable, McCall's *Working Mother* magazine now features a monthly "Guilt" department.) A *Ms.* contributing editor complained that I did not devote enough space to the plight of poor women, though I stated up front that I was not studying that particular group of mothers. She further construed my pointing out that most mothers wound up being primarily responsible for the care of the home and children as advocacy for that unfair arrangement. She was less than supportive of my effort to provide young women with the opportunity to make an informed decision based on reality.

But the collective negative reaction represented less than five percent of those who responded either with a review, comment, letter, or phone call. Although I had aimed the book at young women who had not as yet made the fateful decision to become mothers, I wound up striking a responsive chord in mothers from all over the United States and Canada, Europe, and Australia.

Whatever differences there were among all the mothers who wrote, one message was repeated in nearly all of their letters: "Thank you for saying what I've wanted to say for years, but didn't dare. Thank you for letting me know I'm not alone."

One reviewer called the book "a love story," and one famous pediatrician wrote to tell me that I had performed a valuable service.

When most of the women I talked to asked me not to use even their first names, it became obvious that they shared my feelings that to speak of any negatives in the role of motherhood would cause them to be viewed as evil. We live in a nation where there are over a million cases of child abuse every year and where hundreds of thousands of teenagers, the majority of whom are from "nice" middle-class families, disappear each year, many of whose parents don't even file missing persons reports. Yet we are supposed to believe that everyone thinks being a parent is always wonderful.

Loving mothers dare not speak of how tired they get or of the natural resentments they sometimes feel. They are bound up in a conspiracy of silence that I believe causes some people to have children without any understanding of the responsibility involved.

For a short while in the late seventies, it became almost socially acceptable not to have children. I would like to think that my book, in some small way, had something to do with that trend. But once again, in the late eighties, the drum is being beaten and vast numbers of women are choosing motherhood because they believe the hype about it being fulfilling, and women who might be given to thinking about it once or twice are being pressured not to think at all. The media pressures, the cultural and religious pressures, and new parents who appear to be in the throes of euphoria, represent a combined force that delivers the message that parenthood is "in" and choice is definitely out of vogue. In fact, people who do choose not to become parents are frequently judged selfish and superficial. Well, we are *all* selfish no matter which path we choose. Those of us who choose to become parents expect to derive some personal benefit from having children; we do not do it for altruistic reasons.

As for being superficial, no doubt some who decide not to have children are indeed superficial. But many are far less superficial than people who have children without making a long-term commitment. I know scores of men and women who have chosen not to become parents because they are *thinking* people and truly know, without having experienced it personally, how profoundly the responsibility of parenthood affects one's life. Some are honest enough to say that they aren't cut out for the role and choose to do no harm by being non-parents rather than risk being inadequate parents.

Suggestions that the decision whether or not to have children is no one else's business often fall on deaf ears. As do suggestions that combining a career and motherhood is difficult or that few people can afford to stay home and take care of their own children.

I believe my message is one that bears repeating in the late 1980s. And, judging from my mail, it is one that deserves to be a bit stronger. My mail in fact has provided much of the new material in this revised edition of *Mother's Day Is Over*. Also, in the first edition, I was speaking from experience as a mother of six years. Little did I know that the most traumatic years of parenthood were yet to come. I have added two new chapters—"In the Best of Families" and "The Never-ending Story"—to deal with the teenage years and beyond. I have updated all of the other chapters to reflect changes that have occurred since 1973. And I have entirely rewritten the chapter "Doctor, Lawyer, Indian Chief . . . or Mother" to reflect the present reality for working mothers.

Just after I decided to revise *Mother's Day Is Over*, I received a letter from a thirty-one-year-old mother that I hope will be heeded by women who have as yet to make the binding decision to become mothers:

I bought your book when I was pregnant with my first child in 1976. I had always expected we would have children.

The emphasis should be on the word "expected," because I never actually felt convinced that I *wanted* children. The book's effect on me was that I thought you were being awfully severe, that you seemed to be making the situation a lot worse than it actually was. As I'm sure you know very well, it is quite difficult, if not impossible, to convince most people of the kinds of ideas you discuss. I guess it's typical of human nature to *not* take the advice. People tend to be skeptical of the person who says, "I've already been through this and I've learned such and such so take my advice before you make the same mistakes I've made." The novice comes back with, "Oh, yeah? Well move over and let me give it a try because I'm sure not going to make your mistakes. It won't be the same for me." These were exactly my thoughts. . . .

I had three children in four and a half years. I have gone from being an idealistic, patient, caring, healthy woman to a harried, frustrated, depressed, bitter, sick woman. I can say something to you that I cannot say to anyone I know because it would hurt too much. I love my children because they are part of me, but I do not like them. I do not like them because they have turned my life into a living hell; because I am faced with a lifetime of inescapable, overwhelming responsibilities against a whole world of frightening obstacles. The prospect of this business of child rearing scares me to death and I see no way to do it right or even well.

What it all comes down to is this: I would give just about anything to go back. I would never have had these children. There are simply *not* enough positive aspects to the specter of parenting, there are *no* rewards, *nothing* that could possibly balance the staggering responsibilities and worries.

I was very much influenced by television and all the audio and visual stimulation. But I see now that the influences are so subtle we don't even realize what is happening. It's a rare and enviable soul who does what he believes is right for him instead of what he "ought to do."

But, here we have come full circle, have we not? Now *I'm* the seasoned expert trying to dole out the best-intentioned advice to the unsuspecting, overconfident novice, who gasps a little at what I say and thinks to herself, "It won't be that way with me."

Some readers have said that I don't offer enough of the joyful images of parenthood to lend balance to my thesis that it is not a piece of cake. To those critics I have just this to say: Switch on the television set, leaf through the pages of most any woman's magazine, or even read the family newspaper. The particular "balance" that you are looking for is there, quite overrepresented. The plain truth I aim to present here is that, despite the joys, parenthood is tough. So tough that a surprising number of people regret having made the decision to become parents. In 1976 Ann Landers conducted a survey in an effort to find out how many of her readers might feel that way. Of the readers who responded, an astonishing seventy percent said they regretted it so much that if they had it to do over again, they wouldn't have children.

A few years later a thirty-year-old woman who was agonizing over whether she should become a mother wrote to Ann Landers that she remembered being shaken by that statistic. She felt that the children must suffer, knowing that they were not wanted. She herself had a full-time job and was worried that she would not have the patience to care for a screaming baby. What should she do?

The wise columnist answered that she would not presume to make such a decision for anyone, and that it was strictly a do-it-yourself project. "No matter what you decide," she wrote, "you're bound to have moments of regret, as well as moments of unbelievable joy. But once you decide, don't look back. Stick with it and let there never be a doubt whether it was the right thing to do."

The very best way I can think of to prepare oneself to "stick with it and let there never be a doubt whether it was the right thing to do" is to recognize, preferably in advance, that motherhood is a very difficult job. Had I had a realistic view before I be-

came a mother, I am convinced that I would have been better able
to roll with the punches in the early years. As it turned out, I recognized that difficulty was built into the role before it was too late.
I wrote in a later book (*New Mother's Survival Guide*) that facing
the truth about motherhood when Lisa and Adam were six and
five years old, respectively, was a real turning point in my life.
This is what I said: "Had I continued denying the fact that I absolutely didn't relish the motherhood role, as the motherhood mystique would have you believe every normal mother does every
moment, I surely would have missed any pleasure at all in being
Lisa's and Adam's mother. The day I faced the fact that there
really are terrible sides to parenthood was a new beginning for
me—the beginning of self-acceptance, growth, and the rebuilding
of my rapidly vanishing self-esteem. It was also a beginning for
reaching out and grabbing those joyous times and cherishing them
before they got away or got buried, and a time for laughter mixed
in with the tears." I truly believe that my honest admission spared
me from sharing that view of the seventy percent of Ann
Landers's respondents who said that if they had it to do over again,
they wouldn't have children. If I had it to do over again, I
would—I'd just do it differently from the beginning, basing my
expectations on facts and not on fantasy.

Earlier I said that I would like to think that the first edition of
this book contributed in some small way to women really giving
serious thought about choosing to become mothers and reinforcing those who decided they were not cut out for the role. It is my
hope that this *new* edition, in some small way, will contribute to
lowering the percentage of people who become parents only to regret later having done so. I've said it before and I'll say it again:
Children deserve to be wanted not just from the moment of conception and birth, but forever after. Having realistic expectations,
experience has taught me, contributes to the realization of that
ideal.

There's just one more thing I'd like to say. After the first
edition of *Mother's Day Is Over* was published, I did many media

interviews and gave many talks to parents groups. Invariably, someone somewhere always would say, "Yes, motherhood's a tough job, but there are joys and woes no matter what your job may be." True. There *are* good and bad aspects to any job. But it ought to be obvious that the difference between the job of being a mother and being, say, a lawyer is that should it turn out that you dislike the legal profession, you can change jobs. No woman with a heart, however, can ever resign from the job of being a mother. Not even, as you will see, when the children are grown.

# *Acknowledgments*

Over fifteen years ago, the late John R. Rague, a dear friend, encouraged me to translate my feelings about motherhood into a book. He never doubted that I could bring it off, and never doubted for an instant that it would be an important work. To this end, he launched an all-out offensive, writing and nagging me so much that I felt that the only way to quiet him would be to follow my star. He rejoiced in the publication of that first edition he helped to nurture, and somehow I feel he is looking on today, with a sense of satisfaction that the book he believed in is enjoying a rebirth. I look Heavenward and thank him once again.

Many people encouraged me back then: Alicia Moore, then the Science Editor of *Life,* pushed my words into the consciousness of America by publishing excerpts of my as-yet unpublished book in *Life.* Mark Ross, then an editor of the magazine *Environmental Quality,* gave me much encouragement. My friends Carol Chetkovich and Bob Clayton not only made me feel guilty when I wasn't working on something they felt was important, but helped me type the early drafts. Carol's honest criticism, sometimes a dangerous thing, was an enormous help and made this a better book. A mother named Sharon, whom you will read about, insisted that what I had to say was of the utmost importance to young women and children everywhere.

Carol Eisen Rinzler, then of Charterhouse Books, took an enormous chance on me. I had virtually no publishing history, but she had faith that I could bring the roughest of drafts to final glory. No aspiring writer could ever have had a better editor. Carol guided me, spotted important omissions, knew what were my treasured passages. She was patient, kind, and full of faith. Since our maiden voyage together, I have authored or co-authored a total of seven published books and several dozen articles. It is safe to say that I would not have been able to bring any of them to fruition had it not been for the wise and kind guidance she lent to this then very novice author.

In the present, I have had similar good fortune with the editors of this new edition of *Mother's Day Is Over*. First thanks here must go to Steve Davis of Steve Davis Publishing in Dallas. He was long a fan of this book in its first incarnation, and his faith in the book and in me, along with his meticulous editing, are the very reasons why the revision was ever even considered for publication.

Finally, I must thank James Raimes of Arbor House for his apparent faith in this project, his questioning of detail when that was appropriate, his sensitivity to the subject and the dilemmas of motherhood, and his final editing touch that has made this book a finer product while keeping me on track. It is a wonderfully rewarding experience—especially when the subject at hand is of a deeply personal nature—to have such empathetic support from one's editor. Thank you, James.

*Chapter 1*

# A MOTHER IS

*Young people don't realize that this task—this parenthood busi-ness—is endless. It is twenty-four hours a day seven days a week, and there are no days off from it because there are no days off from worry, concern, and doubt. We went into it with our eyes wide open, and they keep opening wider with every day of par-enthood. I'm not sure that knowing what we know now we would have become parents—paradoxical because, by God, you really do love the little tykes. Maybe that's part of the strain—you try so hard to be good parents and because you care so deeply, you are always aware that you are gambling with [a child's] life. I know that my wife feels this even more keenly, for she's with him all day, as generally a mother is.*

> —A letter to the author from a
> forty-year-old Episcopalian minister

Everyone knows what a mother is.

A mother is someone who makes you wear galoshes when it isn't raining. She gives you aspirin when you have a cold and reads you stories before bed.

A mother is a happy, warm, patient person who effortlessly

*1*

maintains a beautiful, spotless home. She plays games with her children joyously, teaches them constantly, and takes them to the doctor, the dentist, the zoo, the park, swimming, and camping—sometimes all on the same day.

A mother is young and she always looks stunning. She is cheerful, energetic, and always interested in all aspects of her family's life.

A mother is a loving, mature person who is virtually incapable of thinking petty thoughts about anyone, least of all her own children. She harbors no resentment over being unable to read a book when she wants to, take a bath when she wants to, or make love to her husband when she wants to.

Being a mother is normal, natural, easy, and glamorous. Most mothers have blond coifs by Vidal Sassoon, an eternally glorious figure kept that way by Richard Simmons or Jane Fonda, and a dazzling smile.

Mothers are equally happy serving tomato soup, soothing hurts, bandaging cut knees, and turning a little snapper's mud-caked garments into a whiter-than-white wash.

A mother is a good amateur nutritionist, a superb disciplinarian (who need raise her voice only a notch to obtain obedience or cooperation), an interior decorator, a gifted teacher, an expert in first aid, a *cordon bleu* chef, and a wonderful wife with a wonderful marriage.

A mother, in addition to being a paragon in the home, is also a paragon in the world. By day, she dresses for success, and is a doctor, lawyer, accountant, executive. She is fulfilled in her career and fulfilled in her role as a mother. She has a wonderful live-in or a nanny who is "family" to her children, or she has a splendid day-care arrangement that teaches her child how to interact with the world at large. If she is an eighties mother, in the true sense of the term, during the day she swings a mean business deal, runs four miles after work, and on nights and weekends she teaches her two-year-old to read and write. And, she loves every minute of it.

So much for legend.

But the legend of American motherhood cannot be swept away by mocking it, however absurd the cultural images may be. The legend clings and affects all our lives and thinking because it has been carefully fed and nourished for years by the mass media. Films, magazines, the women's pages of newspapers (now renamed the "Living" or "People" sections, or something else that is nonsexist), and especially television have created a pervasive myth that victimizes every mother.

Consider the way mothers have been shown on at least one generation of soap operas. When I was folding diapers and watching the soaps back in the sixties, I would tune in *The Edge of Night,* where I would see Nancy, the mother of a twenty-three-year-old stepdaughter. Nancy didn't look a day over thirty, and she was totally fulfilled by her role as wife and mother. Even early in the morning, children were no bother. Fully and fashionably dressed and immaculately groomed, she saw her family off for the day. Good girl.

On the everlasting *As the World Turns,* Lisa was another kind of person, a sort of supervillainess of the soaps. Yet she was always saved from damnation because she was a "good mother." For all of her problems over the years—an ongoing ordeal for which one can only admire the ingenuity of the scriptwriters— there was never a hint of maternal distress until after Lisa's oldest son grew up and became clued in on his mom's transgressions with (would you believe?) men. No, given the way things are on TV today, I guess you wouldn't have much trouble with that one.

Anyway, that's the serious side of motherhood that was presented during the days when I was launching my career as a mother. By night, the programming was a little different—it was eternally cheerful.

The classic nighttime TV mother who dispensed joy was Donna Reed of the show of the same name. She was very young-looking and lovely and handled her children with a smile and a nod and never raised her voice or her hand to maintain perfect fun-filled family harmony. Cool as twelve cucumbers.

Veteran mothers my own age may remember Joan Nash, the mother of four rambunctious boys on *Please Don't Eat the Daisies.* She did Donna one trick better. Beautiful and totally happy, Joan was also talented: She was a writer. Her problems with her adorable kids were so trivial and so easily solved that there was time left over to put a little extra money in the family coffers by writing about their antics.

By the time we got to Mrs. Brady of *The Brady Bunch,* we started to sense something else about TV mommies: They're rich. Or at least very, very comfortable. Mom Brady runs an enormous contemporary home (not to be confused with the enormous, tastefully decorated *old* home that Joan Nash ran), is aided by a housekeeper who runs a close second to Mary Poppins, and always stays cool, collected, and ravishing while coping with her six well-behaved kids. Speaking of Mrs. Brady in the present tense is not in error—reruns of this show are still going strong.

Another TV mommy who is still around thanks to reruns is Samantha on *Bewitched.* Her problem is to forget she's a witch and just be a regular, beautiful, exquisitely groomed mommy in a regular, large, elegantly decorated house. But she never resorts to witchcraft when it comes to rearing the kids; for her—as it presumably is for all mommies—motherhood is a snap.

TV situation-comedy mothers (the situation-tragedy type are in short supply) are also ageless. On *My Three Sons,* another program still alive in reruns, Katie and Robbie had their absolutely delightful triplets while they were still going to college. But the demands of caring for their little ones only added to their happiness and didn't seem to make a dent in their freedom. They still went whipping off on vacations like carefree newlyweds. Perhaps Katie and Robbie guzzled a lot of Geritol when no one was looking.

And just as they do today, the commercials on television during the early years of my motherhood went one step further. Whether peddling baby products or homemaking aids, they always portrayed happy, immaculate, good-humored families, who were climbing into shiny new station wagons, eating cereal (which never wound up on the floor) in mushy or crunchy togetherness, brushing their teeth with abandon in a spontaneous quest for cavityless good health, marveling over the whitening qualities of monosyllabic detergents, or ecstatically romping through fields of clover while an orchestra hidden in the high grass accompanied them with a tender tune. Commercials for the likes of Mennen baby products, Johnson's Baby Shampoo, and even Jif peanut butter made motherhood seem the ultimate act of creativity and gracious living.

One commercial for Playtex nursers opened with a shot of an ordinary-looking woman feeding an ordinary-looking (and realistically cranky) baby with an ordinary-looking baby bottle. After a few beguiling words from the sponsor—presto!—the ordinary-looking mother and child (and bottle, of course) were replaced by a beautiful young mother and a beautiful bouncy baby, both serene with the Playtex nurser. Its nursing qualities aside, the bottle took ten years off the mother's age and gave her a new hairdo to boot.

To judge by TV commercials, the most serious decision a mother had to make was which brand of peanut butter to feed her family or which cleanser to make her kitchen sink sparkle. And the commercials haven't changed. It would all be laughable if it were not so insidious. For not only is motherhood presented as easy, fun, and vastly fulfilling on TV, but it also is implicit that if life as a mother doesn't work for you the way it does on television, it could easily become so if you'd only buy a bushel or two of the sponsors' products.

It is no secret, even to the densest of us, that products can only be sold if a market is created for them. By reinforcing the myth of perfect motherhood in commercials and on the shows themselves, American business is creating a market for its products. Motherhood itself is sold as hard as any of the individual products—on the theory, presumably, that if you buy the myth, the products that make it all come true will be your next purchase.

Since television networks and magazines prosper on advertising, they are likely to oblige by feeding the motherhood myth. A baby-food manufacturer is unlikely to advertise in a magazine that extols the virtues of remaining childless. Whether advertisers actually control the content of the media may be debatable. What is beyond debate is that the cumulative message of the media is that motherhood is beautiful and a woman without children is an unhappy woman indeed.

As a mother who has experienced the realities of parenthood and has come to take it all quite seriously, I am insulted by the unrealistic and utterly frivolous way in which the mass media present motherhood. The mindless, plastic standards set up on the big and little screens and on the slick, colorful pages of nearly every popular magazine speak neither to the dignity nor to the travail of motherhood.

In the process of demeaning and trivializing women who have chosen (or had thrust upon them) motherhood as their life role, the importance of realistic and meaningful child guidance is ignored. Housekeeping is presented not as a task to be done as speedily and efficiently as possible but as the glory of motherhood. Paradoxically, this false portrayal compounds the problems of parenthood because we come to feel, often without even noticing it, that unless we live up to the media-imposed standards of grace, we are failures as mothers.

Yet how can any of us help but fail in real life when measured against such a giddy standard? As I used to perform my daily janitorial services while coping with two active youngsters, I was confused and distressed by the images that the media constantly flaunted at me. American industry's dandy products did not then, and certainly do not now, turn motherhood into bliss, as the commercials continue to suggest.

Nor does love conquer all, either romantically or in dealing with children. Loving does not automatically equip a human being for the responsibility of caring for a young life (or lives) any more than it removes a parent's aversion to serving time on a PTA committee. Neither love nor sudsier suds can make you like the responsibility, drudgery, or boredom that all mothers know deep down goes with caring for their children.

Many women come to motherhood completely unaware of its drawbacks. And when they discover them, they often feel they are lacking as mothers if they somehow do not relish all the negatives, since a cardinal part of the motherhood myth is that you must *like* being a mother to *be* a good mother.

I suppose there are actually a few mothers around who appear to have satisfied all the media and cultural standards of the perfect mother. They pull it all off. And their kids seem to have no problems.

One such case dates back to my childhood, and I'll never forget her. I was about ten years old when her daughter, whom I will call Erika, came to our school. None of us had ever seen a wardrobe quite like Erika's. Her mother designed and made most of her gorgeous clothes. Her hair shimmered with golden curls (made perfect by appointments at the beauty parlor), and she wore heirloom jewelry and a wristwatch.

Erika's mother looked and carried herself like Grace Kelly. She wore prescription sunglasses (unusual for those days) and would walk down the street on a fall day wearing a camel-hair polo coat, leading the family pedigreed dog on a long leash. The image was made more perfect by the exquisite house where Erika, her mother, and her father lived. ("Mother does all the decorating and made some of the furniture; the rest are genuine antiques.")

Erika made straight A's in school. She had riding lessons, piano lessons, drawing lessons, swimming lessons, and voice lessons. She went to college and became the sweetheart of Sigma Chi, belonged to the best sorority, graduated with honors, married the captain of the football team—I won't even mention the wedding, teas, and all the trimmings—and earned her master's at Stanford.

Years later, and well after I had had children, Erika and I accidentally bumped into each other and reminisced. Things came out. Like the shoplifting bouts that went on during most of her childhood. Like how she had tried to commit suicide at sixteen. Like the nights she sneaked out after her parents were asleep, taking the family car (without having a driver's license) to meet one of many boys. She explained how, many years before, she had changed a teacher's grade book to maintain her straight-A average because if she didn't get all A's, her parents would have beaten the hell out of her. We then talked about her disastrous marriage, her divorce, her psychiatrist, and her generally unhappy life.

Some mothers make it look so good and so easy to bring off that their children never recover.

I have always wondered about mothers who continue to have children long after they have come to grips with the realities of parenthood. I can understand the pressures on Catholic or Mormon women, who really feel they have no choice if they are to adhere to their faith. And I can understand the handful of gifted mothers who are equipped to rear children and who have all the resources—physical, intellectual, emotional, and financial. But what of others who, while their numbers have been declining over the years, continue to have one child after another? Sheer masochism doesn't seem to cover it. Could it be that even in the face of reality, the motherhood myths remain so strong that they persuade some women to try again and again to have a child that will finally make the myth come true?

One mother sent me the following letter:

> We had one child, a little boy two and a half. He had mostly been what is referred to as "a good baby," and we loved him dearly. However, we had had little money when he was born—no color-coordinated nursery, no lacy peignoirs for me to nurse him in. No baby shower—he wore mostly hand-me-downs. He was so undemanding and happy, and so were we. . . . Pressure was brought to bear, however, from family and friends, to have a second child, so he would not become a victim of the only-child syndrome, whatever that is. More im-

portant, I wanted to *do it right.* . . . I had my IUD removed, and one month later the doctor informed me I was pregnant. Thus began a chain of disturbing thoughts and happenings.

Sitting in the OB's office, I was upset by the fact that I was not ecstatic at the news. After all, isn't this what I wanted? I wondered why I was choking down tears that did not spring from joy. The thought of abortion briefly flitted across my brain. Ridiculous! Why am I thinking about abortion? We want this baby, don't we?

Then I was sick for weeks and weeks. Not seriously ill, just the pregnant kind of feeling totally rotten. The housework was neglected; my husband and I fought about only one thing in six years of marriage—my inability to keep house efficiently. I was, of course, reminded frequently of Pearl Buck's *Good Earth* women who squat in the fields, etc., etc.

Then followed classes in natural childbirth. Good, for the most part, but my husband was not as enthusiastic as the books said he should be.

Anyway, on St. Patrick's Day morning we got a beet-red eight-pound girl. She was adorable and delicate and sweet. I loved her on sight, but I couldn't explain my depression.

I had a lovely baby shower. Lots of pretty pink lacy things, but the depression lingered on. My husband continued to bitch about the house. My milk nearly ran out and I went to a La Leche meeting. More tears and depression at all those happy mommies and their fat little babies (mine was so skinny). I loved her so much. I secretly harbored desires of giving her up for adoption to a better mother—she deserved better than me. The depression lasted and lasted—over a year or more. I was beginning to realize I had been a victim of Madison Avenue.

Anyway, Jennifer is two and I have more time to enjoy her now. The house is in a little better shape. Last week I saw a little newborn all wrapped in soft yellow blankets. I started thinking, "Maybe ... maybe I could do it right if I tried again."

And, again, and again, and again, maybe?

Recently, I had a conversation with a mother of nine, the youngest of whom is now in high school. She told me, "Twenty-eight years ago, when I had my first child, having lots of children was the thing to do, so I did it. I never thought about it. But I'll tell you this: I'm completely burned out—have been for a long time. For a very long time I haven't had anything left to give—not even to myself."

Most of the mothers I have spoken to or heard from over the years were neither perfect mothers nor mothers of many children. They were what I think of as typical middle-class women with typical problems and rewards during the course of parenthood. Let us consider three of them, who asked that their names not be used.

One mother is a warm, vivacious, and loving woman whose affection for her kids is as persuasive as the most convincing television commercial. When she was pregnant with the last of her four children, her husband suggested that an abortion might be in order. She wouldn't discuss it—the idea was too repugnant for her to even consider it. But seven years later, she willingly discusses it. She says with conviction that if she had it to do all over again, not only would she have had the abortion, but she would have had no children at all. For her, being a mother has meant fifteen years of fear, guilt, feelings of inadequacy, and the struggle to pursue her own interests against overwhelming odds. She says, "I love the children. I'd die if anything happened to any one of them. But I detest being a mother."

She had never given much thought to what it would mean to be a mother; it just seemed the natural thing following marriage. By the time she confronted the problems raised by her youngsters in high school, she felt as if the walls were closing in on her: "Oh, I know that everyone thinks I have it made, and many of our friends think of me as the epitome of a happy, fulfilled mother. I'm sure many of them would be surprised to learn that they're only seeing the outer wrapper. Underneath I'm constantly surprised and frustrated by all that's involved in doing a half-decent job with the kids. It's such damned hard work, and it's not work that I enjoy. When the kids were younger, I never really felt good—I was almost always slightly ill. The struggle to remain a self has been an arduous one. But what's worse is that, having made it through the drudgery and chaos of handling small children, I'm now moving into the gut-tearing worry of guiding them through their teens."

A twenty-six-year-old mother of two adorable children who could easily have competed with the pretty models in TV commercials, told me, "Nobody ever told me there were rotten sides to it. You just don't happen to think about it. I don't mind changing diapers; changing diapers is no big deal to me—that's minimal. I didn't think about all the other stuff. I didn't think about how hard it would be, how my life would be changed—not just the freedom to come and go as I pleased, but the freedom to put my own needs above those of my children without wondering if it's affecting them adversely.

"My first view of motherhood was that if you do everything right, take care of the kid, change his diapers, and all that, you can make it. Now that I have kids, I know better."

When I asked her if she felt she was equipped for motherhood, she said, "No. Everyone thinks I'm a great mother. Most of the time, I'm even-tempered, I'm nice to the kids, and I really like them. But I don't really want them. I'd be happier without them, but I probably could never have gotten out of the cultural thing of having them. I'm sure that no one would ever believe that if I didn't have children, it would be because I chose not to have any. But I find such joy in them, and I love them so—it's all very confusing."

A mother of two planned children came right to the point: "The kids are great. The only problem we have is that the kids I love got stuck with a lousy mother. I didn't know in advance that I'm not good at this."

These women are only three of the many women I spoke

with who feel they are less than sterling mothers. Yet on the face of it, they are probably three of the most dedicated and proficient. They love their children, and the kids look just fine. None of these mothers go off to work and leave their children with sitters—a reliable way to dredge up a lot of guilt. Why, then, don't they think they are good mothers? Almost certainly, the problem is traceable to the image of motherhood these women carry around in their heads—that great myth that says a mother is a person who loves being a mother, who finds being a mother a snap, who is completely fulfilled by the role, whose children are happy all the time, and whose severest negative feeling toward her kids is one of mild annoyance.

Other mothers I spoke with were more severely afflicted by the myths and realities of motherhood, and the gap between the two. One, for example, who is fairly able to function nearly as well as any TV mother, thanks largely to her psychiatrist and tranquilizers, told me how she felt before she got help: "I thought I knew what depression was—until I really experienced it. God, I tried hard to fight it, but I didn't seem to have the strength. I just simply didn't care anymore. Nothing was very important to me, even the kids, who have always been so dear to me. I just got to feeling that the only reason for me to exist was that the kids needed someone to take care of them. I guess the reason it got to me is that while I had all the responsibility for the kids, the rewards were slim and sandwiched in between what seemed an endless number of crises, enormous confusion, and the increasing feeling that I was a failure as a mother. It didn't help that my husband didn't understand.

"It's odd. When I was growing up, my parents always told me that I was important just because I was me. And now I get the feeling that I'm important only because I'm a mother and the children need me."

Another real-life mother, who never managed to reconcile motherhood with a career because she was never able to stay at anything long enough for things to work out, told me that she felt she was forever batting zero where her personal interests were concerned. Now and then she managed some volunteer work in social welfare organizations, and she went to school, on and off, for *years*—years, because she kept having to drop out to meet what she felt were the legitimate demands of her family. She seemed to be truly fulfilled by her children, but she dwelled on the endless struggle to find a little piece of life that was her very own.

One mother who did pull it all together picked up the threads of her education once her two children were in school all day. She timed everything to coincide with the children's hours of need, but balancing the responsibilities of a family while trying to study nearly drove her mad. She finally got her degree the same week her son got his high school diploma. The price came high.

One mother I interviewed is also a pianist. At the time I spoke with her, she had a little boy, whom she described as being "absolutely terrific," but she told me that if she had known ten years earlier what she knew now, she would have followed up her contraceptive failure with an abortion.

Another who pulled it together is a pediatrician. On the surface, she has it all: a husband who totally shares responsibility, two beautiful daughters, a thriving practice, a nice house, and even loads of pets. But when a younger woman who had dropped out of medical school to have a child asked her for advice on resuming her training, this otherwise composed physician became nearly hysterical. All her years of control evaporated as she screamed at the young woman, "Don't do it! Don't do it!"

On the home front, one of the happiest mothers I interviewed and observed had five boys, who seemed to keep the family in perpetual financial distress. She often would lament that they couldn't afford decent clothes for all the kids. Yet several nights a week, you could find her and her husband elbow-bending at a popular bar in town and having a grand old time of it. Invariably, when she got high, she got sentimental about the children and talked glowingly of the joys of motherhood, starting with the first labor pain. (Actually, this mother didn't spend all her recreational time in bars. During the day, she generally entertained at home, serving generous drinks, whether or not she had any guests.) For some women, it works best to keep the motherhood-reality gap open: It may be the only way they can make it.

A less happy stay-at-home mother penned the following:

> I fell for the whole thing—hook, line, and sinker. I feel so dumb. I feel so taken. And it's too late. Three children too late. A half a lifetime too late. I was a victim of my generation. A victim of the "good life." *I am bitter.* I spent half my life trying to do something I never had the talent or inclination to do. I have wasted half my emotional life in feelings of guilt, inadequacies, anger, frustration, and despair because I could never be the supermother and superwife I thought I was supposed to be. I tried to distort my nature to fit the myth and only succeeded in making everyone around me come on my trip.
>
> I have finally thrown up my hands! My fifteen-year-old daughter is in a mental institution with a drug problem—she's been there since she was thirteen and there is hardly an end in sight. My seventeen-year-old son we sent to a prep school because he was unable to adjust to our moving to a new neighborhood. Now we only have a thirteen-year-old at home with us and I even resent the small demands he makes on us. I can't wait for them all to be grown up and on their own and leave me some *peace.* I don't think I've had a peaceful moment in the last eighteen years. We have fallen into every pit along the way. I feel battle-worn, old before my time, tired, spent, and deceived. We are all victims of the myth.
>
> Why *shouldn't* I be bitter? I went to every PTA meeting, cooked every dinner, went to every Little League game, did everything Supermother should have done, and I have three unhappy, bored children and a ghost of a husband—just as weary as I. Always trying to measure up to the other mothers around me, always falling short, always with the gnawing feeling of guilt and inadequacy. Never really knowing *why!!*

When I look at the devastation of my life, and all those around me, when I see the havoc it has caused, I ask, *"Why?"*

I have tried to discuss this with friends who I know feel the same as I do, but I'm shocked at their resistance to admit it. They seem to be holding on for dear life to the belief that despite all the destruction it was *all worth it.* I suspect letting go of our myth is not going to be easy because we haven't found something of value to replace it yet.

A formerly married mother told me that after getting over the shock of the divorce and the dramatic change in her style and standard of living, she misses adult companionship the way any thirty-five-year-old would. During the week, she works; evenings and weekends she copes with the kids. So, when some man does ask her out, she wants to jump at the chance. Maternal guilt, though, keeps getting in the way, because "the kids really have only me, and I'm gone all day long. I just feel that however much I want to get out of the house or would like to go out with a man, it's really unfair to shunt the children off with a baby-sitter. And when I do, I can hardly enjoy myself because I feel so terribly guilty."

Sharon—and that is her real name—is not a typical mother or a typical divorcée. But her story is important because it did happen to her and can to others. Sharon's sad odyssey began when she married at eighteen. Her husband was a graduate student at New York University, and she was entering her freshman year. Sharon was bright, tough, and intuitive, and when she married young, she looked ahead and saw the future blueprinted: They would be a happily married couple, getting all their respective degrees, finding good jobs, and raising great kids—just like the great-looking, two-child families in the Chevrolet commercials.

It didn't work. One year after marriage, Sharon gave birth to a daughter; fourteen months after that, a son. A year after that, she and her husband separated. He had no money to give her, and her middle-class suburban parents refused to help, saying that she had made her bed and now she could lie in it.

She applied for a job at a public library on the strength of one year of library training at NYU, but she was told, "We don't generally hire women with young children." It was no easier finding work elsewhere. She moved to a tiny apartment on the Lower East Side and continued to seek work. By the time she applied for welfare assistance, she was desperate. Because she and her husband were still legally married, she was turned down.

Truly desperate, Sharon took a low-paying clerical position. She had to place the children in a neighborhood day-care center and hire someone to pick them up at the end of the day because she couldn't get off work to do it herself before the center closed. When she got home, she made dinner, fed the children, left them alone while she ran down to the Laundromat, came back and bathed them, bedded them down—and then prepared for the next dismal day.

Her meager pay simply couldn't cover the rent, day care, and food, too, especially in New York. A resourceful woman, Sharon learned how to steal food while doing the marketing, especially meat, since she couldn't afford to give the children as much as she felt they needed. One day, after months of this grinding routine, she took a good look at her situation and realized that she and her children were trapped in this way of life. The only solution for them and for herself was painful in the extreme: "I knew I was giving them up for several weeks before the appointed time. I could hardly look at them without crying. I'd see their little open faces looking at me—they knew something was going on—and I'd go into the bathroom and cry. Finally I called the agency and told them that I couldn't take it any longer, that I had to do it now.

"I had picked one of the best agencies in New York, and I was told that if I brought them up the next day, the children would be temporarily placed in a foster home until they could be placed permanently.

"The next day I dressed them for the last time and took them to the agency. They were so precious—two little peas in a pod. Anyway, I went up to the seventh floor of the agency—it was beautifully appointed, with nice furniture, thick carpets, and wall hangings. Someone came out into the waiting room, and after a brief exchange, she led them away. The door simply closed and I was alone. It was a few minutes later when I realized I hadn't seen those things on my last visit to the agency."

I asked her, "What things?"

"The bars on the windows. I only noticed them when I wanted to jump. And I knew why they were there—and how many before me had wanted to just make it stop hurting."

The physical and mental well-being of American mothers and the stability of the American family require that we face up to the gap between the myth and the realities of motherhood. Dr. Benjamin Spock, for a long time the nation's most highly regarded authority on child care, notes that the difficulty begins with the fact that ours is a highly child-centered culture. When our media-fed cultural attitudes telling us that parenthood is normal, natural, fun, and easy collide with a child-centered society that makes parenthood a very hard job indeed, a sort of schizophrenia results and leads to the kinds of confusion and frustration reflected in the words of the mothers cited above.

A sober outlook on the world would suggest to us that there is a balance between the good and the bad in life—in a job, in a marriage, in a parent-child relationship. Many women come to feel, as I do, that the scales of motherhood do not really balance out for them. Motherhood does indeed have its rewards. I do not mean to suggest otherwise. But often the rewards are not great enough to offset the difficulties and plain unpleasantness of so much of the job. This is not to say that many mothers who find the job of motherhood unrewarding feel that they have been handed a rotten bill of goods. Instead of questioning the image of idealized motherhood, once they have a truer sense of the real burdens involved, they begin to question themselves. The fault lies in themselves, many mothers feel, and nowhere else.

For other mothers, the rewards are enough. They derive so much joy from so many things about their small babies and their growing children that they are shocked when anyone questions the giving-and-getting ratio. For these joyous mothers, it is very hard to understand how any mother can feel, as a friend of mine did, that "one lousy little smile from a three-month old isn't worth the loss of freedom for these three months or the changing of a hundred dirty diapers every week."

Some mothers don't feel the imbalance until, say, their youngsters are toddlers or perhaps even of school age and demanding in very different ways. Others will sail through it all—infancy, the toddler stage, the "terrible twos," and the elementary-school years, with their myriad demands—pooh-poohing all the way anything I have to say about matching myths with reality. And then, wham, the teenage years blow them away. As one mother of four girls told me, "I loved every minute of it until my first one started high school—it was downhill with each and every one of them from that moment on."

Whenever it hits, the question of "getting as good as you give" is presented in bolder relief. And, when resenting the things about parenthood that one might be expected to resent is heightened by not enjoying enough of the things that one might be expected to enjoy, the whole process can turn into a nightmare.

Motherhood, then, is a career. It has caused many women to seek nothing beyond, caused many others to stifle their creative spirits and their dreams for a career of a different order, and caused still others to wear themselves out trying to do justice to two careers.

In place of the legend and the myths at the outset of this chapter, a different roster of values—and a higher fidelity to the truth—can be offered at its close to define what a mother is.

A mother is being away from home and missing your children terribly only to come back and be greeted by, "What did you bring me?" And finding what you brought (and spent a couple of hours shopping for, nearly missing the plane) broken into a dozen pieces two days later.

A mother is feeling that the children should have a pet—a

nice little dog, say—because all children should grow up with a pet. And then taking the dog to the vet, feeding it, cleaning up after it, nearly breaking a leg tripping over it, keeping it from getting hit by a car, and then looking at the critter one day and thinking, My God, that thing is just as much trouble as another child would be.

A mother is having someone small hovering about you constantly—stepping on your feet, absently fooling around with something useful (or anything at all) and breaking it. Or doing his or her little project inches away from wherever it is you are doing whatever you are doing. Or running in every two minutes and cutting into your thoughts with, "Lookit what I made, Mom," or "Why is the sky blue, Mom?" or "I didn't mean to break the lamp, Mom" or "Mom! There's a big spider in the living room!"—and all the while not losing your patience. Then there's that sinking feeling after the final interruption—the one that goes, "Mom, I love you so much"—that gets to you. To lose your patience just at the moment your child is expressing affection is pain that only a mother can know.

A mother is knowing the dark fear of having a sick or hurt child, feeling your stomach and knees cave in at the sight of a bloody head, feeling the guilt that whatever is wrong might have been prevented if you were better at your job.

A mother is feeling hostility toward the man you love when he speaks sharply to your child and hurts the child's feelings, then an hour later resenting the same child for having triggered another nasty little argument between two grown-ups who otherwise wouldn't be arguing.

A mother is knowing what it's like to have every one of your senses assaulted with questions, noise, and misbehavior until, at the peak of bombardment, you wonder if your mind has deteriorated to such an extent that it will never again be able to concentrate even on a simple thought. It is feeling that where thoughts once lingered, there is now a total void.

A mother is accepting that you must do many things that you

are entirely uninterested in doing, simply because you are a mother. It is knowing not to make comparisons between your relationship with your husband and your relationship with your children. Even in nonegalitarian marriages, the relationship between husband and wife is a matter of give and take toward each other. The relationship between a mother and her children is that she gives and they take.

A mother is feeling the most profound love possible for another human being—or several of them. It is knowing that however much of a disaster you may be as a mother, however much terror you feel over coping with the responsibility each day, you couldn't bear to live without your children.

A mother is also me.

I have two lovely, healthy, intelligent, wanted children. I love Lisa and Adam more than life. I have always tried to take good care of them and struggled to guide them well. But if being a mother means liking the job, then I am a failure at it.

The truth is, I have never liked being a service machine, a janitor, a laundress, a nurse, a room or class mother, PTA stalwart, referee of children's sparring matches, or a guidance counselor when the school system failed to provide that promised service.

I've always been a lousy disciplinarian. I'm nervous. And I detest camping, so my kids have never had the thrill of catching trout (or a cold) in the Sierras—at least not with me along. I lose my cool when they're sick, injured, or have their feelings hurt by other people or even by me. I'm really not very well cut out for the role, and my kids deserved better than they got.

# Chapter 2

# PRESSURE TO BEAR

The eight years before we had children were glorious.

We lived in a tiny, charming house, furnished with an assortment of antiques and junk selected during many happy hours of rummaging through shops and flea markets. The house sat in the middle of a huge lot, and by our own labor we added a swimming pool and, around it, a terrace of 3,000 bricks.

Our home was a paradise, a perpetual retreat.

During those eight years, I worked at a job I liked: I was a secretary to a research physicist. And our home life made the end of the workday yet one more experience to anticipate with pleasure. Each night my husband and I would both race home from work, have cocktails, watch the evening news, and trade gossip on the day's developments while I tried out some new recipe. We had friends, we entertained often, and we traveled when we felt like it. We would go to Mexico, to far-off cities to visit friends, and sometimes, just for the hell of it, we spent weekends in San Francisco, thirty-five miles away.

We also enjoyed going to movies on the spur of the moment, to the theater, meeting after work for dinner out somewhere cozy or fancy, or just spending an hour browsing in a bookstore.

Yet, to our astonishment, we found that friends and acquaintances *pitied* us because we were childless.

If we heard it once, we heard it a thousand times: "When are you going to start your family?" It was always conveyed with an air of deep concern. "Anything wrong with you?" they would ask solicitously. That one was usually addressed to me since it's considered bad form to ask a man (although my husband got some of this from the boys in the locker room). "Have you had tests?" was very common. "I can recommend a good gynecologist" was offered every other day it seemed.

One woman not too subtly suggested at one point that unless I experienced the miracle of having a child, I would never truly be a woman. No doubt, these friends and acquaintances were worried that we might go on living a hedonistic, meaningless, if terribly comfortable, life unless we became parents. I know a few other pitied women who have elected to remain childless. And while they evoke sympathy from others, from me they will have to settle for envy.

One couple we know decided, after five years of marriage and careful reflection, to remain childless. They have a beautiful home, enjoy careers that utilize their talents to the fullest, go camping and skiing as and when they like (rather than forcing themselves to, as many parents do, for the sake of the children), have traveled widely in Europe and the Orient, and are still very much in love after twenty years of marriage. Nothing in their natures suggested that they have neuroses that would lead to their childless state. They are warm and loving and appear genuinely to like children.

Every once in a while, this couple drops in at a moment's notice to visit old friends. Occasionally we are the old friends they come by to see. They seem young and healthy and full of good cheer when they greet us. How sad I am for them, though. They will never know the enriching experience of having to plan such visits three weeks in advance. As another friend of ours, a father of four, put it, "These poor creatures will never experience the challenge of vacationing with four kids, the joy of camping with two other families with a total of ten children to keep them on their

toes. Or the fun of planning an evening at the movies with the arrangements closely resembling in precision and detail the strategy
of the D-Day landing at Normandy."

Then there is my friend and former co-worker Carol. When
I first started putting my thoughts together for this book, Carol
was married and planning a law career. At the time, she was convinced that she could be fulfilled without children. I recall that
when she was asked for the hundredth time why she had no children, she answered, "I'm more of a world saver than anything
else, and it wouldn't be easy for me to save the world if I had children who needed my attention constantly."

The answer she got was: "You should have a child and hope
that *he'll* save the world." Carry that kind of thinking to its logical
extreme, and each generation would defer its ambitions to the next
one—forever.

Carol is now divorced. One can only wonder how much support she would be getting from the old pressure bearers if she had
succumbed and was now a single mother with a couple of kids.

One couple's marriage faced serious problems caused by the
pressure to start a family. The very fact that this was a source of
controversy between them should have served as a warning. He
wanted children, or had been convinced that he did; she didn't, and
had made her feelings crystal clear to everyone since before their
marriage. Some of their acquaintances—all parents, of course—
judged her a vain, cold, and selfish woman. These so-called
friends, with their clucking over the childless state of the couple,
only added fuel to what should have remained a private controversy.

No one suggested that she had confidence enough in her
femininity, and was sufficiently happy with her husband and their
life-style, not to need *more* for fulfillment. Nor did anyone offer
the advice that if he pushed her into having a child she didn't
want—forced her through pregnancy, childbirth, drudgery,
worry, guilt, and abandonment of her career—he would be gambling with their marriage. Besides, he knew in advance, as did ev-

eryone else, that she never wanted to be a parent. I thought it was
a little late to change the ground rules a few years after they had
been agreed upon.

She finally agreed to have a child *provided* that he would
share fully in his or her care. Not even six months after the birth
of their son, he was promoted to a position that required him to
travel two weeks out of every four. So much for that particular
egalitarian arrangement.

At a cocktail party, we ran into some old friends whom we
hadn't seen for a long time and learned that their oldest son had
been married for a while. When I made the standard comment
that it was hard to believe since it seemed like only yesterday that
he was a gangly teenager with braces on his teeth, his mother lamented that children grow up all too quickly. She added she was
hopeful her son and his wife wouldn't wait too long before present-
ing her with a grandchild. She went on to explain that her son's
wife didn't want children, but they hoped to "bring her around."
Apparently our friends thought it perfectly natural for this young
woman to have children she didn't want just so she could please
her in-laws. This attitude, common among potential grandparents,
is suggested by letters to the two famous sisters who give advice in
separate syndicated newspaper columns. For instance, one mother
of a grown daughter, eager to bounce a bundle of joy on her knee,
explained to Dear Abby that her twenty-seven-year-old daughter
had "turned down several good marriage proposals," and went on
to say,

> When I ask her what she is waiting for, she says, "Don't
> rush me, Mom."
> Is there any way I can get her to hurry up and think
> seriously of marrying and settling down? I am fifty years old
> and would like to see a few grandchildren before I leave this
> earth.

To which Dear Abby, a seasoned veteran in dealing with
pressure bearers, replied:

Many moms who have rushed their daughters into marriage see more of their grandchildren than they expected to. (They're raising them because the marriage didn't work out.) If you're eager to see things hatch, settle down on a chicken farm.

Better yet, is the voice of experience that comes from one who succumbed to the pressure to have children to please other people, as illustrated by this sad letter to Ann Landers:

Please tell newlyweds not to have children unless they really want them. My husband and I have been married sixteen years. We have three sons. We didn't want any of them. His parents kept bribing us and we were foolish enough to go for it.

That letter writer went on to say that her "monsters" had effectively ruined her marriage. She and her husband often discussed putting them up for adoption, but were afraid of what people would say.

The newest and most imaginative form of social pressure to have children stems from the feminist ideal that women ought to be able to have fulfilling and demanding careers if they so choose and that women *should not have to choose* between parenthood and a career any more than men should. (I hasten to add that this is an ideal with which I fully agree.) However, while trying to achieve this ideal, many women have been made to feel that they *must not choose* between motherhood and a career. One thirty-four-year-old non-mother who is a corporate vice president described the new pressure this way:

Ten years ago, things were better. When people asked me when I was going to start my family and I explained that I had chosen instead to have a career, while they may have thought I was selfish, they reluctantly accepted the idea that juggling a career with a family would be difficult. Now there is a sense that having a career isn't a good enough reason to forego motherhood because doing both is something everyone can bring off. So, now I get little reminders that I'm "not getting any younger," and kindly suggestions that I may regret never having children.

Furthermore, I have even had people rather crustily imply that all I've accomplished isn't all that great because, "after all, she doesn't have any kids, so why *shouldn't* she be successful?" The message is that I'm neither talented nor hard working. Another message is that I should prove otherwise by becoming a mother.

In view of the importance of parenting and children, this is a dangerously shallow notion. It not only discounts the accomplishments of non-mothers, but it also implies that combining a career with motherhood is a snap, which discredits working mothers of every stripe. Needless to say, retention of the myth that motherhood is easy provides the perfect excuse for husbands and fathers to avoid carrying their fair share of the load.

Why should the decisions of couples or women regarding the establishment of their own families—an area of presumably great privacy—be open to question by relatives, friends, neighbors, or co-workers? People who *have* children are not routinely challenged for their decisions or their contraceptive failures. Why should it be socially acceptable among many people to ask those who remain childless why they don't have any children, but unacceptable to ask breeders why they do? We don't tell other people what kind of jobs they should hold, whom they should marry, or where they should vacation. And it is generally considered rude to inquire into the financial affairs of other people. Yet the breeding habits of the childless or of those with one or two children are somehow considered fair game.

People who try to pressure other people into having children don't seem to consider the possibility that such probing may open old wounds. I know a woman who was devastated by having a hysterectomy when she was just twenty-one years old. A couple I know lost two babies, one right after the other, and they simply can't face risking still another loss. A woman I know is often questioned about having an only child by people who don't realize that her other child—a first-born child—died a few years before. Another woman I know has had four miscarriages. Another experienced a stillbirth. Is it any wonder these women prefer not to be questioned on their reproductive capabilities?

The bad taste displayed by those who don't hesitate to urge, through prying inquiry, others to follow their example and have children may be symptomatic of some disturbance. Or perhaps such people are simply prototypes of what H. L. Mencken called "wowsers," people "tormented by the thought that someone, somewhere, might be having a good time." Consider for a moment that most potent of rebukes that a parent can dish out to a child: "Just wait till you have children of your own."

Nor does the social coercion end after you've had one or two children. We know several couples who have an "only child," and they are constantly harassed. They expect it to continue right up to menopause. "When are you going to have another baby?" becomes all too familiar and tedious. In a letter a friend of mine writes: "We have one baby and would like to keep the number of children to one. Already (our baby is one month old) we are getting pressure about having a second one."

Another woman put it this way: "I've often thought how screwed up our ideal marriage became after our child arrived, but that's not the kind of thing you're supposed to admit, even to yourself, let alone anyone else. I was never an emotional pillar of strength, but I've quickly exhausted my stability in these last couple of years.

"I fear that my wonderful daughter deserved a better mother. I don't deny my deep love for her, but I have denied my deep resentment and unhappiness with motherhood. The result has been frequent bouts of rage and loss of control—outbursts that have frightened me into seeking psychiatric help. Yet most of the advice I get from my bedraggled domesticated friends has been: 'Get pregnant again—you'll be so busy with two children you won't have time for those unnatural feelings of yours.' "

Irene Wilkenfeld, in an article in *New Mother* (August 1985), describes the reaction she got to having just one child:

> The nagging [to have another child] started promptly upon the birth of our daughter, Missi, and persists to this day, fifteen years later.
>
> "It's not fair to the baby."
> "She'll be lonely, spoiled."
> "How can you be so selfish?"
> "It's just not normal."
> "You'll regret this!"
>
> Assaulted by this uninvited advice, my husband and I were left feeling confused and unsure. Still, we refused to be brainwashed into the double-or-nothing approach to family planning. For us, the decision to have a child didn't necessarily mean we were morally obligated to supply her with a sibling. Alone and unsupported in a community that took a dim view of couples who characterized a threesome as a complete family unit, we knew that one thing was undeniable. Choosing to have an "only" was an atypical and unpopular path to follow.

A common whip used on parents of one child is "You really ought to have another baby to keep little Stevie (or Debbie) company." Every time I hear that absurdity, I become nearly hysterical. As battle-scarred veterans will tell you, the way in which siblings keep each other company is rarely as advertised. My own children, Adam and Lisa, have fought with each other since they were one and two years of age.

Some pressure bearers will come back with, "Yes, but when siblings are three or five years apart, they don't fight so much." Really!? For a time we had a boy living with us because it was considered a better alternative than having him and his brother, five years his senior, beating each other to death with crowbars. These boys, from a truly fine family composed of two intelligent and loving parents and four very bright children, have a history of hatred and violence toward each other that would make Atilla the Hun cringe. Lock up the crowbars, and they throw chairs at each other, or break the legs of the chairs and use them as clubs. In our home—apart from the hated sibling—the boy was completely nonviolent.

Don't take my word for it that there is an unwritten law of sibling rivalry. The existence of books like John F. McDermott's *Raising Cain and Abel Too* and Carole and Andrew Calladine's *Raising Siblings* confirms my view that this is a widespread problem.

Some use the myth that only children become deprived and emotionally crippled individuals to coerce couples into having a second child, even though this myth has been refuted by many experts. In 1980, for example, a team of psychologists from the American Institutes for Research in Palo Alto completed a survey of 400,000 high school students. Their findings showed that only children tend to be more intelligent, creative, mature, and socially sensitive than their peers with siblings.

Even when people do go ahead and have that second child, there are no guarantees that the pressure will end. While two currently seems to be a socially acceptable number of children to have, more and more I'm seeing young mommies wheeling two youngsters in a stroller and obviously expecting a third. When Lisa and Adam were very young, I was constantly asked when we were going to have another child. I think we may well see a return to those days.

As a Catholic, once devout, I am acutely aware of a major source of the pressure to procreate that affects Catholics, Mormons, and others whose faiths ban birth control. To be faithful to the teachings of these churches, devotees have but three choices: have babies as the heavens decree; practice the rhythm method of birth control; or abstain (the choice of abstention isn't all that clear—I recall learning in catechism that a wife did not have the right to refuse her husband). The fourth choice, of course, is to break with the Church and use conventional methods of birth control, a course that growing numbers of the faithful are taking. But many others, unwilling to defy the Church, find themselves miserably trapped by their adherence to dogma. Consider these remarks made by a sixty-year-old mother of nine: "Looking back to my time, the pressure young folks got to have kids was unbearable, at least in the Midwest, where my husband and I were living at the time. Besides being surrounded by Catholic relatives who would have been shocked if I didn't get pregnant at least every two years, there was the parish priest. My husband is a much more devout Catholic than I am, so if I had suggested contraception or spacing, he would have been deeply hurt. I love him to this day, and I couldn't disappoint him. The only birth control that ever worked for us was abstinence. For two people terribly in love, it was hell. After about seven or eight months of not touching each other, we'd both lose our heads and I'd always wind up pregnant.

"So the great pressure to have children came from the love of my life. He couldn't help it, the poor dear—he thought he was abiding by the Lord's teachings. Today, in the age of enlightenment, the Church's rules seem insipid—*now* we wouldn't believe such nonsense."

With a bitter laugh this woman added that when she *wasn't* pregnant as a younger woman, she and her husband avoided physical contact as much as possible "to keep me that way. But people still talked, little remarks that implied all we did was screw. It was damned if you did and damned if you didn't."

More and more, though, Catholics are deciding that they cannot reconcile the Church's present position on birth control with either scripture or the problems of parenthood. They are reading books and other publications that hold that not only is the Church's policy a man-made rule but that the Church has not always practiced what it preaches or preached the same thing.

Growing numbers of priests and laymen are adopting more rational attitudes toward family planning. Unfortunately, many Catholics become "enlightened" only after the facts have been painfully demonstrated by their many offspring.

Another mother who decided that the Church's attitude on birth control was both silly and cruel—after she'd had six children—had this to say: "After my last baby was born, I wouldn't let my husband get near me for six months. It was agony for us both, but I was terrified at the thought of another pregnancy. I did some heavy thinking, and I was lucky to have a Catholic friend to talk to. She had practiced birth control most of her married life and persuaded me that the Church's position wasn't logical—probably because I wanted to be persuaded. I still get angry that the Church nearly destroyed my relationship with my husband. What right does a bunch of old celibates have to tell young, healthy lovers that they can't have sex without babies? Sex isn't dirty. It's beautiful. And between a man and woman who really dig each other, it's as close to Heaven as I care to be for now."

This kind of healthy rebellion gains strength from the growing realization that the Church's position on birth control is curiously flexible. If a woman's menstrual cycle is out of whack, she is permitted to take oral contraceptives to straighten it out—in which case birth control becomes a convenient fringe benefit. But who determines how severely or how slightly a woman's menstrual cycle is out of schedule and requires straightening? If your cycle is one day out of line, why shouldn't you do something about it, and derive the benefits in the bargain? Temporary sterility is also sometimes correctable by the sanctioned ingestion of oral contraceptives for a period of a few months. I find this all quite interesting. You can take oral contraceptives to help you have babies, but you can't take them to keep from having babies. It's like sex education in many schools: They may teach you how to make babies, but not how *not* to make them. They teach you how to spot VD symptoms, but not how to cure it or prevent it. That's like showing someone how to start the car but not how to turn it off.

Today, Catholic and Mormon women are not the only ones who are pressured not to use birth control. Fundamentalist groups, such as the Moral Majority and other right-wing organizations, spend tons of money lobbying for things such as Senator Jesse Helms's so-called Human Life Bill, which, among other things, seeks to outlaw many common forms of birth control. To keep the cash flowing in, leaders of these religious organizations must convince their members, and the viewers of such TV evangelists, to keep producing future contributors. The bottom line as it pertains to religion and baby-making was succinctly expressed in a bumper sticker slogan I saw recently: "Forced Pregnancy Increases Church Membership."

The pressure to reproduce directed at young adults is heightened still further by that greatest of the American persuaders— the mass media. Television seems especially insistent on reinforcing the motherhood myths.

When my daughter, Lisa, was a baby, I would watch soap operas while folding mountains of diapers (in those days, one used disposables only for outings). It soon became obvious to me how these daytime dramas, through some of the most bizarre plots ever devised by humankind, attempted to convey the message that a woman's life is not fulfilled unless she bears offspring. And, of course, it was no coincidence that these shows were sponsored by makers of various baby products.

On *Love Is a Many Splendored Thing,* one of the most blatant cases of the idealization of maternity involved the story of a young woman who was in a plane crash and suffered brain damage that produced blindness. Then, as they usually do on such shows, things got worse. Her case was diagnosed as terminal. Her fiancé, nevertheless, insisted that they marry, and after her selfless protests that she would be a burden, she agreed. In a flash she became pregnant.

Fearing that the strain would foreshorten her already waning life, her husband urged an abortion. She would have none of it; she meant to leave him a son, at whatever cost. After six months of pregnancy, it was apparent her end was near. A delivery by cesarean section was the only solution, and a race ensued between the stork and the grim reaper. The stork won, happily, and we all waited for the brave young woman to breathe her noble last. But no! The birth somehow relieved the pressure on her brain (I'm not entirely clear how that worked, unless perhaps her organs were more mobile than most), and her life was spared. As an extra added miracle, the new mom regained her sight. Ain't babies grand?

In those days, any woman on daytime serials who preferred a career to children was viewed as misguided if not actively wicked. And any woman who didn't want to have children was depicted as vain, selfish, cold, more than likely emotionally disturbed, and positively headed for unhappiness and lovelessness.

I will never forget wicked Susan on *As the World Turns*. Susan preferred a career in medicine to motherhood, and her folly produced a great deal of disapproval and the warning that she was jeopardizing her marriage to Dan. It must be noted that Susan, as seemed to be the case with women who weren't interested in motherhood for its own sake, was also a liar and a conniver. Anyway, mostly because Susan was a selfish woman who didn't want to have kids, Dan started fooling around with another woman. Before long, he was getting ready to leave Susan to her medical career and set up a new nest. Susan got the picture and, without excessive remorse, seduced her own husband in an effort to become pregnant. Success was hers and Dan stayed home. Susan, too.

But times have changed, right? That wouldn't happen in the eighties, would it?

On *The Young and the Restless*, Lauren is a singer who has the chance to become a big recording star, so she has decided to postpone having children. Her mother-in-law and mother, however, are less than excited and both agree that she should start her family right away to avoid any chance of her marriage falling apart, although her marriage seems to be going quite nicely.

Lauren's mother says, "In a couple of years, you'll be at the top of your career; a child will be even more of a burden then." The ludicrous message here is that the burden of motherhood begins and ends with having a baby, that motherhood is a temporary affair.

These days, the soap operas have invaded prime time and they've brought the baby-sell with them. On the top-rated evening series *Dynasty,* Steven Carrington, who of course stands to be an heir to the family millions, receives immense pressure from his oil-baron dad to marry and prove he's a man. Marry he does, but given his admitted homosexuality, the union doesn't last long, but long enough for his wife to get pregnant with a male heir to the Carrington name and riches. What is to happen to this child now that he has served the purpose of proving Steven's manhood and perpetuating the family name? It doesn't seem to matter that he will be raised by either a single mother who obviously does not have an ounce of maternal instinct or by a single father who is much too busy building empires to have time for the kid. It's a good thing these single parents can afford nannies and nurses to watch out for their young ones. And, to judge from *Dynasty,* being a parent to a toddler or infant involves only stopping by the baby's room once a day for a hug on your way out the door to the waiting Mercedes.

Then there is Krystle Carrington, the "good woman" on the show. When she is *finally* able to get pregnant by her husband Blake, and thus prove that she is a worthy wife for him, her plans are thwarted by the evil Alexis, Blake's ex-wife, who wants him back so badly that she causes Krystle to fall off a horse and have a miscarriage. When Krystle's doctor informs her that she will never be able to have children, she is so ashamed of herself for being an incomplete woman and an inadequate wife that she becomes practically suicidal. She must have thought that Blake was just keeping her around for breeding. Just as it seems Alexis has Krystle where she wants her, alas, Krystle miraculously defies both Alexis and modern medicine by conceiving anyway and producing a new little Carrington after all, allaying her fears of being an unfulfilled woman.

The parenthood myths are still around in the comedies, too. On the very popular *Cosby Show*, Bill Cosby is Dr. Cliff Huxtable, your average, black, urban gynecologist, who has five children and a wife named Clair, who just happens to be an attorney. The mere fact that he portrays the idealistic egalitarian husband who shares in the housework and child care makes the show an unrealistic representation of American family life. Even today, a woman is more likely to win the New York State Lottery than she is to have a husband and children as willing to perform their fair share of the household drudgeries as Cosby and kids are. Cliff and Clair maintain two obviously thriving practices and still have plenty of time to devote to the myriad problems of their kids, and they make it all look like perpetual fun. Here we have the situation-comedy approach to parenthood: Smile, laugh, make a joke, and the most serious problem becomes trivial and solvable in twenty-two minutes or less. When Cosby was a guest on a recent segment of the *Donahue* show, a woman in the audience observed that, for a gynecologist, Dr. Huxtable spends an unbelievable amount of time at home. "My husband's an ob/gyn, and he's *never* home. I haven't seen him at the dinner table for years."

Most of the working mothers I know have one or two kids and a relatively undemanding career, and they're about to go berserk. How can we be expected to believe both parents can pursue very demanding professions, such as law or medicine, and still have time to raise *five* children?

And yes, the commercials still portray the average family as always cheerful, always smiling, impeccably dressed, living in a quarter-of-a-million-dollar home. A recent ad for Pentax cameras wordlessly depicts in soft focus a sunny, outdoor wedding. The bride never loses her Cheshire-cat smile for an instant because she is so delighted at being surrounded by lots and lots of happy, smiling children dressed in exquisite, spotless, wrinkle-free formal wear. (It must have taken some wardrobe mistress hours to starch all those costumes and arrange the little girls' hair ribbons so flawlessly.) When a very pregnant, smiling mother-to-be comes on the scene, everyone, especially the bride, smiles even brighter. The slogan, in essence, is that you should save all these wonderful memories on film with a Pentax camera. But in order to create a market for the product, the sponsor's implied message is that if you do not happen to be fortunate enough to have loads of wonderful memories to save, you can certainly have your fair share of them if you will only have a flock of smiling children yourself.

As always, commercials for products such as Pampers, Gerber and Heinz baby foods, and Johnson & Johnson baby products still push the picture of perfect motherhood. They feature beautiful mommies with no hardships, and babies that are always clean, smiling, clever, and talented in impeccable settings. Yes, day after day, week after week, year after year, TV continues to deliver the unmistakable message that motherhood is beautiful, easy, and fulfilling.

But no pressure can be compared to the greatest pressure of all toward parenthood—the pressure from within. The bland and unthinking assumption of most women that they must become mothers has been conditioned no doubt by thousands of years of civilization that have made the prospect of childlessness a frightening and lonely one. The intentionally childless wife defies the rules and prevailing myths of every society. Even if legislation were passed tomorrow banning the mass media from depicting motherhood as a state of grace, the long-gathered pressures to reproduce would hardly vanish and perhaps not even be significantly diminished. The lives of millions of women attest that one *can* be fulfilled without bearing children. But until their message and way of life can be presented broadly and honorably, the myth will persevere.

Rationalizations for motherhood are abundant. Babies serve to catch a man, save a marriage, prevent the first child from being lonely, and ensure against loneliness in the parents' old age. But the vast majority of mothers I have spoken with over the years had no reason for having children beyond a sense that, at some point, it was simply "the thing to do." A dozen years ago, young women felt they should have a child after a decent interval of marriage (usually two years). Today, it is looser—some women operate closer to when the "biological time clock" runs out. But the bottom line is that most still opt for motherhood and most expect that it will be as fulfilling and rewarding as advertised.

But babies are not things. They are not doodads or toys to be mindlessly acquired in the anticipation that they will enhance your life as, say, a VCR with Dolby sound might. A baby is not a lark to be undertaken because of a whim, accident, or social conditioning. And certainly not against the backdrop of the untruth about promised fulfillment—a promise that, if it goes unrealized, can lead, and has led, many a young woman to change her mind about the blessings of motherhood after it is too late.

One would think it a civilized and reasonable thing for a woman to discover *before* the fact whether she is suitable for motherhood. If she's not, the discovery ought to be a source of rejoicing rather than a condition to be overcome or a cause of shame, guilt, or sense of inadequacy.

Yet there exists little in the mass media that attempts to convey to a young woman what it means to be a mother. Only a handful of books, my own included, have offered unvarnished job descriptions. Angela Barron McBride's *The Growth and Development of Mothers,* published in 1973, was one such book, but it hardly received the attention it deserved. Another book that was absolutely hilarious and tragic was *Mother's Day* by Robert Miner (1978), about a man who was a mother. It was panned by *Psychology Today* by a male reviewer, who apparently was incapable of understanding what the author was trying to convey simply because he had never experienced the underside of parenthood that every mother knows. Child-guidance expert Eda LeShan wrote *How to Survive Parenthood* (1965), an exceptionally honest and witty book. As I understand it, the book was practically banned before it ever got off the ground. So, while attempts have been made, there is little that is readily available to convey to a young woman what it means to be a mother—little to explain the joy *and agony,* the love *and hostility,* the pride *and fear,* that are all intermingled almost every day. And yet, not to understand as much is to risk a traumatic response when the truth is revealed. What Alix Kates Shulman, author of *Memoirs of a Prom Queen,* called "the terrible weight" of motherhood "and the way it affects a woman's personality" has little to do with the drudgery, financial privation, or loss of glamour that accompanies motherhood. It cannot be described simply by referring to the unpleasantness of red hands roughened from swishing diapers in the toilet or by varicose veins or sagging breasts. What cannot be known ahead of time is the never-ending responsibility, the constant demands, and the nerve-shattering crises that characterize the role at least as much as the joys.

The very sight of my children, Lisa and Adam, from that first wonderful meeting at birth until the present, has always given me joy. The delightful things they have done and said over the years, the absurd presents they have made for me, seeing them grow, watching them discover their world—all of these things are very real. The way they loved me unconditionally when they were young was very precious. When I look at them today, I am swept away by these young adults. I am also incredibly relieved that we have thus far made it through this perilous journey together. I look at them and I see everything that is too important and fragile to be treated as casually and insipidly as our culture does through its pervasive dictum that parenthood is universally right and natural for everyone—and oceans of fun.

I would imagine that no one feels the internal pressures to have children more than the woman who is up against the biological time clock. Many happy, child-free women, even single career women who previously may not have given much thought to motherhood, begin to panic when they reach their mid-thirties. An unmarried, talented, thirty-five-year-old artist and college instructor, for example, told me,

> I'm really inspired by my art. Sometimes I really get into
> a project and pull an all-nighter. I'm at a critical point in my

career now, and all my time, outside of teaching, is taken up with preparing for my first solo gallery showing in New York soon.

But I like children. There was this five-year-old girl living next door who used to visit me for hours at a time, or even spend the night, when her mother was busy. She was a darling child, and I really enjoyed my time with her. When she moved away, it broke my heart.

As a teacher, I feel I have so much to give, so much to share with young people. And I am mature enough now and stable enough that I know I could be a much better parent than I could have, say, ten years ago. I also know that when young kids, one- to three-year-olds, are around, I go nuts. I can't take the noise and the chaos.

Yet something inside of me seems to say, "You'd better have a child now because time is running out." My boyfriend doesn't want marriage or children, and though I'm in love with him, being a single parent has certainly crossed my mind. But I already have *two* very fulfilling careers. I don't even have time to sleep as it is. How could I take on motherhood, too?

Another woman, now in her mid-thirties, beautiful, intelligent, talented, and a health-care professional, has told me that if she doesn't marry and have a child within the next five years, she sees no reason to go on living. She is surrounded by women her own age, younger, and older who are married or single and have children and who are on the brink of burnout, and who tell her she's better off, especially as she has a career. She laments to me that these friends of hers do not have time for her—they have no time to go out, to visit, to talk—but she doesn't put the fact that they have no time or energy together with the reason for it. The pressures, both external and internal, obviously, are so great that they overwhelm logic.

At the risk of stepping on some toes, I believe that having a baby only because time is running out doesn't constitute a good enough reason to bring another life into the world. Some women tell me that they make these eleventh-hour decisions because they fear if they don't have a child before it's too late, they'll regret it in their later years. Perhaps they will. But, there's a chance that they might regret having had a child, too. Of the two, I think it is far more serious to regret having had a child who is alive than to regret not having one at all. Too many people do indeed rue the day they became parents. I pity their children.

When I approached motherhood, I did so with enthusiasm and confidence. I felt that my contact with children had told me all I needed to know—that I really wanted children and that I was potentially a very good mother. What I hadn't actually learned or known would come naturally during motherhood, I thought. My exposure to kids consisted mostly of enjoying someone else's children on weekends. We started baby-sitting for our niece and nephew when we were first married, when they were three and five years old. We made a big thing out of their birthdays and Christmas, took them out on family outings, and looked after them to give their parents a breathing spell—all because we genuinely liked having the kids around.

Seeing these children was easily arranged because they lived right next door to us. They were often hanging around when one or both of us got home from work. But however much we enjoyed being with them, our commitment to them was, of course, of a different order from the kind parents have to their own youngsters. If I had to run errands when I got home and the kids were there, I'd simply tell them to come back later; if they just wanted to fool around after dinner some night, I could say, "No, you can't come this Friday because we're going out. Come Saturday instead." Their parents put in all the work, and we got the gravy. For me they were just two wonderful kids who only added to our lives. We got the part they show on television.

By the time my husband and I had been married for eight

years without the patter of little feet under our roof, the friends-relatives-media-society squeeze had done its work at last. I was able to announce to the world that we were no longer irresponsible, hedonistic, immature, abnormal, sterile, frigid, or impotent. Good old barren Shirl was very pregnant.

Everyone was overjoyed, including this unsuspecting couple. Everyone was indescribably happy that our life would not prove futile after all. We were real people. No longer would we feel left out when the talk turned to toilet-training techniques, PTA politics, and orthodontia.

At the time, it never occurred to us that we were knuckling under to social pressure. And if it had, I doubt that we would have admitted it. In retrospect, we can see now that it was all around us back then and could not fail to have had a conditioning effect upon us. We never once discussed the matter thoroughly. We never weighed the advantages against the disadvantages because it never occurred to us that we might not be cut out for parenthood—or parenthood for us.

To both of us, having kids when we were ready to have them seemed the most natural thing in the world. We put more care and thoughtful examination into the purchase of a new automobile than into the decision to bring two lives into the world.

# Chapter 3

# THE GARDEN OF EDEN

From the moment my doctor revealed the results of my pregnancy test, I was euphoric. That evening, wearing a long, flowing hostess gown, I greeted my husband, Cal, lovingly, sat us down, and, deftly opening a bottle of champagne, proposed a toast to the *three* of us. He did the expected double take and then, in a moment, he was beaming.

While we had hoped to start our family sooner (correcting my faulty thyroid function had taken longer than anticipated), we both agreed that things generally *do* work out for the best. The timing couldn't have been more perfect: We had finished fixing up our little house, we had enough money, and after eight good years together, our marriage was a solid one. Not only would we bring a wanted child into a secure home, but into one where children were truly cherished. We had a marvelous time surprising everybody with our good news. To our friends in Seattle we said, "Gee, we're sorry we can't come up for a visit this summer, but we've really got to tighten the old belt, settle down, and plan for the future." Then we zonked them with it.

When we were asked whether we wanted a boy or a girl, we gave the answer most happy expectant parents give: "We don't care. We just want a healthy baby."

After things settled down, I set about making su
born child would have the very best. I vowed I would
thing *right* during my pregnancy—it would be to the letter. I
picked up a copy of Adelle Davis's *Let's Have Healthy Children,*
just to make sure my diet would be absolutely right, and religously
followed my doctor's advice to drink one quart of milk each day,
eat one serving of meat, and keep the calories down to 1,000 a
day.

I enrolled in a natural childbirth class, as my obstetrician
suggested, and dutifully attended every Wednesday night. The
first evening, our instructor, a registered nurse and mother of
three children, gave us a list of books and pamphlets, recom-
mending that we pick them up to understand better what was
going on. A perfect instructor, she was young, agile, enthusiastic
about both natural childbirth and breast feeding. She had had all
three of her own children by natural childbirth.

We were told that natural childbirth in a normal pregnancy
was fairly easy, provided we did our exercises and learned to relax.
Relaxation was the key to success.

We were also told that the value of natural childbirth was
that it minimized the use of anesthetics or instruments, either of
which could be harmful to the baby. It was possible to have a virtually painless birth without any anesthetic whatsoever. Our instructor pointed out that the only real cause for pain was the
episiotomy—the incision that might have to be made to prevent
tearing of tissue at the moment of birth. Usually all that was required for that was a shot of novocaine.

The class sat wide-eyed as our instructor told us that she had
gotten up off the delivery table after the birth of each of her children and *walked* back to her room.

With the benefits to the baby of natural childbirth and the
obvious ease of that natural function, I would, of course, "go
Read" (a term that was derived from Grantly Dick-Read's break-
through book, *Childbirth Without Fear*—some women "go Lamaze" or "Bradley" or whoever is the current high guru of

natural birth). I diligently practiced my exercises, learned to pant to maximize relaxation, continued with my good nutrition, and just looked forward happily to the big event.

Some of my classmates were less enthusiastic about their pregnancies. Some suffered from morning sickness (I never had a twinge). Some of my pregnant friends would actually go on starvation diets the week before they went to see their doctors just to avoid the disapproval. "Tsk, tsk, they were only fooling themselves," said I, having no trouble with *my* weight.

One of my classmates who was depressed over her "planned pregnancy" confessed that she would eat to excess and then get depressed over her weight gain. One of my friends quit her job early in her pregnancy and spent seven months telling everyone how bored she was. Another friend had morning sickness for four months, overate at the drop of a hat, and confessed to me that she wasn't at all sure she should have gotten pregnant so soon in her marriage.

My only concern rested with preparing to be a real supermother to my baby, and so while some of my less fortunate pregnant friends seemed disturbed about being pregnant, I busied myself with learning all I could about delivery and child care.

Our classes had been under way for about four weeks when a La Leche League representative came around to give a lecture. The purposes and goals of La Leche, a national organization with chapters in many cities, are to educate expectant mothers about the benefits and techniques of breast-feeding their babies, to help new mothers who are experiencing difficulties in nursing, and to supply mother's milk in emergency situations. Their numerous spokeswomen educate the public, and a large volunteer work force of experienced nursing mothers stands ready to go out and help new mothers having breast-feeding problems—a new mother has only to call her local chapter, and a member comes around to help. The La Leche representative that lectured that evening told the class that mother's milk is much more nutritious than formula and that it even provides a baby with immunities against infection. She described breast feeding, reiterating the words of Niles Newton, author of *The Family Book of Child Care* (1957). "Successful breast feeding is so easy! It is simply a matter of holding a hungry baby to the breast and relaxing and letting him suck. Nature does the rest. The more milk the baby takes out of the breast, the more milk the body puts back into the breast," she pointed out, and she assured the class that "anyone who truly *wants* to nurse her baby can do so—it is, after all, the *natural* way to do things."

Then she described her own experiences. Her baby had been delivered naturally and the birth had been totally painless. Her husband had accompanied her to the delivery room and he was a full participant in the birth—a revolutionary idea at the time. She said it had been the most beautiful experience of her life. Then she told us of the joy of caring for her baby in her hospital room instead of leaving him in the nursery. This, too, was rather unusual at the time since few hospitals allowed either fathers in the delivery room or rooming in; today, however, both practices are so common that they have now become "must dos" for new parents.

The lecture reinforced my decision to breast-feed my child. There had never been any real doubt, because I wanted to do everything right. And now I had even more proof that breast feeding was natural, easy, good for a new mother, and *so* good for the baby.

When my obstetrician asked me if I would be nursing the baby, I responded enthusiastically and affirmatively. He wagged a very long index finger in my face and said, "Okay, but plan to bottle-feed, too. Otherwise you won't be able to get away from the baby for any length of time."

"But, Doctor, why would I want to leave my own baby for more than four hours?"

During the last two months of what was a fine and easy pregnancy, I got even more serious about the impending arrival. My husband was delighted. He often referred to my "nesting instinct." With joy and love and beautiful new baby furniture, I put the nursery together. But it didn't stop at the baby's room. I tore our house apart, gave it a thorough cleaning, repainted the interior, rearranged the furniture, shampooed the carpet, stripped and waxed the floors, washed and ironed the curtains, and packed my suitcase. I reorganized kitchen cabinets for the baby things, and cleaned out my sewing cupboard to use it for the higher purpose of storing baby clothes.

I continued to read my books, do my exercises, go to classes, and practice going with the contractions of labor pains, and panting. About a month before the baby was due, I went on a tour of the hospital so I'd know where everything was and, more important, where my husband was to take me when the time came. During the tour, along with about thirty other pregnant women, I saw more films concerning the miracle of birth and child care and received a free gift packet of all sorts of things, including formula that this new mother would never need.

At shortly after 10 P.M. on February 17, 1965, the contractions started coming at regular intervals, and I was pretty certain that I'd be a mother before morning. After talking to my doctor and being assured that I wouldn't somehow magically deliver the baby while sleeping (so relaxed and prepared was I), I went to bed.

At 3:15 A.M. on February 18, I nudged my husband and told him to wake up, get himself together, and take me to the hospital.

Once we got settled in the labor room, the contractions started coming furiously, and they were HARD. I hadn't expected such intense pain, and I kept trying to go with it, employing the breathing technique I had learned in the class and faithfully practiced. My husband had never seen me in any pain, and he was obviously disturbed.

It isn't unusual for a first-timer to have intense pain, but to someone standing on the sidelines it can look scary, particularly if that someone has been assured by his wife that all her preparation was going to make matters move along simply and painlessly. While my husband looked forward to the baby, there was no way that he would have traded his wife of eight years for an infant he didn't know yet. The labor-room scene put that kind of question to him. It also introduced something else.

I forgot all about him. When my doctor came in to assess the situation, he took one look and ordered a sedative for me. While I was going down for the count, I asked him if I'd be able to do everything naturally. I was concerned only about the delivery of my child. I was asleep before I caught his answer.

The sedative had an interesting effect. I would sleep soundly between contractions, waking up only while the pain lasted, and then immediately drop off. My first failure at being the Perfect New Mother came when I welcomed the anesthetic. I wasn't going to "go Read" after all. While suffering body-racking contractions and genuinely wanting relief, I felt disappointed and ashamed that I didn't have the stuff to do it naturally. (The instructor in my class had said, "Anyone who really *wants* to *can.*")

I thought of the other women in my class and wondered jealously how many of them were going to be able to do easily what I couldn't. And I remembered the woman who came to class after having a baby a few days before: She described the birth as one so easy "they almost didn't get me to the hospital on time." Then, after feeling maternal inadequacy for the first time and setting aside my concern for my wounded vanity, I had my first taste of maternal fear and guilt. I started worrying about what effect the anesthetic or instruments would have on the baby, and if forceps could be harmful if required to help my "unnatural" delivery. My baby wasn't even here and I'd let him down already.

Shortly after the production started, it was over. At 9:15 A.M., I was the mother of the most beautiful baby girl I'd ever seen. My fears and guilt over not having natural childbirth were forgotten when I first saw Lisa. I thought I'd explode with joy as I looked at her. Petal pink, lots of black hair and lovely eyelashes, and oh, so tiny and perfect. Later that day, hand in hand, my husband and I walked to the nursery and stood transfixed, looking at our lovely baby through the glass.

We were enchanted. I thought for a moment about a close friend who had confessed that she didn't feel anything for her new baby. How terribly sad. Her pregnancy had been as easy as mine. She was working when she got pregnant, kept working until a month before the baby was due, glowed all through it. When I visited her, the baby was about two months old. She said she was desperately tired, couldn't stand the work of taking care of a baby, and saw the baby only as something that was turning her into a miserable machine. My friend had said that she felt unnatural—why hadn't she felt a rush of love for the baby when she first saw her, and why hadn't she felt it yet? She was ashamed to admit her feelings even to her husband.

During our hospital stay, I lived from one feeding time to the next and for the two visiting periods when I would get to see Cal. He was growing increasingly eager for us to leave the hospital. Me, too. It was time for us to start being a real family.

It was wonderful to be home. Lisa went to sleep nicely and we enjoyed a quiet dinner, alone together for the first time in nearly a week. After dinner, I reviewed some material on breast feeding and infant care until it was time for another feeding. Things went beautifully, and I noted with pride that I had lots of milk. Taking care of Lisa was going to be a snap. When one of the doctors saw my baby for the first time, he said, "Boy, are you going to have fun. Taking care of her is going to be just like playing dolls."

By the time the 10 P.M. feeding rolled around, both mother and baby were so relaxed that, moments afterward, both were sound asleep.

The next day, Cal went to work, and Lisa and I were on our own. I was a little anxious about taking care of her without any help, but I was feeling marvelous and, after all, mothering *was* natural and as old as the human race.

When Cal got home, he was great. He spent most of that second evening at home holding Lisa and giving me encouragement. It had been a good and easy day, but it was nice to have company and moral support.

After she had her six o'clock feeding, we just enjoyed having Lisa with us for a time, and then we reluctantly agreed we should put her to bed. We might as well have simply moved the cradle into the living room because it seemed as if one of us were checking on her constantly. It started out by our going in to take an extra little look at her; as the evening progressed, we realized that we were actually monitoring her.

On one occasion Cal caught me in the act. I was gently pinching Lisa's foot. My explanation, "I just wanted to make sure she was still breathing. She was awfully still," was met with stern disapproval. I caught him doing the same thing the next night.

We agreed that this sort of hovering was going to make the baby nervous and reassured each other that she would be just fine. In fact, as Cal said, she would probably be greatly relieved that we quit pestering her.

Two weeks after her birth, our precious little girl started losing weight, and I panicked. I called the pediatrician. By the time we got there, Lisa was weak and rapidly becoming ill. The doctor weighed her and gave her a thorough examination, and then asked me if I was still breast-feeding. After I said yes, he said, "She's starving," and instructed me to back up each feeding with formula. He told me my milk had apparently dried up and suggested that if I gave her formula and continued putting her to my breast, my milk might come in again.

In a matter of days Lisa was thriving, and I was nearly back to my normal happy state. But before that, I was scared, disgusted, and ashamed. I had put my child through this misery to prove a point, to satisfy my own vanity; in an effort to be the Most Perfect Mother, I'd nearly starved our baby. I felt so very inadequate. I had let my child down by not being able to give her the benefits of mother's milk. And I had compounded the failure—no, crime—by being too dumb and too vain to realize what was really going on.

One day after I'd acknowledged that I was a dismal failure on more than one count, a woman from La Leche League—a celebrity of sorts, I guessed—appeared on a daytime television talk show. As I bottle-fed my baby, she spoke right to me: "Breast feeding is so easy, fulfilling, good for the baby, and good for

Mother, too! When my baby gains weight, I know that *I did that,* I'm responsible for the fact that he is thriving. That's my own accomplishment. I did it all by myself. Any woman who loves her child can do the same."

It was some time after the fact, when the disappointment and feelings of guilt had dissipated, that I pondered the pervasive attitude that says that any woman can do everything naturally if she *really* wants to. This illogically leads to the conclusion that when a new mother can't earn her marks, either in the delivery room popping out the baby or with successful suckling, it's because she loves her child less than her friends who can. It makes no sense to me to measure a mother's love for her child in such terms. One of the worst mothers I have ever known successfully breast-fed all seven of her children. She was so bad that she put her eldest child, when he was just fifteen, out on the street.

If breast feeding is so easy to bring off, then why is there a need for a whole organization with chapters virtually everywhere to help women accomplish through instruction and encouragement what is "so natural and so easy"? If it's that easy, why does Dr. Spock devote nine pages to breast-feeding problems? How does Niles Newton's description of the ease and simplicity of this natural function reconcile with eleven pages describing the many difficulties that can surface? Why are there now entire books (*The Breast Is Best* by Penny and Andrew Stanway, *Parents' Complete Book of Breastfeeding* by Susan Trien, and *Breastfeeding Success for Working Mothers* by Marilyn Grams, for example) devoted to this "easy" process? Breast feeding may well be very easy for some mothers—maybe most. But that fact should not be used as a club to coerce new mothers into feeling that they must adopt the method or brand those who don't or can't as dismal failures. It's not a great failure, but in its sometimes cultist context, it can be one of the early, unnecessary ones that can start the ball rolling for the inadequacy trip that each new day of motherhood can compound.

Some mothers who have nursed quite successfully never

really wanted to. One such mother said to me, "Of course I breast-fed my child. I had to—all my friends did, and I couldn't be a misfit, could I?" Still another admitted, "I hated it—I was trapped by the baby. Being successful at it doesn't mean you'll like it." And a woman who disdained the fad fanfare said, "Personally, it didn't make much difference to me. I did it for the baby."

Summing up the pressure some of us older mothers had on us to do everything naturally, one woman told me, "Thank God, I had to have a cesarean. It gave me a marvelous excuse for not having natural childbirth, which I didn't want that much in the first place. Having the decision taken out of my hands made me feel less guilty about not doing it for the baby, and I could hold up my head in front of my pro-natural-childbirth friends."

That was in 1965. In the eighties, however, the religion of natural childbirth has reached such proportions in some quarters that my friend might well have trouble avoiding judgment for flunking. In a fascinating article in *Parents* magazine, September 1979, author Tim Paulson, who was eager to share in the birth of his child, explains his feelings when things didn't go as he and his wife were led to believe they should: "I had a hard time at first believing that progress wasn't simply a question of mind over matter. It seemed that Jane ought to be able to force the baby out if she strained hard enough. I found myself whispering encouragement, as if I were cheering on a marathon runner who was only halfway through a race." He then explains that, despite all of his cheering and despite his wife's reluctance to accept sedation or other medication, not only was there not going to be a "natural" birth, but if mother and child were to make it, there would be a cesarean section. Happily, mother and child—a beautiful baby boy—made it. Paulson continues:

> Many expectant mothers today are victims of what Jane and I came to call "feminine machismo." They are going to deliver their babies without pain, without drugs. They are going to be stronger and more fearless than their mothers

were. They are going to enhance the quality of the birth experience.

"I don't know what these disciples of natural childbirth are trying to prove," my mother told us during her first visit to see her grandson. After two short labors and easy deliveries . . . my mother's last two pregnancies had ended with cesarean deliveries. . . . I realized that I had never once heard her complain about having had the cesarean. There had simply been "complications." A cesarean section was just another way to have a baby. My mother was impatient with our sense of disappointment. . . . We should be thankful we live in an age when mothers and babies don't have to die in childbirth. . . .

Our mothers were right in emphasizing the product rather than the process of delivery. But knowing intellectually that we were lucky to have a healthy baby has not prevented occasional relapses into disappointment.

How sad. A perfect diamond is a precious jewel whether it is delivered in a Rolls-Royce or by a messenger on a bicycle. But then, even without having had a cesarean section, I know from whence the Paulsons speak. For at least a dozen years after Lisa was born, whenever the subject of her birth came up, I automatically felt one stab of disappointment and another of guilt. I stopped feeling that stab when a friend who had a very easy delivery with both of her children told me, "The one thing the instructors of natural childbirth classes fail to teach expectant parents is that whether you have a natural birth, forceps delivery, or a C-section is often a matter of luck. There is too much emphasis on the idea that if you do everything right, you'll deliver naturally, so obviously, when you don't deliver naturally, you've done something wrong. I think people ought to be taught to hope for the best, but to accept whatever comes."

Lisa was a wonderful baby, and the three of us got along beautifully. I'd weathered the breast-feeding storm, and then an interesting thing happened. I ran out of powdered formula, but I had some liquid formula that I'd brought home from the hospital. Everything went swimmingly, but the baby's bowel patterns changed radically. I couldn't imagine why. Babies have lots of bowel movements every day, so I didn't notice an unusual increase until after about three days, when it started getting worse. Then she developed a diaper rash. This, of course, made her very fussy, and made me feel that I was doing something wrong—maybe the laundry, or maybe I wasn't changing her often enough or using the right powders and lotions. As the diaper rash got worse, she became fussier, and I became more upset and guilty about whatever it was I was doing, and we seemed to be caught in another downhill cycle. I called the pediatrician and reported the changes in her bowel patterns, and he seem unperturbed. Then I called and discussed the diaper rash, and he made a few suggestions. I tried them all.

Monday we dashed over to the doctor. "Lisa has diarrhea. That's why she's dehydrated and has a diaper rash" was the pediatrician's proclamation. Then he asked if I'd introduced any new foods or juices in the baby's diet, or if any changes had taken place. I assured him that I had followed all of his instructions to the letter. Finally, bewildered, he wrote out a prescription for something that would stop the diarrhea and said, "She's not really sick. Not yet, anyway, but diarrhea can be debilitating. Already she's lost a little weight, and we can't have that."

Lisa was marvelous through it all. Sure she was fussy, but she was still cheerful and sweet, and surprisingly, she slept through the night.

The next morning when I got her up for a diaper change and her "breakfast," she was still having the same problem. For the next few days, the diarrhea lessened, but it didn't clear up. I called the pediatrician; he was genuinely puzzled, and we agreed that I should bring her in again.

That evening while I was fixing dinner, I started rearranging the cupboard where I kept the baby things—I suppose in an effort to keep as busy as possible and thereby subdue my fears about

Lisa. I was putting away the new cans of powdered formula I had picked up that day and was considering our dilemma when suddenly a light went on. There was something wrong with the formula I had been using. I had switched from powder to liquid, using the same brand. That was the change in her diet. It wasn't even a real change because it was supposed to be the same stuff in a more convenient form.

Lisa dear, for the first time in your young life your incompetent mother did something right. She dumped all the liquid down the drain, made a whole new batch of powdered formula, told a dismayed pediatrician that she was a lucky genius, and progressively started compensating for a month of hell.

In three days, Lisa started looking like a real baby again, a little thin, but healthier. Her diarrhea and diaper rash were over, for the most part, and our trip to paradise was rescheduled. As I came up from a month of feeling greater terror than I had ever felt in my life, a level of inadequacy and guilt never before imagined, I pondered a question: Is original sin meant to be regarded as innate in man as a direct result of Adam's sin? Or is it really the shame felt by a new mother when she commits her first innocent sin against her new child?

# Chapter 4

# THE JOYS OF PARENTHOOD

"Good God, Shirl, are you sure? What will people *think?* Lisa isn't even five months old, and pretty soon you'll be busting out all over . . ."

I wasn't only sure, I was delighted. Once I had gotten over the rough spots of taking care of Lisa—the fear and guilt of our bad beginnings nearly forgotten—I'd thoroughly enjoyed her. Our little girl had become such a delight that I was certain that another baby would only add to our happiness. I assured my self-conscious husband that people would only think good thoughts, and hardly think we were sex maniacs. "After all, Cal, people *do* get together after they have a baby. No one's going to think we've been behaving like impetuous teenagers. Everyone's going to think it's great."

And they did. Everyone expressed joy that we would have another baby soon. Many of our friends told us how relieved they were that we were not going to burden Lisa with being an only child. And there was much talk of the good genes that couldn't help but produce another lovely child.

Caring for Lisa and the house had become such a simple routine that I felt certain another baby wouldn't complicate matters. If things continued as beautifully with Lisa, and I brought the experience of her early babyhood to a second child, having two kids would be just as easy as having one.

In many ways I was quite correct. The months with Lisa before our next child was born were a breeze; she was almost never ill, she wasn't fussy, and she was loads of fun. She was a beautiful, healthy baby. She had a sense of humor, and she was busy discovering her world; just looking at her or being with her provided reason to have another baby. She became more delightful each day and easier to care for. And every day we loved her more. She learned to crawl and started to investigate every corner of the house, but her mom was way ahead of her. I totally child-proofed our house.

Like my first pregnancy, my second was perfect: no morning sickness, no aches and pains, no incredible weight gain. I didn't attend classes this time around because I'd done that and I knew pretty much what to expect. Instead, I went out and looked for a larger house. I found one that was ideal for a growing young family. There were three large bedrooms, two modern baths, and an enormous all-electric kitchen with room for everything, including playpens. We left our tiny palace with reluctance—it was our first home, however small and inconvenient; we had put it together ourselves and we had shared many happy, loving hours there.

My second baby was due on Valentine's Day. The day before, my father searched the San Francisco peninsula to find just the right gift for me, and then he proudly delivered it. He found a *blue* Valentine heart, and he gave it to me with these words: "This is to hope that you'll even it out and have a boy. It's nice to have one of each."

Hey, Dr. Lamaze. Hi, Dr. Read. Guess what I just did? I just had a natural delivery. Know why? Because I had stretched my undersized birth canal just a year before. That's why.

One hour after we had arrived at the hospital, Cal and I were having breakfast together in my room and calling friends and family. My parents were flabbergasted when I got on the line and said, "We just had a son a few minutes ago—his name is Adam."

Adam was born on Monday, February 14—right on schedule—and on Wednesday morning we were being tossed out of the hospital because we both seemed hale and hardy and they needed my bed.

When we got home, I prepared dinner in advance, got Adam settled, made formula (no way was I going to put this kid through what Lisa suffered), breast-fed him for a while, backed it up with a bottle, and then called my sister, who had kindly kept Lisa while I was in the hospital. When she indicated that they would happily keep her for a few days, I said, "No, I've missed my little girl, and I want her home."

I could tell right away that Adam was going to be very different from Lisa in many ways. A mother conjures up images of what her baby will look like, and I had based the image of my second baby on what Lisa looked like at birth. But instead, Adam was a very blond baby, and beautifully so. To this day he remains a genuine platinum blond. His skin is very fair, and he has enormous deep-blue eyes. He has always been adorable, but in a way much different from Lisa. They've both always been beautiful and healthy. But they look—and are—so fascinatingly different.

When we brought Adam home and greeted our baby daughter, we were prepared for still another pleasant and uneventful year, particularly since I wasn't about to make the same mistakes with this baby as I had with our first—I had learned too much the hard way.

The birth of our daughter just a year before had introduced me to the genuine joy of motherhood, but it also had introduced me to the sting of failure that hurts so much when you really want to do everything as well as the rest of the gang—just as well, that is, as they tell you they did. But more important, a new mother wants to do everything right for the baby.

Adam was about to introduce me to another dimension of parental joy, but before he could do so, his sister put my stomach in my shoes.

On the day we brought Adam home from the hospital, our one-year-old baby girl dived head first off her changing table, with Mom standing right there. I had been restraining her with one hand and reaching for a diaper with the other when I felt her slip. Suddenly she was on the floor and she wasn't crying, a fact I didn't notice right off because little Adam was loudly exercising his lungs. I scooped up Lisa, who started to cry as I leafed through my Dr. Spock to check for symptoms of concussion. It's amazing how many different thoughts the human mind is capable of handling simultaneously. While looking for the appropriate section in the book, I was yelling to my husband to call the pediatrician, rocking Lisa, and feeling a rush of terrible guilt that she had slipped from my grasp. And fear! My God, was I scared!

The pediatrician assured us that Lisa would be just fine. "These things happen all the time," he said. How comforting to know that I could look forward to a whole string of things like that.

As soon as we had recovered from our near hysteria over Lisa, we noticed that Adam was breathing funny. We listened as he rasped away, wondering what in the world could be wrong. Then a strange thing happened: He choked and then vomited up some mucus. I didn't know what to make of it, so naturally I called the pediatrician. He assured us it was nothing, that normally this mucus is expelled while the baby is still in the hospital but that not infrequently it took a little longer. What a relief! Now he would breathe normally.

But he didn't. Not then, and not six months from then. We found ourselves behaving with him much as we had with Lisa, when we used to hover over her while she was sleeping. On the other hand, if he didn't make that strange noise, we thought he had drawn his last breath. For months I feared that one morning I would wake up and find a dead baby in the cradle. The first night Adam slept clear through, instead of waking up refreshed from an uninterrupted sleep, I jumped out of bed in a panic to see if he were still alive.

I found his breathing not only unnerving, but a source of almost constant anxiety, an undercurrent that was always there. Always. That edge of fear that his respiratory system would fail.

As had happened with Lisa, each day Adam was with us, our love for him deepened, and he brought his own sparkle to the family. As my love for him grew, so did my concern and my realization that now that he was here, life would be unbearable without him.

Adam's next contribution to my education (in things not mentioned by those who say how much fun parenthood is) was noise. Unlike Lisa, who cried for a reason, he just cried.

He cried, and I worried. He cried loudly, urgently, and most of the time. If he cried because he was hungry, he would just continue while he was eating, after he was finished, and after he was burped.

I thought there must be something wrong with him. Maybe it had something to do with his strange breathing. But the doctor could not find anything wrong, not even colic. So I worried. And Adam cried.

It is not just that it is difficult to hear above all the racket; it is difficult to think even simple thoughts. With Adam's constant crying, I found it difficult to do anything more complicated than heat his bottle; closing a pin on a diaper became a major technical feat. On one occasion he cried incessantly because he had a diaper rash—I accepted his noise as my punishment for maternal incompetence, until my sympathy (very real in the beginning) deteriorated into anger.

Occasionally when it got bad, I would put Adam in his crib and go sit outside. The trade-off was a few moments of peace and quiet for the guilty feeling that I was being indifferent to my baby's troubles.

One of the most dubious joys of parenthood is learning that you are capable of feeling annoyed by a tiny baby. Sometimes I would hear myself saying, "You're not being *fair*. Here I am trying to take care of you, do your laundry, and make a nice home for you, and this is how I'm treated," to two kids whose vocabularies consisted of "gurgle" and "da," respectively.

Trailing closely behind petty feelings like that was the constant fear that perhaps somewhere along the line I *was* doing something wrong but just couldn't figure out what it might be.

During one of Adam's stormy sessions, I had what I'll loosely term a telephone conversation with another mother. Adam was screaming at the top of his lungs when she called. Her voice was being drowned out by the strains of another baby at her end of the line. "How's it going?" I asked. She told me.

"After listening to ten solid hours of an infant crying, my nerves are shot, and if I didn't have the responsibility of taking care of this baby, I swear I'd get drunk." What little voice she had left broke while she talked. She had consulted their pediatrician, who assured her there was nothing wrong with the child. Just a little indigestion. "Don't worry, Mrs. Smith, the baby is just fine."

Comforting words like that go a long way toward relieving a mother's concern for her child; they say nothing of how to alleviate the suffering of a mother who is slowly being driven out of her mind.

"You know," my friend continued, "when it first starts I really feel sorry for Cindy because I know she hurts. But after it goes on interminably, I just get nervous and tired and sometimes I don't even like her. And then I feel horrible about feeling that way." To my suggestion that she ask her mother to help out she said, "That's not really fair—she's more than willing, but why should I put it on her?"

Monday morning quarterbacking helps neither a fussy baby nor a mother in absolute agony, nerves taut, bathed in guilt. Someone is always hanging around in the wings with advice like "The baby cries a lot because she doesn't get enough love" or "If you'd breast-feed the baby, she wouldn't get indigestion." If breast feeding satisfies the breast-feeding advocate, someone else is sure to suggest that the breast feeding is probably the *cause* of the baby's problem.

I recall that when one friend's baby had colic, absolutely everyone had an opinion about the cause. The opinions boiled down to one: Good mothers don't have bad babies. That was a great help as she sat at the kitchen table, her head in her arms, sobbing her heart out, while her child continued to wail. This perfectly healthy young woman with a fine strong baby ultimately became so exhausted and overwrought that she started hemorrhaging.

One woman could readily afford to deposit her baby with a sitter or hire a nurse to come in. She said there were times when she detested the "thing" generating all that noise. Yet she didn't have the heart to leave him with a nurse while he was feeling so terrible.

To know your child is in pain is agony. To know you can't do a damn thing about it makes it worse; it isn't possible to get your mind off the problem while your nerve endings are being ravaged by the sound of loud wails. As sociologist Jessie Bernard notes in *The Future of Motherhood,* 1974: "Industrial engineers have long since learned the hazards of fatigue in the factory or plant; they are now alerted to the health hazards of noise 'pollution.' If the biological stresses to which the mother-child relationship exposes women could be measured in the laboratory, monitored and recorded, they would be shown as enormous. A crying infant, as any sleep-starved young mother can testify, can be devastating as can the noisy play of children of any age."

It is quite possible for the tenderest and most loving mother to feel absolute hatred for a child who has been making that terrible noise for hours on end. She can hardly be rational after listening to that, knowing she can neither leave it nor turn it off. The most intelligent of mothers finds it confusing to hate someone they love who is in pain. They feel guilty and unnatural when they do. But it is not an unusual way to feel.


As the children grow, the strains of caring for young babies are gradually replaced by other trivia and different crises. The constantly crying baby turns into a toddler who cries only a "normal" amount from bumps on the head, cut knees, and being said "no" to. But the "noisy play" that Dr. Bernard speaks of may cancel out any gain. Less frequent diaper changes simply mean that a mother has a little extra time to clean up messes, sweep up piles of glass that once may have been lovely vases, and follow her child around ensuring that he doesn't destroy himself in the process of destroying the house.

The first order of business when a mother notices that her infant is becoming a crawler, and will soon be a toddler, is to child-proof the house. That proved to be my forte. All sharp objects, breakable items, potential poisons, and table lighters were put away. The electric range had all of the controls at the back—out of the reach of children. Pens, pencils, and sewing gear were tucked so far away that even I had trouble getting to them.

Not only was I efficient and diligent in making our home a safe one for children, but I was efficient about my household routine, structuring it around my children's naps. I was extremely well organized, and I found that the drudgery associated with caring for young children was really not as bad as I had anticipated.

The one thing few people realize is that when there are no children in the picture, depending on the neatness of the adults, housework generally takes a finite amount of time. With a baby, that amount of time will expand depending on the needs of the baby. When you have a baby, if he or she naps a lot, you usually can still get most of your chores done in a reasonable length of time. If, however, you have a sick, fussy, or demanding baby, you may be lucky to get the bed made and a few loads of laundry tossed in before it's time to start thinking about dinner.

And once the babies turn into children, the routine gets considerably more complicated as the little ones spend less time sleeping and more time getting into mischief, until doing the housework, laundry, writing checks to pay bills, and preparing meals can seem formidable tasks.

When Lisa and Adam were young, I recall that my day started on a positive note, with the delightful sight of Adam, hair as white as the pages of this book, amazingly beautiful devilish blue eyes, and a funny grin missing two teeth. Beside this vision was still another vision, Lisa who was (and is) beautiful, adorable, and fascinating.

From this delightful beginning, it was inconceivable that the average day would ultimately give way to hostility, resentment, and absolute fury. But the schizophrenic facts I had to adjust to when I was a young mommy were that, although I adored my children and could be totally pleased by just the sight of them in the morning, by 6 P.M. that same day, I could feel like heaving them through a plate-glass window.

The first discordant note began with our difference of opinion about bathroom togetherness. I didn't like it. My husband couldn't tolerate it. The kids insisted on it. My firmness in the matter was generally rewarded with semiprivacy, and while I was inside, they would bang on the door, whine, talk, scuffle with each other, and ask questions while the water was running. Gathering up all of my Dr. Spock–inspired parental sense, I would try to reason with them, and, after a few minutes, I would realize that, although my normal speaking voice had risen several decibels, my volume wasn't sufficient to beat out the competition.

With the bathroom ordeal out of the way, I would trudge to the kitchen to see about breakfast. While I was putting together the breakfast, the kids would take apart the kitchen. While my hands and eyes were occupied with the dangerous practice of cooking around children, the children would occupy themselves with crawling on the drainboard, getting into the cookie jar, running the water, and "helping" me as much as possible ("But, Mommy, I want to help"). As soon as I could safely extricate myself from the cooking process, I would again draw on the wisdom of Dr. Spock and coax them off the drainboard and encourage them to enjoy breakfast.

After the routine argument about who was to sit where, their father would make his appearance, survey the mess and chaos, and grunt his irritation.

Once the kids started to eat, they were very serious and very quiet. It was always toward the end of any meal that things would get into full swing—gargling with their milk, chewing vigorously with mouths open wide (or, as they would say to each other, "showing your food"), laughing, pounding, shouting, pushing and shoving, or whatever else could be contrived to annoy, while we would try to point out that such behavior was rude and unacceptable. No one heard. The theme had many variations.

The gargling, chewing, etc., would continue and Adam would choke. This was very frightening, but he'd been doing it for at least five years. I would pick him up, turn him upside down, and he would work it out (so to speak). The rest was easy—Mom cleaned up the mess. Or, the gargling and other nonsense would continue, Lisa would color her doily and chatter, and Adam would simply vomit on the breakfast table. Or, Dad would reinforce Spock with a yardstick. Or, Mom would reinforce Spock with a yardstick.

Then we would get dressed. The ritual invariably consisted of Lisa crying that her favorite dress of the week was in the hamper. Somehow, we always managed to find an adequate substitute, and she would acquiesce through tears. While this was going on, Adam would put his shirt on backward, and because he put his shoes on first, the next hurdle required getting his jeans over his shoes.

After the kids were set for the day, I would do the dishes, make the beds, and load the washer. Then, after I managed to throw some clothes on, I would tackle the household chores. Interspersed with scrubbing floors, making beds, or whatever, were demands that would range from getting a glass of water to rushing a bleeding child to the doctor. It could start simply: I would hear the water running. It was in the bathroom. No, the garage. Then there was the sudden realization that it was in both places and I could only manage one at a time. They used to have me at either end of the house. Or, I would hear crying. Adam? No, Lisa. No, both. Are they hurt? Who is hurt worse? Who needs the most immediate attention? Sometimes there would be a chorus of other kids going all at once. And this seems to be a good place to note that the mother of two children very often supervises four, five, or six kids all at once—they're called playmates.

Or, I might be retrieving my purse from the toilet, wondering which of the little darlings put it there, and get a funny, sinking feeling. It felt less funny when I took the laundry out of the dryer and discovered that my best permanent-press clothes were dried with my new lipstick, tossed in by innocent hands.

I would be comforting a hurt child, putting a Band-Aid on a knee, or inspecting a bumped head when I would hear a crash in another part of the house, and once again be pulled apart by the simultaneous needs of my children. One would be high in a tree, the other climbing on the roof. And so it went.

All the while, through the drudgery and the continuous, simultaneous, child-generated chaos, there were the never-ending requests for water, food, cookies, Scotch tape, paper, and anything else they thought they wanted. Naturally, there were the inevitable battles between siblings close in age, often triggered by something monumental: "He touched me"; "She took my bubble gum." I'll never forget taking Lisa in for emergency treatment after Adam hit her over the head with a coffee can.

Sometime in the course of the average day, lunch time would be signaled by the appearance of Adam and Lisa with three friends. The friends had been invited for lunch, which meant that we would have to have a private chat—one delivered at least 500 times—about inviting friends to lunch without asking Mom and about compounding the error by asking in front of said friends. Denial of these guests inevitably resulted in tears and shouts of "You don't love us."

After lunch, we would return to more of the same, punctuated with interruptions by students selling magazine subscriptions, more playmates at the door, Scouts selling candy, Fuller Brush men, Avon ladies, and phone calls telling me that we had just won a full-color photo of the kiddies for only six dollars and asking when we will be coming to the studio.

This brings us up to about dinnertime.

The National Safety Council tells us that the majority of home accidents take place in the early evening while mothers are preparing dinner. If I failed to get a head start earlier in the day, cooking became a major feat. The children were hungry, curious, talkative, and constantly underfoot. And, like moms the world over, I am sure, I was pretty tired at that point. *This had to be the worst part of the day.*

Dinner would usually be some variation of breakfast and lunch. This was when I heard that I was a terrible cook, the food I served was just "icky," and that Jeffie's mom served "real good hamburgers" every night.

After dinner there would be some television, followed by an argument over taking baths. After that was settled, the kids would have their baths, sloshing water on the floor, the ceiling, and Mom, all followed by reluctance to get out of the tub because they were enjoying themselves.

Finally, we would get them dried and combed, all teeth brushed, and coaxed into their pajamas, and then we would go through the debate about going to bed. That settled, they were kissed and tucked into bed to go to sleep so quickly one wonders why—as with the bath—they argued about it. *This had to be the best part of the day.*

The day with the children always ended as it began. With a sense of utter awe at the miracle of them, and an overwhelming rush of love as we took that last look at two sleeping angels.

It could be said that there is nothing unique about the daily routine I've just described. That is precisely the point. There is nothing unique about it.

Parenthood can be a lot of work, the associated drudgery can be boring as hell, the rewards can be minimal, and the terrors associated with caring for an infant when inexperienced very serious. But it doesn't end there. That is only a tiny beginning—the first deposit in the negative bank account of accumulated disappoint-

ments, fears, guilts, and inadequacies a mother feels. If the drudgery is glossed over by society in its hot pursuit of turning every
young female adult into a mother, that sin of omission pales next
to the failure to tell the truth about far more serious matters.

How unbelievably petty my routine sounds. And yet, life is
made up of small things. Taken one by one, each frustration or annoyance is trivial, but the opportunities for all the feelings of guilt
and inadequacy are there: Am I letting them watch TV too much
because I want them out of the way? Will anything bad happen if I
don't bathe them for three days because I can't face the fight?
How could I possibly have let myself not brush their hair? Am I
being a dreadful mother because I let them have candy before dinner? Is dinner nutritious enough? Will they starve or grow up ane-
mic because I can't face the hassle of shoving food down their little
throats? Every action, every act of discipline, every Frito given or
not given, is contributing to what they will become. Am I doing it
right or wrong? And how can I remain reasonable when the petty
frustrations seem to be destroying my ability to reason? And, if I
find the job for all these reasons an unpleasant one, am I a bad
mother?

The annoyance of simultaneously scrubbing a toilet and
being nagged by a child cannot be compared to the fear and inadequacy one feels when a child is hurt or sick. I have described fearing concussion in a one-year-old, but getting through that didn't
prepare me for future incidents. No mother can be so prepared;
instead, she only becomes more and more sensitized by the dan-
gers as time passes.

One very cautious mother, for example, sadly learned that
her efficiency nearly cost her both her children. Having completely child-proofed her house, putting all medications and cleaning compounds in a locked suitcase on the top shelf of her closet,
she was sure her children wouldn't be able to ingest a lethal dose of
anything in *her* house. But when a baby-sitter carelessly left al-
lergy medicine on a counter, she learned that you can never be too

sure. She didn't know it was in the house until she found the empty bottle. Suddenly the children's listlessness that morning took on a new meaning. She got in touch with her pediatrician, who said, "You can't take any chances. They may not have taken anything, then again, they may have—and if vomiting doesn't bring anything up, we'll have to pump their stomachs."

Luck was on this mother's side. She had moved swiftly enough so that the vomiting did the trick. "They had taken enough to put them to sleep permanently," she told me, "and the fear I felt at the time and the sympathy for the two I was forcing to vomit is indescribable. To say nothing of the guilt."

"Oh, but that won't happen to *me*," you might be saying. "That only happens occasionally." Really? According to the *Ann Landers Encyclopedia*, every year 100,000 children are poisoned by aspirin alone.

Careful and cautious mothers are scarcely immune. No one ever knows precisely what the neighbors are up to. The family with the prettiest yard on the block, for example, may be a menace to your child. A friend of mine reported that her two-year-old ate a poisoned snail that had crawled over from a neighbor's yard. Our next-door neighbor came rushing over one day to report that he had been spraying with dangerous pesticides and Adam had gone into the yard to retrieve his ball. I immediately took my son into the house, lathered him up, and scrubbed him from head to foot. I worried about the incident for days because two days later our small dog died from pesticide poisoning, and I found dead baby birds on our patio.

One day, when he was three years old, Adam disappeared. The police combed the area for one agonizing hour before he was found by some neighborhood boys. One minute he was in our fenced backyard, and the next minute—gone! I was terrified. Thirteen years later, he was hit by a car. I thank God every day that it wasn't just an inch to the left. And of the years sandwiched in between, I could write volumes of the near-misses my children, especially Adam (there really is something to "snails and puppy dog tails"), have experienced.

I could write many more volumes on the sorts of things you don't think about when you don't have kids. For example, one father pointed out that he had never thought much about hammers until he saw his two-year-old with one—the little boy was ready to hit his four-year-old brother on the head. A mother tells of her little boy running into the house with his head bleeding. It seems that he and a playmate were digging in the backyard. She had no idea where they got a pickax, but they did, and a fight broke out. The result was a visit to the emergency ward. How many near-misses have all of our kids had while riding their bikes? How many of us have cringed as our children have chased toys or pets into the paths of oncoming cars?

Somehow, most kids survive. At what cost to Mother? Even on good days, her conditioned reflexes have her sitting on the edge of her chair—anything can happen.

A friend told me that sometimes when her kids are playing at someone else's house, even as old as they are now (eight and six), she can't relax for very long. Not hearing them about, not being reassured that they aren't getting into some trouble, always leaves her slightly uncomfortable.

"Oh," you say, "she must be a lunatic." But years of worrying about children, feeling guilt and fear, start to accumulate, becoming a habit. And unlike most bad habits, it can't be broken because it has pure love as its foundation. A woman who does not care about her children does not feel these things. But most mothers do care and thus most mothers experience such feelings.

"Oh, but what are a few accidents now and again? That's life." True. So are illnesses. And when one is effusively describing the joys of parenthood, these things are rarely mentioned.

Did you know that a young child can run a fever even when there is no infection? And a high fever frequently can be more dangerous than the illness, if any. Every mother I know has labored, at least once, to get a child's temperature down, sometimes without knowing what caused it, because a high fever can cause convulsions.

One mother found it out when it happened to her six-month-old baby boy. She had taken him to the doctor, given him his medication, and he seemed to be getting better. She put him down for the night, comforted that he was improving. A short time later when she looked in on him, she found him in the middle of a convulsion.

Although parents become fairly "seasoned," the anxiety is always there. One young woman insists that mothers with especially healthy children suffer even more when their kids are actually sick. "They're sick so seldom," she says of her two children, "that even a mild cold or temperature terrifies me. I always worry about brain damage." In describing how she reacts, she says, "I'm useless. I'm no good in a crisis when the kids are sick. I just can't handle it." Added to the worry, there is always the nagging feeling that a better mother would have prevented this particular illness somehow.

One couple I talked to admitted taking shifts for one week because their three-month-old baby had a slight cold. They were too frightened to leave him unattended. Night after night they took turns sitting up in a chair in the baby's room.

Incidentally, for those who might believe that breast-fed babies are totally immune to colds, flu, and other illnesses, it's interesting to note that a number of mothers who nursed their babies said that when their children got sick for the first time, they were still nursing them. (To lay another old wives' tale to rest, my doctor's warning that breast feeding is by no means a surefire method of contraception has been borne out by two very unhappy, very pregnant, breast-feeding friends.)

The way mothers react to their children's illnesses can be summed up in the words of one pediatrician when he said, "In most cases, mothers wind up being sicker than their children just from their own anxiety."

And children are not the only members of the family to get sick. Someone once said that mothers appear unusually healthy because there's no percentage in their being sick, at least not until their kids are teenagers. If her illness is severe enough, a mother can get someone to help out. But usually it's just a bad cold or a simple little 101-degree fever that doesn't quite justify paying money to a sitter. *There are no sick days off for mothers.* As one mother said, after recovering from a bout with the flu, "What was I supposed to do? Walk into my baby's room in the morning and tell him I was sorry that I was sick and wouldn't be coming in to work today?"

I have a friend, a kind and patient woman, who painfully and skillfully raised two now-grown children. Looking back, she lamented that "if only I could have afforded a little help, it would have been easier—I could have been a better and happier mother. No one ever helped me."

When I mentioned to her one day that a friend was agonizing over a serious problem with her two oldest children, she snapped back, "Well, she has money; she can afford all the help she needs." When another friend was suffering from a physical illness caused by nervous tension, she was unrelenting: "What's she got to be so nervous about? She's got money and only one child, and all the nice clothes anyone could want."

There are three important things I want to say about my friend's value judgment.

The first is something I say to any young woman who is contemplating being a mother, and in a subsequent chapter I will spell this out in detail. For now, *make sure you can afford it,* or every pitfall of parenthood will be more painfully aggravated.

The next is that, even if you are incredibly wealthy and have only one child, you may experience just as much trauma as a mother of four who is struggling with a diminishing budget because—and this is another thing that few people ever talk about—*we are all different.* We are unique individuals, each with a different threshold for pain, anxiety, and stress. What may cause you to go off the deep end may be something that another person can easily take in stride. Know that when you are tempted to judge.

Finally, being able to afford a housekeeper, a baby nurse, nice clothes, and vacations doesn't let the mother off the hook. "The buck stops here" is as true for a mother as it was for Harry Truman. Take the kids out of homemaking, for example, and the tasks are a snap, as I noted above. But take the homemaking out of the responsibility associated with caring for kids, and you're still left with an enormous, tension-filled job. The straightforward general maintenance is not all that time-consuming. Ask any working woman how much time it takes her to keep things up, and ask any childless couple what is involved.

The buck that stops here is the one that no housekeeper or baby nurse can take for Mom. When your child is doing poorly in school, no amount of floors waxed for you is any comfort. It just means that you don't have to wax the floor while you are worrying. When your child is running a 104-degree fever, it doesn't matter one bit that you can afford to take off for a weekend trip or a vacation. When your child has just been brought home by the police, unless you are hopelessly superficial, looking at a healthy checking-account balance is no help.

No maid or housekeeper can relieve you of the ultimate responsibility of guiding your child or relieve you of worrying about your child. No hired help can always be there to get up in the middle of the night; go over to the school when there's a problem; take your child to the dentist, doctor, Scout meeting, Brownies; and attend the PTA meeting for you.

No one who scrubs her own floor, is dying for a day out of the house, or is just exhausted should be asked to feel sorry for someone who has trouble with the servants. I do suggest, however, that anyone who feels that pain-free parenthood is ensured simply because she can afford to pay someone to take care of the drudgery had better think again. She'd better know, just for openers, that the domestic labor force is a declining one.

A woman with help sums it up nicely: "In the final analysis, no one but you can raise your child or children the way you feel is proper. No one but the parents can possibly feel the pain associated with the doubt, fear, and guilt of that responsibility.

Whether it be a question of toilet training or your choice of spiritual guidance, having a housekeeper and nurse may relieve you of some of the drudgery, but ultimately the parents are responsible for the orientation and happiness of the children and their impact on society. And that's a very heavy trip."

# Chapter 5

# HI, I'M MOMMY.
# FLY ME TO THE
# CUCKOO'S NEST.

When Adam and Lisa were six and seven, I wrote the following:

> While I'm sitting here writing, there are four kids playing in another room. If I recorded the audio accompanying their "playing Scrabble" (that's what they tell me they are doing), there would be shrieks, thumps, crashes, chatter, doors slamming, the sloshing of liquids, occasional laughter . . . and constantly. Not a single second contains only the sound of my typewriter. And today is a good day because they remembered to turn off the television set when they quit watching. It will soon grow very quiet, however, and that is the signal that they have now begun to misbehave seriously.

> But for now, all this racket is setting the stage for this mother to have a real case of nerves by about five o'clock. The racket is stacked up next to the three fights that I broke up within the last half hour, jumping up every two minutes to answer the phone or the door, or to get the dog back into the yard so she doesn't get pregnant or hit by a car, the numerous requests for food, water, juice, Coke, and chewing gum in between the breakfast routine, the lunch routine, and my daily

janitorial chores. I'm now starting to view another day slipping by—another day when success or failure will be measured by how depressed or nauseated I will be once we somehow get through it. Another day that I will set against all of the others, nearly identical—with the knowledge that tomorrow will be the same.

My reaction to that moment in time was, of course, exaggerated by the fact that I was trying to concentrate on my writing. It was a momentary outburst at the extreme frustration I felt at being constantly interrupted and driven crazy while working against a deadline.

People who do not have children cannot have any sense of what it is like to attempt the work of writing, or any work, under the conditions I described. They may also make the assumption that once children get past a certain age, those kinds of stresses fade away.

As I write this, more than a dozen years have passed and Lisa and Adam are adults, still living at home. In addition we have living with us Steve and Matt, both friends of Adam's. Steve works full time and Matt is a student. Four young adults. Terrific young adults. I adore both Steve and Matt and often forget they are not my very own.

But . . .

While I'm sitting here writing, there are four young adults watching a videotape in another room. If I recorded the audio accompanying their "watching," there would be shrieks, thumps, chatter, doors slamming, the sloshing of liquids, the scraping of chairs, slight conflicts over who is wearing whose shirt and who stole whose beer out of whose dresser drawer, and raucous laughter. Not a single second contains only the clackety-clack of my word processor or the sound track of the video.

Earlier in the day—Saturday—they were coming in and out of the house, asking me how they looked, what they did with their books, how they should have their hair cut, when the computer might be free, what's for dinner, where's the coffee, what I'm writing, *why* I'm writing it, where's the hair dryer, and could they borrow five dollars for gas. "Here, anything. Take it and go."

Before they all collected themselves to watch the video, and my fingers were poised just above the keyboard, Adam entered the room to give me a long, detailed, and unsolicited discourse on what is wrong with my car and why I should sue the folks who were supposed to have fixed it. I could not very well ignore him. Just before he started in, I had received a call from Lisa, who was stranded and needed a ride. At some point, on resuming work, it seeped into my consciousness that Matt and Adam were tapping out rhythms on their bodies and on the kitchen table. I had no idea how long they had been doing this before I realized that it was driving me nuts.

But things are better now than they were when Adam's rock band regularly practiced here, destroying my hearing and the neighbor's nerves. The police came by so frequently in those days that I got to know the officers on a first-name basis.

While some women are able to cope with the never-ending stress of motherhood, many don't fare so well. For the woman who finds it extremely difficult, the results can range from an uneasy feeling that makes her wonder if she isn't just going slightly crazy to a life of horror and self-hatred. I have known many women who have never shown the slightest sign of anxiety until they had children to care for. Often, for reasons unapparent to them, these mothers are suddenly thrown emotionally out of kilter. One mother I interviewed had this to report:

> When I was first married I spent two years getting my master's degree and another year and a half working as a medical social worker. I then had a very wanted son and seven months later got pregnant with another wanted son. However, I remember when I was eight months into my second pregnancy I felt great fear of not being able to cope with two

young children. It was at that point that I began being afraid
to drive on the freeway because I was afraid I would pass out
(which was an irrational fear since I commuted seventy miles a
day to and from grad school and forty miles a day to and from
work). When my younger son was eight months old I began
having anxiety attacks, so I finally went to a psychologist, who
really helped me realize that I was so tied to my family (going
to Safeway was my big outing) that I was afraid of losing control of my own life.

One friend of mine discussed her situation with me at length.
This is what she had to say:

> The first time I noticed I no longer had "nerves of steel"
> came while I was calmly sipping a cup of coffee in a friend's
> kitchen. I had taken my children, two and three years old, to
> play with my friend's little four-year-old boy. It had been a
> nerve-racking drive on the freeway, but I managed it
> neatly—or so I thought. In any case, while Linda and I sat
> talking, her doorbell suddenly rang and I understood the ex-
> pression "I jumped out of my skin." I did just that.
>
> I was rather surprised. But because I have a long history
> of keeping cool during confusion and clamor and being able to
> work calmly under pressure, I attributed it to the freeway with
> the kids, maybe that second cup of coffee, or a combination of
> the two. I didn't recognize it as the first signal that I was grad-
> ually becoming jumpy and tense—the first step toward deep
> depression. The roots of all of this can be traced back to the
> very beginning—the day I first felt anxiety about a new baby,
> and the rush of conflicting emotions and fears that apparently
> all new mothers have. From that point, I just started building
> my negative bank account, while I still appeared to be fairly
> calm for a few years.
>
> To illustrate how the geometric progression took hold,
> and how quickly it can work, I can recall a friend saying to me

in the midst of a batch of kids generating noise and confusion, "Jean, I don't see how you can stand it. You're so *calm.*" I also remember commenting sincerely that it really didn't bother me. But just a few months later, the jangling of the telephone could set my nerves on edge, the sound of something dropping could make my skin crawl, and more and more I was feeling that sudden twinge in the pit of my stomach over very trivial incidents.

Now, four years later, I can hardly be described as calm or serene, and it is doubtful that I ever will be. The best that can be said is that I make a valiant and successful effort to maintain control; I've learned many tricks to keep my head and body in good shape, but the trip has been an arduous one, punctuated with very dark days, when I feared I was losing my grip entirely or would become physically very seriously ill.

While I mistakenly assumed that I was adjusting to child-generated confusion and noise, I was instead becoming sensitized to it, a fact that made itself known for the first time the day I reacted so strongly to the sound of a doorbell. The truth is I was becoming sensitized in a number of different but interlocking ways. The real difficulty comes in recognizing that something is happening and then knowing what to do about it. For me, this was very difficult since I've always enjoyed good health and an overall sense of well-being.

So, one day came that held the answer to my new jumpiness and nervousness. That was the first time I noticed tingling sensations in my legs and arms, quickly followed by numbness. I wasn't at all relieved at my assessment of the situation and I made an appointment to see a doctor, fully convinced that I was very seriously ill. I seemed to have the symptoms of Parkinson's disease. I also considered that I might have a brain tumor or a grave neurological disorder. After the doctor examined me briefly, we returned to his office and I expressed my fears.

He laughed. Then he gave his diagnosis: "Nerves."

*Nerves!?* Since when do nerves cause all of these physical conditions? I could understand the upset stomach and headache, but some of the other symptoms seemed almost like seizures. And besides, I'd always been quite calm. Surely something else, something physical, was at work. I'd always believed that even under great stress people could talk themselves into semi-tranquility at least—by just refusing to give in.

At least partly convinced that the diagnosis was correct, I accepted the doctor's prescription for tranquilizers, but firmly resolved not to use them unless I couldn't function otherwise. A couple of years back, a friend of mine told me that she'd learned how to cope with her maternal responsibilities, as she produced a bottle of innocent-looking white tablets from her purse, saying simply "Equanil." I recall my reaction—I thought she was weak.

For better or worse, I kept my promise to myself by not taking the medication as it had been prescribed; instead, I took a pill only when my physical symptoms got in the way of taking care of my responsibilities. Generally, I'd cope with a few dizzy spells, some visual problems, and continually sweating palms and feet; but when I drove the car, I recognized that it was only responsible to take something that restored my coordination. I found out later that driving on tranquilizers can be dangerous. I was so afraid of getting hooked on these hated tranquilizers that I actually damaged my physical health by allowing all that adrenaline to course through my body constantly; at the same time, I reached another milestone of sorts. I felt incredibly guilty about having to take tranquilizers to perform even simple tasks, like driving, and at the same time I was living with the gnawing fear that the situation could get even worse.

That fear was reinforced on one lovely Saturday afternoon during the summer when I nearly lost consciousness. I was convinced I was having a heart attack. I became weak, my heart was pounding, and I broke out into a cold sweat. Too

weak to do anything else, I simply went to bed, resolving that
as soon as I could muster the strength, I'd call my sister or a
friend so that there would be someone on hand to look after
the kids, who were luckily at the home of a playmate. Fortunately, I'd done the right thing at the right time and within a
half hour I felt better.

Like my friend, I've taken tranquilizers, but always with the
feeling that it was still another piece of evidence that I was a very
imperfect mother. I've learned that I'm *far* from being alone.

Another woman I talked to, an affluent, seemingly serene
mother of teenagers, told me that what motivated her to go back
to school and prepare herself for a teaching career at the commu-
nity-college level was that when her kids were still fairly young,
she developed what appeared to be a heart condition. Her physician told her flatly that there was nothing wrong with her heart, or
with her physically at all for that matter, but if she didn't get herself out of the house and away from the kids, she'd be in very serious trouble. It was difficult to believe that this confident,
intelligent woman had been reduced to the level she was describing. While she felt guilty about what she termed her "unsuitability
for motherhood" in the past, she had come to terms with it many
years before. As she put it, "I felt guilty about pursuing a career
and leaving the kids with sitters, and it was very difficult to bear
the responsibilities of a home and family while working full time.
But had I not, the kids might not have had any mother at all."

Another mother I talked to, on the other hand, is a mother
who never left home:

It finally got so bad that one day I just passed out. I'd
been taking tranquilizers for years and hating it. I gradually
was attempting to make it on my own with my ultimate goal
being to quit relying on medication. I realize now that I picked
a lousy time to try. We had holiday houseguests, the kids were
on their Christmas vacation, and it was pretty hectic. Anyway,

one day I just started hyperventilating like mad, and then I was out like a light. The next day I did two things: I took a tranquilizer when I first got up, and I made an appointment to see a psychiatrist.

It took only one visit with the psychiatrist to fully understand the level of my problem, and what needed to be done. I continued with sedation, and I learned to force myself to relax to the extent that when it really got bad, I'd just say, "The hell with it." That may sound simple. It isn't. Oh, yes, I also reinforced my entire program with vitamin therapy and plenty of rest. Things are a lot better now, but of course, one of the kids is in college and the other two have become fairly independent and I can see the light at the end of the tunnel, and I know that in about five more years, I'll be fairly free from the picky details of raising kids.

Still another woman I talked to is the mother of four planned children. She said that if she had to do it over again, knowing the realities of coping with four youngsters, she would not have *any* children. In discussing her two-year bout with severe anxiety, she said it all converged in one day: "Oh, nothing really special happened. But suddenly I just had to get away. I walked into our bedroom and locked the door, then went into the shower, closing the door behind me, and sat on the floor for a very long time, doing nothing, just sitting. I was coming apart at the seams. You know, I always thought I was fairly stable, but when the children were small, my hands would shake, I would have fits of depression, cry for no apparent reason. I finally went to see a psychiatrist. It helped."

I've known few mothers who haven't suffered from anxiety, tension, depression, stress, or emotionally induced trauma in varying degrees. Nearly all the mothers I've talked to rely on something external to help them cope with the difficulties of raising children. For some it's alcohol, for others it's tranquilizers, while others use food. The healthier coping devices include a job, volun-

teer work, regular respites from the children, exercise, or medita-
tion (hard to pull off when there are constant interruptions). Most,
however, also take a large dose of guilt for *needing* something to
help them cope.

While some of the mothers I know and have talked to
seemed to benefit from visits to a psychiatrist, it should be noted
that not all troubled mothers fare quite so well. For a while, I
worked as a trained lay therapist on a parental stress hotline. Many
overwhelmed mothers dialed our number in desperation because
they had consulted professionals and spilled out their stories of
being pushed to their limits only to have their therapists respond
with a total lack of comprehension. One woman told me that her
therapist said, "Come now, it can't be all that bad." Another told
me that her psychiatrist flat out didn't believe her. The saddest of
all was a distraught mother of six- and seven-year-olds who, in a
wavering voice, said that when she told her psychiatrist she felt she
wasn't cut out for motherhood and couldn't cope with its demands,
he told her she was probably not fit and suggested that she give
her kids up for adoption. I suggested that she not be so hard on
herself and that she hire a sitter a couple of times a week and get
away. I suspect, however, that given her emotional state, she was
beyond hearing anything that didn't reinforce her conviction that
she was a bad mother.

The plain fact is that most people who haven't been mothers
have little understanding of the many factors that can drive a
mother quite mad. Because the realities of motherhood are so diminished and hidden from general view, even some mental health
care professionals do not understand that what is culturally perceived as the happiest state imaginable for women can be cause for
serious emotional disturbance. They don't seem to realize that
there are variables peculiar to each individual situation, as opposed
to the happy, plastic state put forth by the media. As an illustra-
tion, a distraught housewife writes:

> I've been to three psychologists, two of whom told me I
> needed to divorce my husband. The other one sat there and

said "What do you want me to do? You have a long time to serve your sentence." I am thirty-two years old, my sons are eight, five, and three. I love them, and they drive me crazy. I've got loads of guilt complexes, ranging from my kids to a total inability to organize my time to get anything done. I feel like a vegetable. I'm convinced my mental capacity is diminishing daily through lack of stimulation and a voluntary shutdown as a defense against the effects of three young children.

In *The Future of Motherhood,* the sociologist Jessie Bernard said that far more housewives are likely to suffer insomnia, depression, and nervous breakdowns than working women are, and she feels that housework "may have a deteriorating effect upon a woman's mind, rendering her incapable of prolonged concentration on any single task." Further, she pointed out that the housewife generally does her tedious job in isolation, unlike her predecessors (previous generations of mothers), who shared manual chores with members of an extended family: "Far fewer than expected of the working women and more than expected of the housewives, for example, had acutally had a nervous breakdown. Fewer than expected of the working women and more than expected of the housewives suffered from nervousness, inertia, insomnia, trembling hands, nightmares, perspiring hands, fainting, headaches, dizziness, and heart palpitations. The housewife syndrome is far from a figment of anyone's imagination. . . . In terms of the number of people involved, the housewife syndrome might well be viewed as public health problem number one."

While I certainly agree with Dr. Bernard, I've just got to say that I've never known of a single case of a housewife who had no children who suffered from any syndrome. Housework, per se, never drove me nuts. What has driven me nuts and continues to drive me nuts is being denied the opportunity to go about my business—no matter what it may be—without either constant interruptions or without a sense of dread, waiting for the interruption or the crisis to occur. It is the care of the children or the presence of children that makes housewifery a crazy-making situation.

What is crazy-making, I think, is the pressure to get certain tasks done within a context that virtually guarantees such to be an impossible goal. I have a friend, for example, who is the mother of a grown son who lives 3,000 miles away. This woman does not work outside the home. She is a housewife. She takes care of her husband, cleans her house, gardens, cooks fantastic meals, decorates her home, sews her own clothes, plays tennis, reads books, paints pictures, does volunteer work. She is far from being driven mad by housewifery. There are no children in her home.

# Chapter 6

# SCHOOL DAYS

"Just wait until the kids are in school" is something struggling mothers of toddlers often hear. The rest of the sentence is conveniently omitted. Whatever respite is provided by having the children away from the house for a few hours every day is balanced by still another dimension of parenthood novice mothers are ill prepared for.

For a mother who has been taking care of preschoolers at home without help, there is certainly no question that, when the children are in school, her hours will be shorter. Not that much shorter in many cases where schools are on half sessions through high school, but shorter all the same. The fantasy of many mothers—that when their children go off to school, they will live a life of freedom and leisure—is only partly true.

Many mothers who assume they will march blithely off to work when their children are in school find that children get sick, schools declare vacations, and there is, of course, summertime.

Whether a mother works outside the home during the day or inside, she soon discovers there is a larger-than-imagined number of time-consuming school-related activities. The housewife is especially vulnerable to pressures to become involved, as there is a general assumption that housewives don't do anything, even when they clean their own houses and have other children at home. The working mother is usually exempt from most daytime activities (except special events), but is expected to participate in evening functions. Fathers, even in this egalitarian age, are not *expected* to participate, but are applauded when they do.

Furthermore, the demands generated by having children in school are frequently not only time-consuming, but emotion-consuming as well. A child's life may not be warped if you change a diaper less often, but as a child grows, the acts you perform with and for him or her seem to take on a greater urgency. It is difficult enough to meet his or her emotional needs at home, but the assumption of most parents is that the school will see to the education, at least, of the child. All too often that assumption proves unwarranted.

One New York mother told me that in California we have it all. True, ours is considered to be a good school system. Palo Alto ranks somewhere near the top in the nation and is an exceptional system, especially if your children happen to be either budding geniuses or "educationally handicapped." (God help you if they're average.) But, even the best system in the state is wanting because, periodically, there are bad teachers with tenure who cannot be fired. The mother of three boys, herself an elementary school teacher, said, "To assume because our school system is one of the best that each and every teacher is first-rate is a mistake. You get bad teachers in good systems and good teachers in bad systems."

But most parents don't indulge in statistical analyses of school systems. Most of us are concerned with how our children are doing, how we are doing, about our children's inadequacies, and about our inadequacies as parents. Many mothers have complained that their kids can speak Spanish or French but don't know how to read English. Two college instructors have told me that a growing number of their students, although bright, are "functional illiterates." In the recent book, *Illiterate America,* Jonathan Kozol indicates that fifteen percent of recent graduates of urban high schools read at less than a sixth-grade level and that over a million U.S. teenagers between twelve and seventeen cannot read above the third-grade level.

Parents complain, in increasing numbers, that the schools are attempting to mold the morals of their children and that the parents, unskilled at the task, are having to teach basics. (As religion in the classroom becomes more of an issue, I'm betting these complaints will multiply.)

When I sent Lisa off to school for the first time, she had one year of nursery school under her belt (to prepare her for kindergarten; today, two years is nearly a requirement). The only other preparation I had for this phase of her life, and a year later for Adam's, was that I had gone to school. Drawing from my own experience, I assumed my children would, in their early years, learn the same things I had—the basic tools. The matter of my morals, sociability, chess, music lessons, or philately was pretty much left up to me and my parents. The matter of teaching me how to read and write was left up to those whose training and skills were equal to the task—the teachers.

At the time Lisa started school, there were approximately two dozen kids in our neighborhood who attended the same elementary school. There were two teachers teaching first grade. I will call them, for the sake of this discussion, Mrs. A and Mrs. B. Those who went to Mrs. A's class learned to read; those who went to Mrs. B's class learned to read with home assistance, or with special outside reading classes, or they simply didn't learn. As one seven-year-old girl told me, "My brother had Mrs. B and she didn't teach. I'm sure glad I got Mrs. A."

Lisa was in Mrs. B's class. I tutored her every night, but I'm not a teacher, gifted or otherwise (that's why I didn't choose it as a profession), and my help to her was, at best, dubious. The next step for her was a remedial reading class—unheard of for an average or bright student in my day.

One of the areas where I honestly feel that I failed my kids was in helping them with their homework. And, more and more, I learned that once the children are in school, so is Mother once again. Every night one hour of my time was set aside for helping them with reading, math, spelling, and other lessons. We tried to adhere to a specific time each evening to ensure that the homework didn't get neglected. Once I got into a routine of helping them, I really didn't mind too much. But for one as ill equipped as I was in the teaching of young children, this was slightly more than a challenge.

An informal poll I conducted revealed that most of the mothers had no idea that they would be required to help their children with homework; in fact, they had never given it a thought until it was presented to them as part of their maternal responsibilities. Most of those who indicated that they were fairly conscientious about helping the kids with their studies conveyed an attitude of resigned reluctance. Many mothers just somehow never got around to it, and one or two did all of the homework themselves. A few others said they felt it was the school's job to educate their children.

One mother said that she didn't help her kids because she didn't understand the work, and the kids thought she was stupid so they didn't even ask for help. Still another said she didn't help because there were four kids and it was just too much, even if she and her husband divided them up. Another, echoing many, told me she helped but, "It's a real drag and I resent it."

At the time, almost none of the mothers I knew worked outside the home. Today, most do. In talking with mothers who held outside jobs, I found an even greater reluctance to help with homework for many of the same reasons, but compounded by the fact that their evenings were filled with household chores necessarily deferred during the day while they were at work.

The issue of homework is one that points up a major difficulty for many mothers in raising children. I would be less than candid if I said that I did not resent having to help my children with homework. It was not enjoyable, and I resented the school for forcing me to spend time in a way that I found unpleasant. More important than the time was the pressure on me not to fail my children, to make certain that I was doing all that I could to help them grow up well. Similarly, I resented the time it took to involve myself in school activities. But most important was my feeling that my concern for my children's well-being was constantly being measured by the degree to which I participated.

I did not like baking cookies for carnivals, delivering treats, serving as a room or class mother, attending school board meetings, going to open house, or running telephone trees. I couldn't volunteer for car pooling because, fortunately, I had no car at the time. The PTA was a drag; parent-teacher conferences scared me. In fact, participating to the limited extent I did during the elementary-school years was torture, though I can honestly say that there are no other people in the world for whom I would have made such sacrifices.

But I did feel incredibly guilty when I either chose to or had to say a firm no to a teacher when she asked me to participate in some program involving the kids. On one occasion, Adam volunteered me to serve as a monitor for a field trip (without first asking me about it), and I simply could not do it. Some friends of ours were moving here from the East; they were driving, but the movers were expected on that particular day, and they were to call me when they got here. I might have to supervise the unloading and placement of the furniture. I couldn't very well say to these people who were counting on us, "Gee, I don't know what happened. I had to go on a field trip." I know the teacher shared my opinion that I was being a real dud of a mother, but what mattered more was my son's disappointment.

The telephone tree, a project for which I said a firm no more than once, was generally used to galvanize us errant parents into action on short notice. But most school functions were announced in advance by little notices that got lost in the accumulation of papers, bills, grocery lists, and appointment reminders that make up Mom's desk (or space on the drainboard, actually). As one mother of four put it, "What really overwhelms me about raising children is all those goddamn notes and little slips of paper they bring home from school." Some of them were veritable pamphlets, but most of them were precise little reminders that asked you to *do* something. And when the school asked you to do *anything,* you felt you must. When Lisa and Adam were six and five, respectively, I had a two-inch-thick folder of these tiny consciences on little pieces of paper, representing only one school year's worth.

Once, when I was working full time outside the home and Lisa was in kindergarten, I received a call at the office from her school. I had my usual reaction of, "My God, something terrible has happened"; the call, however, was to inquire if I had received a notice inviting me to a mother-daughter fashion show. I resisted the temptation to tell the caller that the notice must be sitting next to my invitation to the Mad Hatter's Tea Party and instead simply said, "I haven't seen the notice." I explained, guiltily of course, that I worked full time and couldn't come. The teacher, who must have known that, because she called me at my office, was most convincing when she expressed her sincere disappointment that I would not be joining them in this and other similar functions. I think I got my first inkling then of how primary-school teachers, whether they themselves are mothers or not, disapprove of working mothers. The teacher's disappointment, however, was no match for my daughter's. I felt a little guilty when I talked to the teacher, but it really hit home when Lisa let me know how she felt. I promised her that I would participate in the next function at her school, no matter what.

But before I had the chance to make amends, I was invited to a tea for the mothers at the nursery school—Adam's school. The little kids had baked nut bread for the occasion, and Adam was terribly excited about the event. So I went, with Lisa feeling really out of sorts as she said, "You go to Adam's school, but never to mine."

Even a fairly conscientious mother finds it difficult to believe that she is doing enough if she cannot attend every school function. After missing one or two, the teacher's cordial "Glad to see you, Mrs. Radl; we missed you last time" brings home the guilt.

A good example of what I mean is open house at the school, which, in our case, took place two to four times per child each school year. Generally, you find out about open house when you have just vowed that you will not leave the house for a million dollars because you just had one of the rottenest days of the year. Then, in they come: *"Open house tonight, Mama!"* At that point in the scenario, your husband looks at you with utter dread, proclaiming that he won't budge, he's out on his feet, and *he* has just had one of the rottenest days of the year. In the end, you both go to open house because you cannot bear seeing a child hurt over your apparent lack of interest, and because, "Mommy, I've made a special drawing and cleaned out my desk just for your visit."

There are many time-consuming things that occur once the kids are in school that have less to do with their being in school than with their being of school age. For Adam, for example, there was Cub Scouts; for Lisa, the Brownies. Quite a while before they signed up, I heard that mothers of Brownies were expected to participate fully or the children couldn't join. So, to avoid depriving my daughter of something she wanted very much, I participated as much as I could. Ditto for Girl Scouts for as long as she was interested. My own mother's participation had consisted of buying my uniforms.

Other mothers told me, "I participated, and it was torture." There was a lot of work, a large commitment of time, and more important, the obligation to do specific things at specific times added to an already full schedule of child guidance and family obligations. Those mothers who served have said they were pressured into it by a combination of guilt feelings and such comments by their children as "Jennie's mother *likes* to do these things. Why can't you be more like Jennie's mother?" One mother who was very active in the PTA told me that what motivated her was that teachers generally treated the kids of PTA stalwarts better than the kids with mothers who resisted involvement.

Parents strong enough to withstand the pressure to get them to serve as leaders can't escape the "homework" that goes with children's extracurricular activities—another inevitable and unanticipated aspect of parenthood that gradually becomes accepted as part of child rearing, although in reality it has nothing to do with it at all. As one mother told me, "In addition to having to help the kids with their schoolwork, my son's scoutmaster called me and

asked if I couldn't please help the boy with his knots." This lady
knows from naught about knots, so how could she help? By learning about knots first, which she did, of course, to avoid feeling
guilty. "It's not that one specific thing is a lot to ask. It's that I
have four children, a husband, and a dog. All of them have needs,
and I can ignore the dog, but not the rest. Every single special
extra from homework to knots can add up to many hours each
week, until I have a long list of things to do, all trivial, that hangs
over my head—the knots, the PTA meeting, the cookies for the
carnival all become part of one heavy burden."

And, speaking of cookies, let us not forget the matter of Girl
Scouts selling them. Inevitably, Mother becomes involved at several levels. First, because it really isn't a good idea to allow little
girls to go knocking on strange doors, Mother must also go door
to door. Next, because most little girls aren't the world's greatest
bookkeepers, that chore falls to Mother. Then, there is the matter
of delivering the goods as ordered. This is when Mother finds out
that some of the customers have changed their minds—they
wanted peanut butter instead of mints, or they've gone on a diet
and don't want the cookies after all. This is when Mother learns
what is meant by "eating a loss."

A mother who had one son told me, "No sooner had we finished with Cub Scouts—I was a den mother—than, the next thing
I knew, we were deeply involved with Little League." And another, a mother of three sweet daughters, felt that parenthood was
lovely and easy before her kids were in school, before they reached
that special age when they have social activities. From that point
on, she found that she had to run over to the school at least once a
day to deliver a forgotten lunch or a misplaced homework assign-
ment or raincoats.

There was, during my time, an assumption that Mother was
always available. I was astounded one day, for example, when the
school nurse called and asked me to drive over with an aspirin for
Adam because he had a headache. When I related the incident to
my husband, he said, "You should have told her to send the bus
for it."

"Making sure that dinner preparations are well under way before school is out is imperative," one mother told me, "because I spend the afternoon carting the kids to and from their various music lessons and Scouting activities, to the library, the doctor, the dentist, the orthodontist, and the variety store to pick up binders, paper, pencils, or whatever tools they desperately need for their schoolwork."

Then there are the activities *at* school.

One mother of two girls described it this way:

> The big problem I had was that they wanted mothers or fathers to come in twice a quarter—eight times a year per child. With the first child I couldn't go because I was working, and it was like, well, I was sending her to school to get her away from me, so she could get out in the world alone. Besides, I had enough of kids at home. Since I worked, I got out of it by promising to make some smocks for the kids; the teacher said the school would supply the material. After I said, "Sure," they never asked me again nor did they bring me the material. Even the smocks, or the promise of them, didn't keep me from feeling guilty though, because my daugher wanted me to come and all the other mothers went. Even if *all* of them don't go to everything, the kids whose mothers don't go to a particular function always feel that everyone else's mother went. The guilt is there because if every other mother is doing it and your child wants you to be there, you feel it. If no one else did it, then there wouldn't be any guilt feelings.

> My mother used to go to PTA meetings, and she helped out at things, but I don't remember asking her to, and lots of other mothers in my child's school have the same memory. I think this sort of thing with the schools is a kind of reinforcement that we are a child-oriented society. But this thing—this *fad*—could be bad, because we might have children more dependent on their parents. The whole idea of going to school is not just to learn, but to get away from Mommy, now isn't it?

Another mother expressed these feelings:

> I'd like to know who came up with the idea that we need
> to coordinate the parents with the school and the school with
> the child, and so on. It must be considered to be better that a
> child have a "medium" environment than have all school or all
> parents. I never had my mother in *my* kindergarten. I never
> had my mother all the way through elementary school—the
> teachers didn't want the parents there. It's a new trend. To
> me, all of this interacting with the schools hasn't been all that
> beneficial. When the kids get in first grade, as long as you ask
> your child what he is reading, you can find out directly from
> your child. If I feel guilty for not doing some of the things,
> imagine how mothers who work—who have to work—feel
> when they can't participate.

It's easy to say that these mothers were simply rationalizing
away their desire to have their children in school and, thus, away
from them. The reaction of many people is to say how selfish
mothers are who want time for themselves and who, admittedly,
would like to have their children out of the way at least some of
the time. (Many women who were unable to work before their
children were in school find it easier to do so afterward, making
the logical assumption that as long as the children are *supposed* not
to be with them, then it's okay to be away from them.) Are mothers selfish to want the school to take the children off their hands
for a while? Perhaps. But presumably the children do have to get
an education, do have to mix with other children in order to grow
up. Is the only acceptable definition of a good mother one who
wishes with all her heart to be with her children at all times?

Throughout most of Lisa's and Adam's school years, I was
home, so I went to virtually every function at the school because I
felt it was important to the kids for me to do so. I also did so to
avoid feeling guilty. During that time, I wondered how mothers
who couldn't go to anything felt? I wondered how their kids felt?

Sometimes a mother is ill, or she may have another child sick at home, or she may be a working mother. If she is particularly interested, she is disappointed, and to her own disappointment she must add that of her child. It is easy for her to feel that she is the only mother in town who is letting her child down.

The *time* taken by school-related activities pales next to the *toll* they take on some women. Spending time at school is not merely baking cookies and tying knots. It is learning precisely how much is expected of you and having others evaluate you, your children, and your ability as a mother.

One young woman, who sadly is probably not much of an exception, found herself caught in a vicious trap. Her husband had become ill and could not support the family, so she worked to put food on the table and pay the rent. For many reasons, she did not feel she was a very good mother, but having to take a job and leave the family home each day only added to her already poor self-image. Because of her job, she could not attend most of the school functions or participate in the PTA, and sometimes she found it difficult to attend even the all-important parent-teacher conferences. When she finally worked it out with her employer so that she had time to attend one or two events at the school, she found, after a few attempts, that she couldn't do it. Couldn't because she was frightened. By this time, she had missed so many functions, even important meetings with the teacher, that she felt she was truly a bad mother; she was convinced that her son's teacher thought so, too, and that the other parents viewed her with disapproval. She went to a few functions, and with each one she became progressively more nervous and self-conscious, feeling more and more out of step with what was going on. On those occasions when she made a monumental effort to go to a conference, tea, or PTA meeting, she would feel frightened and inadequate. She took the teacher's "Glad to see you" not as a gracious welcome but as a criticism of her failure to be more active.

The last function this mother attended was a parent-teacher

conference to review her son's progress and his problems. This already anxious and self-conscious woman dragged herself over to the school for an anticipated ordeal to find the teacher obviously distressed over this "problem child." Instead of beginning with a review of the child's academic progress or a discussion of his strong and weak points in specific subjects, the teacher marched over to his desk and flung it open. "Look at this. It's a mess." According to the mother, it was indeed that, with papers and books and pieces of pencils and all sorts of garbage mixed up together. The mother nodded, while the teacher went on, "And he doesn't sit still during class. He chews pencils, and then he breaks them up into little tiny pieces, and really, Mrs. L., it is driving me out of my mind." The boy's mother was too nervous to do more than mutter, "I know." The teacher's diatribe became even more furious as she ticked off all the child's bad qualities (he didn't seem to have any good ones), and finally she said, "Mrs. L., this boy is incorrigible. You must take him to a psychiatrist." Mrs. L. said simply, "Why?" At this, the teacher just screamed, *"Why?"*

This mother knew better than anyone that the boy was rapidly becoming a problem, and she felt that the teacher behaved in a completely understandable manner under the circumstances. She blamed herself and her situation for all of her son's problems.

Well, in retrospect, I don't. In fact, I think this was a mother who was caught in a terrible web of circumstances. The teacher was well aware that Mrs. L. had to work because Mr. L. was paralyzed from the neck down, a sad fact that meant he not only couldn't help care for his son, but required care himself. I further think that any teacher worth her salt would have been compassionate toward both mother and son and would have, as was not so unusual when I was a kid, taken this particular child under her wing.

But instead, as often is the case, the teacher scared the hell out of Mrs. L. Teachers look us over and judge us, and often, when they aren't judging us, we feel that they are. And we believe they possess extraordinary expertise in judging our children's morals, manners, and psyches, and we sometimes mistakenly look to them for all the answers.

On teachers as experts on children, Joseph and Lois Bird write in *Power to the Parents:*

> A parent-teacher conference or welcoming talk at the school open house takes on the flavor of shop talk at a psychology convention—if psychologists talked in nothing but cliches. ("I am happy to say, Mrs. Smith, that Johnny seems to adjust well to competitive situations and is able to establish comfortable relationships with his peers, although he does seem somewhat insecure when called upon to assert his individuality and natural creativity.") Teachers who face thirty children in a classroom—and have no more experience or training in diagnosing and treating psychological problems than the school custodian—"authoritatively" analyze young Jimmy, who has been sitting in the sixth seat, third row, for five weeks. They then advise Jimmy's parents. Of course, Jimmy's parents have been living with Jimmy for nine years, but the teacher "by reason of her training" is better able in five weeks to psych out thirty kids than their parents are. Of course, if the teacher is a bit insecure in her diagnosis, or if Jimmy is a problem in the classroom she feels she can't handle, she can send him to the counselor. The counselor or school psychologist then can approach Jimmy's poor academic performance or misbehavior on the playground as a neurosis. There is a very real fear on the part of many parents that they will do the "wrong" thing, i.e., psychologically damaging, if they take action on their own without first seeking the advice of the teacher or if they ignore the teacher's advice.

What is so terribly sad about this whole situation is that often the teachers are wrong, and we parents don't always trust our best instincts but instead go along with whatever these experts recommend, often to the detriment of our children. And, to the detriment of ourselves, the message we internalize is that *our* children are the ones with the problems.

It is our confusion, I think, that makes us so ready to pin the label of "expert" on anyone who works with children, or seems to know more about guiding them than we do. If we are having problems with our kids, that seems to be enough reason to believe that we don't know what we are doing.

Like many mothers, I felt inadequate to the task of disciplining and instilling values, and so I found myself giving great weight to every word the children's teachers uttered. I found myself asking for advice from a divorced woman who had never had children of her own, and then feeling guilty when she implied that I didn't spend time with my children, didn't provide enough enriching experiences, didn't help with the lessons.

Over the years, I have talked to, and heard from, many mothers who would do virtually anything the teacher recommended, from simple help with their children's lessons to seeking psychiatric treatment or drug therapy to calm down their "hyperactive" youngsters. As one mother reported, "My son's teacher, who took a psych course in college, is younger than I and has no children. Yet she explained how sibling rivalry, my husband's indifference to school activities, and the part-time job I held last year were causing my child deep emotional disturbances that were interfering with his ability to learn. At the time, I hung on her every word. Looking back, I realize that in an effort to do the right thing, I was grasping at straws."

"Whenever I talk to my daughter's teacher," one mother told me, "I come away from the meeting first feeling inadequate, of course, for not helping her more with her schoolwork, being a disaster as a tutor, and not spending more time with her. But more than that, I leave with an impression that the teacher thinks I have no responsibilities except for Lucy. That I don't have a husband with needs, another child with needs, a house to clean, or an obligation to myself."

For the elementary grades in our district, parent-teacher conferences replaced report cards, so when Lisa and Adam were in elementary school there were an unusual number of them each year. The regular ones took place four times each school year (for each child), and then there were other conferences that were called for special problems. I used to prepare for these meetings as if I were either going to play Lady Macbeth to an audience of thousands or go into court to face murder charges.

To an already anxious mother, any problem her child has is magnified out of all proportion, and each conference, each unpleasant or worrisome session, provides more negative information to add to the store. Here are some excerpts from a session I will remember until I go to my grave.

TEACHER: Let's discuss her physical disabilities.

MOTHER: Physical disabilities?

TEACHER: Yes. They're quite severe, and you don't seem to be doing anything about these problems. What, for example, have you done about her hearing?

MOTHER: I explained all that to the school nurse. She has allergies, and when they're raging, it affects her hearing as well as her respiratory system. I give her a decongestant three times each day, and—

TEACHER: Well, she talks too much and too loudly.

MOTHER: (Incredulous.) Lisa talks too much and too loudly? Why, on my last visit I was told that she was shy, quiet, and didn't participate in class.

TEACHER: Well, she talks too loudly and I can't do anything with her. When it occurs, I bring her up in front of the class and make her sit on the floor so that perhaps she can be shamed into better behavior—encouraged by having the other children looking at her.

MOTHER: (Speechless.)

TEACHER: And what about her vision? Haven't you gotten her glasses yet? It's been quite some time since we advised you of her problem.

MOTHER: (Muttering.) We were on our way to get them today.

TEACHER: Good. When do you think they'll be ready? (Sighing.) Frankly, Mrs. Radl, try as I may, I really can't find any strong points in Lisa.

MOTHER: Oh.

TEACHER: And the thumb sucking. It's gotten so much worse. Since I started teaching this class in January she's gotten worse every day. And she gets her papers wet with her thumbs, and when I speak to her about this, and her other, uh, problems, she starts sucking her hair. . . . She needs a good deal of help . . . perhaps a surrogate mother . . . uh . . . to help her over the rough spots. . . .

Today, although I am a nonviolent person, I think I would belt a teacher who spoke to me that way. I would belt her once for treating me so badly, and I would belt her six times for abusing my child. The best I can do retrospectively is to never forgive her.

But that is now. Back then, I took my clammy hands and feet, throbbing head, and water-filled eyes away from that meeting just as fast as I could. My failure as a mother was obviously crippling my child intellectually and emotionally for life. My friend who had kindly driven me to the school turned to me and said, "Shirl, I've never seen you like this . . . so upset." My reply was simply, "You've never seen me immediately after a parent-teacher conference." My thoughts, however, went something like this: My poor baby, how are you ever going to feel good about yourself when you've got a lousy mother and you've got a teacher who not only thinks you're a real dud, but humiliates you to prove a point?

Oh, my . . . we lousy moms can just hurt all over for our hurt children, but we're so inept we can't do what we should to keep them from hurting.

The double bind with my darling daughter was that I had long tried to follow the pediatrician's advice about her thumb sucking, a not-unheard-of habit in a six-year-old. He said to ignore it. But after that dreadful meeting with that dreadful teacher, I conjured up a picture of my poor little girl sitting up in front of the class feeling grossly self-conscious, vigorously sucking her thumb, kids giggling at her, viewing her as some sort of freak. And I felt guilty and sad—not because the thumb sucking offended me, but because my child must have felt terribly insecure. I felt guilty about my delay in getting her glasses even though the reason was that I had been without transportation, and that very day my friend was so generously carting me about to right the wrong.

A number of years after this incident occurred, I spoke with a psychologist, who told me that there exists a breed of teachers who have an innate sense of just where a mother's vulnerability may lie and who get off on sticking it to them. Lisa's first-grade teacher just had to be such a teacher.

In any case, the detail, trivia, and tedium that attend child rearing build up to the point where the total task of adequate mothering seems most formidable—because of the minutiae. We—I and the many mothers who have shared their views with me—have had the experience of becoming overwhelmed by an accumulation of small obligations and enormous responsibilities, and very often we have retreated from the whole combination. After this hideous meeting with this wretch of a teacher, I felt that all the tiny transgressions were symptoms of overall benign neglect.

Before I had children I smugly thought that mothers over-reacted to parent-teacher conferences. My sister, for instance, seemed to spend half her life at the school and the rest of it brooding about what I thought were trivial problems with her children. After meetings with her kids' teachers she always seemed depressed or agitated. *I*, on the other hand, would take matters more in stride once *I* was a mother. But I soon learned what it's like to be called over to the school because "Lisa doesn't jump rope as well as Sally and Karen," because she sucks her thumb, chews her hair, talks too loud, laughs too much, doesn't talk, doesn't laugh. And Adam: "He's too intelligent, Mrs. Radl; he said 'shit' seven times in four days, talked back three days ago, hit Bobby with his lunch box, doesn't defend himself. . . ."

At the time the kids were in elementary school, I didn't have the good sense to realize how bad the situation really was. It took time. And just when I started to say, "Hey, wait just a minute," I started learning that the older the children get, the worse it gets. The only thing that improved with age for this family was Mother, but that improvement came very late.

In any case, many middle-class mothers I talked to had real horror stories that made my early experiences as the mother of schoolchildren seem trivial by comparison. It is bad enough that we must insecurely ask teachers for advice. That frequently the advice they give proves so far off the mark is terrifying.

One mother, for example, told the following story:

> My daughter, who is now a straight-A student in college, was judged by her second-grade teacher to be extremely slow. I was frantic, thinking, of course, that the girl was retarded, but after I calmed down, I realized that I knew my daughter pretty well and she could, after all, read quite well—not exactly a symptom that supported the notion that she was either slow or retarded. I just let matters slide, and she did quite well in school, much to the surprise and, I suspect somehow, the disappointment of her teacher. But then a couple of years later, the school nurse and one of her teachers got me in a corner and talked to me about Sarah's speech impediment—she lisped. They recommended that she have surgery. I agonized over that, but decided to wait. After I had her teeth straightened, the lisp disappeared without surgery, and I realized that I had been right in thinking that it's pretty difficult to articulate when one's teeth are parallel to the floor. She's fine now—very fine—but these are only two incidents where the school could have guided me into erroneous decisions that might have marked my daughter for life.

Another mother told me that she regretted her decision to go along with her eight-year-old son's teacher when it was suggested that the boy be left back in the first grade. The child was not a slow learner, but the teacher gave his "immaturity" as the basis for her recommendation. Where once the child was simply immature, he went on to fail miserably in all of his subjects, and in view of his past performance, this was indeed a surprise. As a preschooler and first grader, he was a fast learner, seeming to grasp skills more quickly than most children his age. He had a marked talent for drawing and painting, a fine sense of humor, and showed apparent ability at the piano. These are not exactly the qualities possessed by an unintelligent child, but he was simply not learning anything at school. After he was held back, his self-esteem eroded and he began to feign illness to get his mother to keep him home from school. At this point, his mother and his teacher were at wit's end. The teacher recommended that the mother get in touch with the school psychologist. She tried to reach him for months but was unable to make contact. She then took her child to a private counselor and reported to me that it made her feel good to talk to someone, but four sessions at fifty dollars each didn't get her son beyond trying to dodge school.

A footnote is in order here. In junior high school, this boy cut most of his classes, but managed to graduate to high school, where he continued the pattern until, ultimately, he dropped out during his senior year.

Still another mother told me, "The school experts told me that my son was hopelessly mentally retarded and recommended that we put him in a special school." The experts advised this boy's hand-wringing parents that he would never progress beyond the first-grade level, or that of a six-year-old. The child's first-grade teacher gave the mother the name and address of a "place for this kind of child"; the mother visited it, she became physically ill, and then she just sobbed. She took him to doctors, psychiatrists, and counselors, and finally learned from the boy himself that whenever the class was to have a spelling or math test, the teacher didn't give him and two other children the material to study because she only gave out the study tools to those she had determined could actually do the work. After two years of utter misery and many bizarre experiences, this poor woman put her son in a private school. He's no Albert Einstein, but he *did* graduate from high school and go on to vocational school.

The most extreme case I have ever heard of was that of a boy in his first year of junior college. The dean looked him right in the eye and said, "Your IQ is under eighty; obviously you cannot continue attending classes here." The young man in question was graduated with honors and then picked up a master's degree in education at Stanford University. Stanford is hardly regarded as a school for mental defectives.

One mother I know has harbored deep guilt for years because she did not follow the advice of her son's fifth-grade teacher and seek professional help. The boy is now a man and in his twenties and married. He had marital difficulties and his mother wondered if that might have been prevented if she had heeded the advice of the all-knowing fifth-grade teacher.

Educator John Holt, in his book *Freedom and Beyond,* cites an extreme example of parent-teacher interaction, but one that is only the tip of the iceberg. He tells the story of an acquaintance of his who, in a state of agitation, came to him for advice. The man had a friend who was having a terrible problem with her child at school. The child was getting good enough marks, but he was behaving so badly that he disrupted the entire class. The teacher had already called the mother several times, and it had been suggested that the child be taken to a psychologist and perhaps be given drugs. Holt describes the man as emphasizing that the mother was growing frantic, and the school was demanding that something be done:

> . . . with visions of a thirteen- or fourteen-year-old boy on the rampage, hitting out in all directions, I said, "How old is the child?" His wife said, "He is six."
>
> "Six?!" I thought to myself, what in the world can a six-year-old do in the classroom that can throw all these adults

into such a panic? . . . What this six-year-old was doing to
cause such an uproar was only this—he likes to get up out of
his seat from time to time and go talk to his friends. He re-
fuses to stay seated. At first, I could hardly believe my ears.
Was it really no more than that? Apparently, that was all.
Otherwise, as my friend described him, the child was lively,
sociable, attractive, and had many friends.

My friend said to me, "We think the child may be hyperactive." I assured him, on the basis of what he had told me,
that he was almost certainly not "hyperactive," and that in any
case, such a diagnosis could only be made by a very few highly
specialized people on the basis of elaborate tests, which the
child had not been given. There was no question at all of the
child hitting other children . . . throwing tantrums. He just
likes to talk to people. I tried to convince my friend that the
only problem was that this lively, energetic, and personable
kid had had the bad luck, like many other kids, to get a first-
grade teacher who like many other teachers believed that six-
year-olds ought to spend a large part of their waking hours
sitting down, motionless, and quiet. . . . This child may all too
soon find his way into the hands of experts who will find something they can say is wrong with him. (A month later, I
learned that he was being given drugs, which had "solved the
problem.")

John Holt and Joseph and Lois Bird did not relieve my para-
noia about elementary-school teachers as much as talking to a
young married couple—teachers and parents themselves. The
young woman summed up the advice she constantly gave to parents: "Just tell the teacher you agree completely, admire him/her
greatly, and will leave no stone unturned to comply with his/her
recommendations. Volunteer for everything, and then beg off with
a sick headache—in fact, sometimes when you volunteer to do
something, you will find no one will ever follow up, and you're off
the hook."

Her husband had this to say: "I watch my co-workers get a charge out of making parents feel rotten about both themselves and their kids—they really do enjoy it, you know. Where else can they wield such power?"

One of my worst flaws (some call it a virtue) is that I tend to assume the best about most people until I have reason to feel otherwise. It is an offshoot of that great American principle "innocent until proven guilty." Thus, it took me a while to become really jaded about the school system in general, and various teachers in particular. I have now experienced fourteen years of dealing with the public (and one private) school system, and I can say, without any qualification whatever, that school systems can do more damage to children and their parents than any unsuspecting mother of an infant could possibly believe. This particular bias of mine was reinforced when I worked with Dr. Philip G. Zimbardo, the world's leading authority on shyness. In interviewing young adults for our book *The Shy Child,* over and over again we heard tales of how severe shyness began during the school years. We concluded that the public school is a veritable breeding ground for shyness.

To correct the problems caused by Lisa's negative first-grade experiences, she was put into a program for "educationally handicapped" children. The same year, our son demonstrated that he was a true deviant, if not a mental case, because he was avidly interested in electronics, motors, all things mechanical, and music. He wound up in the same program. It is impossible to convey how terribly painful it was to sit with the school principal, several teachers, and a psychologist and learn that my children were "learning disabled." Naturally, I believed that they were the only children in the school to be so labeled. I recall walking out of that meeting in such a daze that I shouldn't have been allowed to drive myself home. (By then, I had a car.) I recall feeling that I was a total failure as a mother. I recall searching my mind, my soul, and my heart to determine where I'd gone wrong. It was only much later that it was revealed to me that *many* children were so labeled, and that such labeling was necessary to obtain funding for special education teachers, whose job it was to teach children to read and do math when their regular teachers failed to do so.

After "special ed," Lisa and Adam did quite well in school. In fact, Lisa reached a point where she became an A-B student in junior high school. Adam did not do so well. His problems may or may not have had something to do with the fact that his sixth-grade teacher threw chairs across the room and that he, sensitive soul that he was, became quite terrified of her. (According to Adam and his friends, this teacher once broke a child's leg with a flying chair.)

By the time Lisa and Adam got into high school—Palo Alto High School, one of the best in the nation—they became lost in a sea of 2,000 students and became rather petrified of school in general. Paly High, as it is fondly called, is a school wherein the teachers tend to pigeonhole students. If, for example, you are a Stanford professor, your kid has an edge. If, on the other hand, you are not a Stanford professor, your kid is average, and if he or she smokes an occasional cigarette, your kid will be classified as a "burnout." To make matters worse, as one teacher pointed out to me, when it comes time to justify the budget, teachers want all the kids they can get in their classes, but come opening day, they want to drop as many kids as possible. This particular teacher also told me that the very teachers who will judge a kid because he or she smokes a cigarette will look the other way when some kids smoke dope—because a hit of grass will mellow out a kid enough so that he or she won't disrupt the class.

Yes, of course, I am angry and bitter. Here's why: My four-teen-year-old five-foot-tall daughter was dumped into a garbage can by "preppies" and not one teacher intervened. That same girl loved biology and did all of her lessons, and her teacher dropped her from the class. My child came home from school and gave me two grades to look at. When I asked her where the others were, she told me she had been dropped from the classes—that was the first time I had word that such had taken place.

When it became apparent that one of her parents had to make sure she had her classes set, I tried to contact her counselor. After three weeks of tracking him down and pinning him down and making specific appointments, he never showed. Eight weeks into the school year contact was finally made. It was too late.

After said daughter asked to have courses of independent study and was turned down because "You're not mature nor are you bright enough," she was finally given a chance to prove otherwise. After taking one course of independent study, she won an award for achievement.

During my children's years in junior high school and high school, I had meetings, often initiated by me, at the school on the average of once a week, which hardly speaks of parental indifference. I would call the school and then go over and stalk the halls looking for counselors or teachers. After three years, I found one counselor, one teacher, and one vice-principal who were willing to help. By then, it was really too late.

It was also too late to do any good when I learned that to ensure that your son or daughter got into the appropriate classes, it was necessary to accompany them to school on the first day. I recall asking my then sixteen-year-old daughter if it embarrassed her to have her mother tagging along on registration day. She said, "No way. I need you with me or I won't get into my classes." I would have nearly expired from embarrassment if *my* mother had felt it necessary to accompany me to school on registration day. As was the case with my peers, my mother visited my high school on two occasions—the day of the Senior Girls' Tea and graduation.

I was by no means alone. I've talked to dozens of other bitter parents who went through the same thing. A handful of them were frustrated enough and affluent enough to take their kids out of public school and put them in private school. We just kept believing in the school system, probably because we didn't know what else to do and couldn't afford private school.

I spent a chunk of my life at the school, but it was time spent in vain. Up and down Lisa would go. By the time she proved herself, it was too late. She was heartbroken that she wouldn't be graduating with her class. Like some twenty-eight percent of the kids, she learned too late that she didn't have enough credits. It was then that she told me she didn't want to be a dropout and was willing to repeat her senior year. But, she was eighteen, and the school is under no obligation to carry a student beyond the age of eighteen. She then asked if we would send her to private school. Ultimately, we transferred both kids into a private high school and they passed all their courses (it was, by the way, a tougher school) with flying colors and graduated.

My experience with the public school system has taught me that anyone even contemplating having children would do well to figure the cost of private schooling into the budget.

# Chapter 7

# MOLDING YOUNG MINDS AND MORALS

*We live in a computerized society, one in which we are
warned not to fold, spindle, or mutilate. But mothers and children
are repeatedly folded, spindled, and mutilated in an effort to make
them fit into institutions and ideas designed to serve large numbers
of people rather than individuals. When dealing with numbers it
is inevitable that a hypothetical norm becomes the standard against
which everyone is measured. Deviations from this norm present a
problem, because they require special thought and attention. As a
result, it is automatically bad not to conform to the norm. Differences are undesirable. It is not "normal" to be different. This is
the message given to mothers about themselves. Diversity and differences in development are not readily tolerated by those whose
function it is to serve the needs of children, but the onus is shifted
to the child and, by implication, to the mother. The idea is that if
the child doesn't fit in, there is something wrong with the child. If
there is something wrong with the child, something also must be
wrong with the mother.*

—Elaine Heffner, *Mothering*

When my children were babies, I saw Dr. Lendon Smith,
"The Children's Doctor," on a television talk show. He said that

toilet training was unnecessary, that if the parents used the bathroom, the children would follow their example and use it, too. I took his advice and it worked for us. I didn't have to spend hours in the bathroom and in discussions of the subject with my little kids, there were very few accidents to take care of in training pants, and my nerves—and perhaps the psyches of my children—were spared a lot of wear and tear. But sticking to my plan was difficult.

For one thing, it was so easy I felt that I was copping out. For another, I had lots of advice. To accomplish this "nontraining," a mother is told to keep her child in diapers until the child lets her know that he or she no longer needs to wear them. So, here I had a two-year-old still in her diapers. I could put my kids through college if I had a dollar for every time I heard the questions, "Is that child still in diapers?" "When are you going to train her?" "Have you read Spock?"

A friend of mine followed Spock, or rather she tried to. Spock, like other experts, states that children will be trained first to have bowel movements, then to urinate in the toilet. My friend's son did just the reverse, and it drove her nearly mad. Since he had skipped phase one and moved right into phase two, she was confused about how to proceed, fearing that he might just never return to phase one.

To the inexperienced mother, striving to do well and to do the best for her child, the conflicting views of the child-guidance experts and the well-meaning advice of friends ("My Stevie was trained at a year") and grandparents ("Your sister was trained at four months") on everything from toilet training to the best brand of baby food serves only to confuse. Raising a child is an extraordinarily complex and challenging job, and not only are most new mothers completely untrained for it, but their on-the-job training is almost always conducted with advice that is neither useful nor helpful.

It was bad enough when my children were young, but the situation has grown steadily worse over the last few years. The new "pregnancy chic," or baby boom, or whatever you want to call it, has spawned an entire growth industry consisting of courses, books, and fads. The last time I counted the number of child-guidance books on the market, there were well over 1,600 of them. The last time I looked at the new releases, there were books telling young mommies how to exercise their babies, how to teach them to read at six months of age, and how to toilet-train them in one day. (There's even one that shows you how to teach your baby to program a computer!) While there exists total recognition that most mothers must work or want to work, it should be noted, there is little recognition of the fact that the time required to be a "good mother" seems to have increased in direct proportion to the decrease in time available to become that paragon. Furthermore, if motherhood is as easy as television paints it and everyone else says it is, why are there so many books written to tell you how to do it?

The value of many of these guides, I think, was best expressed by one mother, who told me, "When things get bad and I don't know how to handle a particular situation with one of the children, I often sit down and read Spock, Ginott, or Salk. After a half hour's reading I feel better. I still don't have an answer, but the momentary escape of reading distracts me enough to carry me over the frustration and rage I feel on such occasions."

One child-guidance specialist who never did provide *me* with the answers to my questions on discipline was, I admit, one who never failed to entertain or amuse me. He is long gone, but his books live on, and in their recent incarnations, he advises mothers that when a child throws a cherished object across the room and smashes it to smithereens, a mother should calmly say, "Things are not for throwing. Balls are for throwing," and then serenely hand the child a ball. Right. I just happen to have a ball to toss at my fingertips. I give it to the kid and he throws it across the room and knocks over a lamp.

This specialist also advises that when a child mischievously breaks a window, a mother should calmly inform him, "Windows are not for breaking." I recall the day when I looked at the jagged shards of what was once our plate-glass window, and I must admit that my sense of humor and goodwill failed me.

One widely read manual told us that the best way to make sure our children understood what was expected of them was to talk it over with them at length. Did you ever try to talk over *anything* at length with an obstinate two-year-old? If you ever gave it a shot, you know that it's a self-contradictory proposition.

At the same time that I was advised to give children lengthy explanations, another well-known expert proclaimed that parents mustn't become argumentative and verbose, or give long explanations because, "If the parent talks too much, he [or she] conveys weaknesses—at a time when he [she] must convey strength." (An aside: Early experts always referred to the parents as "he," though they generally directed their comments to mothers.)

Not only have experts traditionally disagreed among themselves, tending to confuse and bewilder parents, but it is not unusual for experts to contradict themselves. For example, when guidance was uncomplicated, a very famous pediatrician warned parents that threats tend to weaken discipline, and therefore suggested that we avoid threatening to take away a child's bike, for instance, to keep him from riding it in the street. This expert went on to say that if such drastic action was necessary, a parent should give a child a fair warning. But how does one differentiate between a "threat" and a "warning"?

Once my children left the what-do-you-do-for-teething-pain stage, every time I looked for an answer to a particular problem in the dozen or more different child-rearing manuals on my bookshelf, I was left with the feeling that our children's problems must fall outside the normal range and that, with its varying moods and emotions, our household was totally abnormal. At the time, four people and one dog lived here; playmates drifted in and out; salesmen and friends called up and came by; one person was shaving, while other people were dressing; one person was cleaning up breakfast dishes or emptying the garbage (guess who), while other people were getting ready to go to the office or to school; some days it rained, some days the TV went out, some days someone was sick, some days dinner was late. But I came away from reading all of these guides that were designed to help me with the sense that the people who read them must be mothers of one child (or mothers who never find themselves with more than one child at a time needing attention); that a mother's sole function is to serve and guide; that she is devoid of any emotion save overwhelming love for that one child who has just committed that one act on that one page of that one manual. (The father lurks in the background, where he provides vague support and encouragement for the mother, and brings money home.) The family lives in a world where events never converge, no variables are involved in the care of the children, life remains stable, and the perpetual backdrop is an enormous white room in which the mother and child do nothing but interact.

If the experts agree on one thing, it is that parents should be "consistent" in their discipline and guidance. Consistency, however, is a state of perfection, and perfection is not a human condition. Perhaps it can exist in the sterile world of the child-rearing manuals, but it doesn't work in real life.

One day a child can break a glass, and his or her mother will say, "That's okay, accidents happen." On another day, when the washing machine has gone out, the children have been misbehaving, the phone has been ringing, Mom has had a bad session with a child's teacher, and one of the kids has broken her eyeglasses, she can fly into a rage at the final assault on both her senses and her possessions. A mother, not being a robot, is incapable of consistency.

The range of problems a mother must deal with in guiding children goes from the absurd and trivial to the very serious. How she handles a given situation at a given time depends not only on the gravity of the problem but also on a great many variables.

When the children were in elementary school, we had a steadfast rule that they had to come directly home from the bus stop to check in and change their clothes. The rule was for their safety and my peace of mind. Lisa broke the rule once and was lost for three hours. I called the school and all of her friends' homes. Then I combed our neighborhood. With growing panic, I called the police. Before the squad car arrived, I saw her. Tears were streaming down her face. I could see that whatever was troubling her was deeper than the prospect of a confrontation with an angry and scared mother. What should I have done? Admonish her for being late when she was already obviously miserable? If I had, would I have ever found out what was troubling her so I could help?

By deviating—departing from the rule of consistency—I learned that our daughter had gone to play with a girl who had just moved into the neighborhood and some older kids had started calling her four-eyes, teasing her about her glasses.

Yes, I was distressed that she had disobeyed an important rule and caused me to worry, but I could still feel her hurt. And I was disturbed that the teasing would counteract all I had done to ensure that she regularly wear her glasses. I think I handled things just right, however inconsistently.

As an aside, I would be remiss if I did not point out that one of the unwritten details of the job description of mother has to do with combing the neighborhood in search of children. When Lisa and Adam were small, I kept a list of phone numbers tacked to the wall near the phone and almost every evening at around dinner-time I had to make a number of calls to locate one or the other of the children. When that failed, I went out on foot, and when that failed, I got into the car to go looking. It could easily be said that proper guidance or discipline would have guaranteed that the children would always be home on time. Well, easier said than done.

In any case, hundreds of examples of the consistency rule come to mind. A more recent one concerns Adam, who when he was nineteen years old, borrowed my car to go to a rock concert. I told him he absolutely had to be home before midnight. He was four hours late. When he walked through the door, the only emotion that came to the surface was *pure relief,* and that gave way to hearing, and really listening to, his explanation for this violation of the rules.

Who can be truly consistent when matters of the heart are involved? Despite my warnings about the pitfalls of parenthood, I have a long-standing love affair with my children. That they, on the one hand, can enrage me, while on the other, are two people I love more than life, is a crazy fact that has always made being consistent an elusive goal. No child-rearing manual can tell us precisely how to deal with everyday problems as a cookbook can tell you how to put together a lasagne casserole. There are no prescriptions or perfect recipes.

I recall a day when Adam and Lisa were about seven and eight and they and two friends were planning a carnival in our backyard to raise funds for muscular dystrophy. Realizing how important it was to them that it be their very own project, I resolved not to interfere. The four children set about cleaning the patio area and putting everything into shape, and in their excitement "forgot" my warning not to move the marble table (partly because it was too heavy and partly because they might drop and break it). After they had worked for about an hour, the four little kids appeared in the doorway, eyes cast downward.

"We're sorry. We forgot. We dropped the table." They disobeyed me, and it's hard to believe that not one of the four remembered the warning. But what do you say to kids who were trying to raise money to help kids less fortunate than themselves? Feeling sad at the loss of the first piece of furniture my husband and I bought when we were first married, I said, "It's okay, kids, don't worry about it."

I can honestly say that most of the times when I've compromised consistency for the sake of responding naturally, I was absolutely right. The times I feel the worst about are those times when I let the experts' views overrule my finest responses.

Whether you're determining what sort of toilet-training methods to use or deciding what to do about a teenage daughter's contraception, in the end you are alone. The experts do not help you, and the responsibilities are harrowing. How do you instill values? How do you answer youngsters' millions of questions intelligently? How do you, in short, make yourself a good mother? What counts, what doesn't? What is your job, what is the school's job, and what is best left to chance? How do you ensure that your children will grow up to be decent and content human beings? In our society, the care and training of children is, despite claims to the contrary, a mother's responsibility. And mothers find it an onerous one.

Answering the myriad questions that little children ask can be exhilarating sometimes. Sometimes it can be very boring. At other times it can be infuriating. When you're trying to add up a bank statement and your child asks you why the grass is green, it's hard not to succumb to a feeling of annoyance. How much must you do to keep from feeling that you're failing your children in some way? How much time can you take for yourself without feeling selfish, without feeling that you're neglecting them, without feeling that they may sense a rejection of them on your part? How much "enrichment" is enough? If you don't particularly want to go to the zoo or to the museum, are you causing them to suffer in some way? The children themselves offer little feedback. Mothers are frequently distressed when children fail to appreciate utterly the nice things that are done for them. It simply isn't human to be totally selfless. And because there's no way to look into the future and behold your child at twenty-five and feel assured that you've done a good job of raising him or her, the doubts and fears abound.

As they grow, there are teeth to be brushed, toys to be picked up, social amenities to be observed, and millions of things to learn. While all of this is going on, children, being the wonderfully curious creatures they are, get up on roofs, climb trees, take things apart, and generally get into one hell of a lot of mischief in the process of learning about their world.

And as they grow and learn, so must we. Each day brings surprises, instant tests for us to pass or fail. And each child is a brand new experience with foibles all his own. One of the most closely guarded secrets seems to be that all children are not born alike.

One mother, whose four children range from seven to eighteen years, finds herself dismayed at both the experts and herself:

> You'd think I'd know pretty well how to handle most situations by now, but I don't. Each child is entirely different in temperament, intelligence, and interests. If my oldest daughter, for example, asks permission to do something and I want to give it some thought before I answer, she accepts that decision. But the next child in line not only continues to argue her case, but a final "no" answer is construed by her as a "maybe," and a "maybe" as a "yes." I had always assumed that my first child would be my most difficult because essentially I'd practice there and bring vast experience to my caring for and guiding subsequent children. That just hasn't happened. Whatever I learned with each of them, other than the basics, applies only to each on an individual basis. I'm sure if I had another child, guidance would be just as much of a mystery to me as it always has been.

And a mother of two boys, nine and five, told me:

> My husband drives me up the wall with his running commentary on how I raise the kids.
>
> He comes home quite late, sees the children only on weekends really. They are, in the curious way of children, quite good when he's around. It's funny, isn't it, how they're so good and well behaved with baby-sitters and relatives and Daddy. Every woman I know has commented on the way you'll walk in the door, be congratulated by the sitter on how adorable and easy to get along with your children are, and

then, five minutes after the door is shut behind her, be in the middle of deciding which one to hit over the head first.

On the occasions when the children are difficult and balky and I feel called upon to discipline them, my husband will tell me that I'm really not doing it at all well. If I yell at them, he'll suggest that it would work far better to reason with them. If I reason with them, he'll pitch in with his opinion that I'm not being strict enough with them, and that what they really need is a spanking. Of course, the insidious thing is that I always feel that he may be right. If my childless great-aunt, whom I haven't seen in twenty years, were to butt in with her ideas on child rearing, I'd probably think she was right. Spock may be right, and all the other experts may be right. Anyone, in fact, can be right, because I certainly can't say that I am. Sometimes one thing works and sometimes another thing works. Sometimes I think I'm doing the right thing, and sometimes I know perfectly well I'm doing the wrong thing. And the whole time I'm dealing with them, I feel totally inadequate to the task—totally unhelped by any of the experts.

When I consider myself to have punished them rather too severely, I feel guilty as hell. What am I doing to their little psyches if on Monday, Tuesday, and Wednesday I say nothing about their smearing paint on the playroom floor, but on Thursday I come in and give them a thorough dressing down because Thursday has been a dreadful day and I've just come home from the dentist?

Most disciplinary situations are not covered in the books. It's quite easy to decide that you'll punish your child if he takes something from a store or deliberately breaks something. But what do you do when he's fighting with his brother and you think, but you're not entirely sure, that he's at fault. Punish one? Punish both? Leave them alone? And what about those times when something gets broken purely by accident? And that thing happens to be something that you valued quite

highly? Sometimes you can be quite rational and shrug it off
and say something along the lines of "Please be more careful."
Other times your impulse is considerably less reasoned. And
you scream or you spank or you take away television privi-
leges for three days because you're only human and you're
angry and you're lashing out in anger.

Another woman, the mother of three daughters, ages eleven,
eight, and four, recalls:

> I think I'd been a mother for about two weeks when I
> realized why parents spoil children. It's so much easier that
> way. Just give them what they want and they'll stop bothering
> you. I remember when my first child was a baby. If she cried it
> seemed much easier to give her another bottle. But that led to
> the problem of whether that was good or bad for her. Would
> she expect it all the time? Was she getting spoiled? What was
> better—to feed her or to let her cry? I remember vowing be-
> fore I had kids that I'd never bribe them and I'd never
> threaten them. And after being a mother for eleven years I've
> discovered that the only things that seem to work are bribes
> and threats, and every mother I've ever spoken to has admit-
> ted that the only things that work are bribes and threats. But
> every time I say, "If you clean up your rooms, I'll let you have
> lollipops," I have the guilty feeling that I'm doing the wrong
> thing—that I'm not giving them a proper outlook on life.

And the mother of a son age nine and a daughter age seven is
also concerned about spoiling her children:

> The very word "spoiled" says an awful lot. It implies that
> you'll do something to make them not good. Of course my
> children are spoiled. For one thing, because I work I'm less
> likely to be hard on them. I'm with them such a relatively
> small amount of time that I want that time to be pleasant for
> them. I don't want it to be full of "nos" and "you can'ts."

Also, because I work, I think they're spoiled in terms of material possessions. I buy them things and take them places out of a sense of guilt to make up to them for my working. I suppose in the end my problem, and that of a lot of mothers I know, is that I want my children to like me. And how can they like me if I keep doing things to them that they don't like?

On the other hand, I'm constantly concerned that they are being spoiled, that they're growing up with the wrong set of values. But when I stop to think of how one goes about instilling values, I'm totally at sea. We live in an age where some of the experts speak out for permissiveness and other experts call for strictness. We've all heard enough for and against both sides to make us confused. To say that I should just do what comes naturally is absurd. What seems natural one day seems totally unnatural the next.

I laugh when I hear about consistency. And yet, my concern is with the responsibility I hold for molding them. If anyone had asked me before I had children to write a five-hundred-word essay on how precisely to mold children, I'd have been at a complete loss. It simply didn't occur to me that the responsibility would be as great as it is. And I'm still at a loss. I do what most other mothers do—I do what I can and I pray for the best. But I'm never quite free of the nagging worry that my best is far from good enough.

One mother zeroed in on the unpleasantness of actually carrying out discipline:

One of the nicest things about going away alone with my husband is that I spend the entire time saying, "Yes, let's do that," or "Yes, why don't you," or "Yes, I'd love to," in rather sharp contrast to the constant "nos" I deal out at home. I suppose there are a hundred reasons why I like to go away alone with my husband, but one of them is certainly that I feel a hell of a lot less rigid as a person. I'm not a person who likes to discipline and deny. My husband has pointed out quite accurately that when we're away from the kids even my voice sounds different—it's younger and warmer and considerably more pleasant.

Another mother, whose two girls are now grown, reminisçed about raising them this way:

> The thing I remember the most is how terrible I felt when I did things I'd sworn not to do. I suppose I was particularly sensitive to that because I hated the way my mother had raised me. I remember how unfair I thought it was when she punished me totally out of proportion. Once she practically beat me up because I'd pulled down some curtains, completely by accident. And yet, I'd find myself behaving in an equally irrational way with my children. I'd vowed to be rational, reasonable, sensible, and fair with them in a way my mother had never been with me. I found myself being totally unreasonable and unfair more times than I care to recall.
>
> I remember thinking how stupid it was of her to buy me off—how demeaning, almost. And then I'd find myself buying my children off. I remember how, before I had kids, I'd see mothers in supermarkets shame their kids into tears, scream at them, behave in an absolutely vulgar, disgusting, and altogether unreasonable way. I remember thinking how I'd absolutely never, ever, ever do anything like that. But I did. And I had young women look at me in the same way I'd looked at mothers before I had kids.
>
> But the thing that galls me the most is how I assumed I'd be so much better a mother than my mother was to me—and how I wasn't. Now my older daughter is pregnant, and I wonder what promises she's making to herself that she's going to find herself breaking in a couple of years.

The frustration, pain, guilt, and fear accompanying what we not-so-rational mothers inflict on our children in the name of training and discipline is well illustrated in the following letter included in *Between Parent and Child* by Dr. Haim Ginott:

> If I leave anything unsaid I know that you will be able to read between the lines. You were very kind to come to our church to conduct a discussion group for parents. While it was not completely satisfactory to me because I never learn enough on the subject of raising children, one thing that appealed to me was the statement that you knew that no parents deliberately did things to injure their children emotionally. Rather, they did so unwittingly. Not one of us willingly would do anything to cripple our children spiritually, morally, or emotionally, and yet we do just that. I cry often inside for things I have done and said thoughtlessly and I pray not to repeat these transgressions. Maybe they aren't repeated but something else just as bad is substituted, until I am frantic for fear that I have injured my child for life.

This letter struck a familiar chord. How many times I've felt that I've really hurt the children, how many times I actually have hurt them, I do not know. I only know that I've done nearly everything on my mental "I will never" list. I'm bitterly amused when I reflect on my attitude before I had the kids. I was very quick to say and think, "But it will be different with me."

Now then, if you are tempted to say that, too—"It will be different with me"—I couldn't agree more. Not only will you be faced with the old guilt-engendering and confusing experts who contradict themselves and one another, but you will quickly discover the new ones who carry on that tradition. Moreover, you will discover that a number of these new experts have expanded the job of molding young minds and morals rather dramatically.

The two major areas of conflict and expanded responsibility have to do with preschool and early learning.

For at least two decades, there has eixsted the widespread

belief that young children should attend preschool. The thinking has been that preschool provides them with regular opportunities to interact with their peers, helps them to develop social skills, and readies them for elementary school. And now along comes expert Burton L. White to tell mothers that children can and should be prepared for school by their parents in their own homes. In an interview (*San Francisco Chronicle,* December 20, 1984), White said, ". . .there aren't any transitional benefits to preschool. And the socialization they talk about is horsefeathers." White dismisses the argument that many mothers don't have time to serve as preschool teachers to their young because they must work outside the home by saying that these mothers could stay home if they reordered their priorities, even if staying home meant a family had to live on welfare.

Meanwhile, of course, there are numerous experts on either side of that particular fence. On the one hand, there are those who agree with Dr. White, while, on the other, there are those who say that working mothers are happier mothers and their children derive certain benefits from that fact alone; others say that the children of mothers who work are likely to be better socialized and more independent, even ahead of their peers whose mothers are home. I have even heard some authorities go so far as to say that mothers who stay home with their children all day "smother" them.

The other roaring debate of the eighties is over the "super-baby movement." The dean of this movement is Glenn Doman, founder of the Institutes for the Achievement of Human Potential, located in Philadelphia. In an interview (*Times-Tribune,* January 27, 1985), Doman said, "The younger a child is when he learns to read, the easier it will be for him to read and the better he will read. Children can read words when they are one year old, sentences when they are two and whole books when they are three years old—and they love it." In the other corner we have Dr. Martin Ford, assistant professor of education at Stanford University, who views the superbaby movement as dangerous: "If you push people beyond what their developmental status allows for, you're asking for trouble. You can create a situation where children don't enjoy learning or see it as something they have to do for social approval."

Whether Doman is right or Ford is (and I'm voting with Ford), the entire superbaby movement promises to make the job of molding young minds a far more demanding one for those who succumb to it. James Traub, in a fascinating article, "Goodbye, Dr. Spock" (*Harper's,* March 1986), covers the ground from parents scrambling to get their kids into the "right" play group or the "right" preschool to Doman devotees. A typical example is the Barnes family: "Now Mrs. Barnes teaches four-year-old Christopher from nine to two, while seven-year-old Vikki attends the on-campus, accredited International School. Then Vikki gets Mom's undivided attention, Dad comes home from work, and the parents teach both kids until bedtime. It's a full-time job, raising Better Babies: when the Barneses decided to teach their kids *Romeo and Juliet* they bought the material, made costumes and props, and acted out the entire play."

As Traub points out, the good old days of simple parental pressures are a thing of the past:

> A baby is a bundle of unrealized destiny. . . . When I was a baby my parents made no greater provision for my growing mental abilities than to read to me, as their parents probably had read to them. It never occurred to them that they could, or should, do more; like their other middle-class friends, they simply assumed that I would have more or less the same gifts, and face more or less the same large prospects, as they had. . . .
>
> Now my brother is himself a father. . . . He and his wife braced themselves for the arrival of their newborn with no fewer than twenty-five books, among them *The First Twelve Months of Life, The First Three Years of Life, The Complete Book of Breast Feeding, How to Raise a Brighter Child,* and, of

course, *Baby and Child Care.* . . . To stimulate Rebecca's visual faculties, they plastered her room with wallpaper featuring a gaudy parade of animals; a mobile dances above her crib. Rebecca is already, though ever so gently, in training.

Rebecca has to keep up, and the other toddlers-to-be have to keep up with her. Theirs is the brave new world of the better baby, a world in which the calm New England certainties of *Baby and Child Care* sound suspiciously like the counsels of mediocrity. It's hard not to feel, all things considered, that Dr. Spock is getting out of the business just in the nick of time.

# Chapter 8

# SPARE THE ROD

*In one widely read book on child behavior, the authors tells us that some three-year-olds enjoy wandering about the house late at night while the family sleeps, exploring places and things, perhaps getting something to eat from the refrigerator, and maybe sleeping the rest of the night on the living room sofa. . . . We agree there are some three-year-olds who might enjoy such nocturnal adventures, but the authors then go on to tell the concerned parents that this is really nothing to be concerned about. All the parents need do is to make sure the front and back doors are locked so the child can't wander out into the street. And put the knives and poisons out of reach. This may be normal, expected behavior of the three-year-old, but what the experts don't tell you is the normal expected behavior of the three-year-old's mother as she cleans up the mess of spilled milk, sugar, breakfast cereal, and tries to remove the lipstick he has used to decorate the living room wall.*

—Joseph and Lois Bird,
*Power to the Parents*

In recognizing that parents are occasionally capable of anger, Dr. Spock says:

Sometimes it takes you a long time to realize that you are losing your temper. The child may have been putting on a series
of irritating acts from the time he appeared at breakfast—
making disagreeable remarks about the food, half deliberately
knocking over a glass of milk, playing with something forbidden and breaking it, picking on a younger child—all of which
you have tried to ignore in a supreme effort to be patient.
Then at the final act, which perhaps isn't so bad, your resentment suddenly boils over, and it shocks you a little with its ve-
hemence. Often when you look back over such a series of
exasperating actions, you can see that the child has been asking for firmness of punishment all morning and that it was
your well-intentioned efforts at overpatience that made him go
from one provocation to another, looking for a check.

But he doesn't tell us what to *do* about it. Nobody does. And
nobody explains that sometimes it isn't that a parent is intentionally ignoring a child, but instead she has temporarily tuned the
child out and is suddenly brought back to attention while everything has been working on her at a subconscious level.

"I watch with horror as I behave in a manner diametrically
opposed to my most profound beliefs. One day after I had just had
it up to here with everything, I sprawled out on the sofa to relax
with the newspaper. As I sat there, wearing my peace medallion
and lamenting all of the violence in the world, the kids started
scuffling while watching TV. After the boy hit the girl, I jumped
up and belted him, yelling, 'Stop hitting, I can't stand violence.' "
This confession came from a sweet, easygoing father of two young
children—a Methodist minister who counsels those with family
problems.

One friend, the mother of three young boys, got so angry
when her oldest son broke a new toy that she threw all of his little
cars and trucks on the patio and jumped up and down on them
until they were in pieces. The boy just looked on aghast while she
told him, "If you can't respect your toys, then you can't have
them."

A divorced mother of three children wrote to tell me, "I love them so much and miss them badly on the three days a week that I work for our living. But when I am with them, I scream, slap, smack, and have even *kicked* my children."

The mother of a teenage girl admits that she broke a bed while chasing her daughter around the room in an effort to mete out disciplinary action because the girl had just hurled insults at her. The broken bed only inflamed her more. What had pushed her beyond the limit was that she had tried to teach her daughter respect and felt, at least momentarily, that it had all been in vain.

The late Haim Ginott also recognized that parents get angry: "When we lose our temper, we act as though we had lost our sanity. We say and do things to our children that we would hesitate to inflict on an enemy. We yell, insult, and hit below the belt. When the fanfare is over, we feel guilty and we solemnly resolve never to render a repeat performance. But anger soon strikes again, undoing our good intentions. Once more we lash out at those to whose welfare we have dedicated our life and fortune."

Fine. But how do we handle it? How do we keep from behaving like lunatics when our kids are just begging for discipline? Why do they beg? Is it for attention? What, if not the spanking they are asking for, do we give them? Will just ordinary attention do the trick? If we don't really let them have it, will we be too permissive and therefore damage them emotionally? When we are enraged, how do we call upon remembered advice?

There are no blueprints.

I once saw one of the best mothers I know slap her child across the face while hovering over him in rage, totally shaken at what she considered absolutely intolerable behavior. It was a painful sight. What made it even more painful was that although the child looked healthy and normal, he was terminally ill. The agony on this mother's face will be etched in my memory forever.

This mother and I share an abhorrence for this form of discipline. We are both nonviolent and share the view that face slapping robs people of their dignity. It would seem to be impossible that

anything could happen that would make us subject our children—
of all people—to such humiliation.

And yet, when Lisa was just seven—tiny Lisa—I slapped her
across the face for balking at taking a bath. Moments later, the
remorse, love, and empathy for her hurt and humiliation welled up
in me painfully. My guilt was completely deserved because she had
merely triggered an explosion that had been building for hours.
Ironically, Adam had been particularly obnoxious a few moments
before and was dealt with appropriately. But Lisa took the brunt
because her act was the final trivial incident of that particular day.
I was pushed beyond my tolerance level.

I knew very well, when my children were young, how important it is to gently, but firmly, push a child in the right direction
and that very often counting to ten or making him or her stand in
the corner or sending a misbehaving child to his or her room can
get the desired results. And yet all too often this reasonable
method of dealing with children is completely forgotten when
Mom has simply had enough of their arguing, nagging, shouting,
or back talk. And the fuse gets shorter as the physical and emotional fatigue gets longer. My own behavior in these instances
didn't do much for my self-respect, but at the moment of rage,
Benjamin Spock was a complete stranger, and my self-respect was
not even under consideration.

Where were my reason and self-respect on a lovely Sunday
afternoon in December when I told Adam and Lisa at ages six and
seven I was leaving them for good—that they'd just have to find
another mommy—and put on my coat and walked out the door?
Did I do that? Unbelievable.

After I had done the dishes, made the beds, and stuffed a load
of clothes in the washer, Daddy tripped off to run some errands,
the children went out to play, and I sat down to work on a project
that was hanging fire. Minutes later the kids were back in the
house, asking for potato chips and chocolate milk while pulling on
the Christmas tree and mutilating several packages. Correcting
the situation, I returned to my project, but before I got settled

down, they started wrestling on the living room floor, knocked over an ashtray, and kicked the antique carved chest. After I meted out the appropriate punishment, they became very quiet.

While I was congratulating myself on my disciplinary expertise, the silence was broken by the sound of a quart of milk hitting the newly waxed kitchen floor. And from that point on, things continued to deteriorate until I finally exploded. I spanked them, put them to bed, and announced I was leaving. I stalked out of the house amid mournful sobbing and pleading and frightened questions about who would take care of them.

Oh, I came back. In five minutes I was back in the house muttering something about having forgotten money for bus fare. They begged me to stay. The rest of the day and evening they were little angels.

That I could be driven to demonstrate such utter hostility and hatred, making those two little beloved children insecure in the process, is despicable.

A letter from a suffering mother appearing in a "Dear Abby" column also hit home. The woman wrote that she had hollered like a fishwife at her ten-year-old daughter as she was leaving for school. She went on to say that it was over a trivial matter, that she was so ashamed of herself, and that her daughter's feelings were obviously hurt. The woman was sick at heart at her behavior and felt pain for her hurt child.

I've been there, too. I have sent off not one but two children to face the day feeling bad about themselves. One morning when Lisa and Adam were about eight and seven and I was trying to get them ready for school, they kept dawdling, and the clock kept ticking away. I was tired, I prodded them to eat their breakfast, get their clothes on, and get moving so they could get to the bus stop on time. Finally, I blew my top.

After things cooled off, and I had bid them good-bye, I watched them walk off, hand in hand, heads lowered, knowing that their day had started with them holding back tears.

My God, what a terrible mother. And although I never for-

got how bad I felt that day, I have repeated that transgression
more times than I like to admit.

When my children became targets for my wrath, I tried to
find comfort in the words of Dr. Ginott: "There is a place for parental anger in child education. In fact, failure to get angry at certain moments would only convey to the child indifference, not
goodness. Those who care cannot altogether shun anger." But I
couldn't relieve my guilty fears.

The irrational behavior of parents, particularly mothers, is
sometimes humorous, often sad, and—many of us fear—emotionally damaging to small children. But what is even more disturbing
is a parental reaction that none of us is prepared for, and when that
happens, it strikes terror in our hearts.

A good friend and former co-worker, Bill, the father of three
boys, startled me with his honesty. Bill was an unusually good father to his youngsters, and I don't mean just in terms of participating in Little League, PTA, or Scouts—rather, he really
participated. When they were babies, he would get up for the
middle-of-the-night feedings, change their diapers, bathe them,
and put them to bed. As they grew, this kind of participation continued. He was an unusual, sensitive, and loving father.

One day we were chatting, and naturally the conversation
got around to his boys. Quite suddenly Bill said, "There's a fine
line between honest discipline and child abuse, and it's frightening
how often I find myself at the threshold of crossing over." This
came from a man who is gentle and kind and who has always loved
his children deeply and unconditionally.

My own way of handling things has been to walk away when
I felt my head filling dangerously with rage—rage I never expected to experience. Before I had children I had been virtually
devoid of a temper. In fact, I cannot remember ever hitting another person in anger, even when I was a child. Perhaps "walk
away" is not honest. I have *run* from the house more than once
because I was genuinely afraid that if I laid a hand on one of the

kids, it wouldn't stop there. I have reached the threshold of violence only a few times, and the sheer terror of my own rage has kept things in check.

Years ago, I watched my gentle mother kick a box around the kitchen for several minutes. She was so enraged at my younger brother that, as she kicked the box, she called to my father to "get him out of my sight—if I touch him I'll kill him." She meant it. Yet she adored my brother, and she was never one to spank any of us very much.

Another woman, a seemingly sane one, broke several yardsticks over her son in fits of rage. After a time her fury and guilt showed up as muscle spasms so severe she would occasionally pass out. Fortunately, yardsticks are too fragile to cause lasting damage.

A friend of mine used to regularly hurl her cat across the backyard when her kids were young and driving her mad. She confessed that at times, she, peace-loving, gentle, and nonviolent, had such feelings of hostility toward her children that she dared not discipline them for fear of where it might lead. She reasoned that it was better to throw a cat across the yard than to throw a child out the window.

Scores of mothers, and a few fathers, have confessed to coming very close to battering a child, to momentarily feeling such anger, hating a child so much, that maiming or killing him or her would be almost a pleasure. These parents have held their emotions in check, and while they have not hurt their children physically, they have built up a huge storehouse of guilt, shame, self-hatred, and fear—fear that just once they won't stop at the threshold, but will slip slightly over.

And statistics tell us that this fear is not at all unfounded. Over a million children are physically abused each year in the United States. The vast majority of those children—about ninety percent—are victims of what the child-abuse experts call "situational abuse." Situational abuse is defined as that which occurs when an otherwise stable parent becomes so overwhelmed with stress that he or she loses control. And most experts agree that *every* parent is a *potential* child abuser.

In 1973, I organized a Parental Stress Hotline in my community to reach out to overwhelmed parents and to help prevent the sort of child abuse that is preventable—that is, situational. It was an eye-opening experience. Child-abuse experts, such as C. Henry Kempe, Ray E. Helfer, Brand F. Steele, Carl Pollock, and Vincent Fontana, have conducted numerous studies that indicate that child abuse cuts across all socioeconomic lines. Based on the calls that came into the hotline in this affluent and child-centered community, I must concur that abuse, especially situational abuse, has no respect for status.

Parents—especially mothers, since most of the time they are primarily responsible for the care of the children—from all walks of life called the line. Comparing notes with workers on hotlines in other parts of the country, I found the pattern was the same. And so were the stories:

> The baby wouldn't stop crying. Nothing I could do would make him stop. At first I felt sorry for him. And then sympathy deteriorated into rage. I caught myself just in time. I was about to put a pillow over his face to make him stop.

> I spent the entire day cleaning the house and trying to be patient as my two- and four-year-olds took it apart as fast as I could put it together. Just before my husband was due home from work, the four-year-old climbed up on the drainboard, got into the cupboard, pulled down a jar of mayonnaise and dropped it on the floor I'd scrubbed that morning. I was cooking dinner, the phone rang. I just snapped.

> I'd been trapped in the house without a break for three months. Just me and the kids. They were driving me crazy, my husband didn't understand. This day was especially terrible because of all of the mischief and the noise. So, when the baby cried, I hit her.

It was when he flung his orange juice at the wall that I went out of control.

I'd wanted this baby so much. I thought he'd make me happy, bring my husband and me closer together. So, we adopted this child. We went to all the trouble and expense. I see now that I expected him to be a superbaby and me to be a supermom. Why else would we go to all that trouble? Things were great for the first couple of years. But he wasn't a super-baby and that meant I wasn't a supermom. It all fell apart when, after I knocked myself out day after day, he wouldn't mind. It wasn't at all what I expected, and one day I just blew sky high and beat the shit out of him. I did it again and again, no matter how I resolved not to. And then I blacked his eyes. I'm scared to death of what I might do next.

Statistics show that the incidence of child abuse is high among parents of adopted children. Is it because they have such high expectations and feel cheated if they "haven't gotten their money's worth"? Or is it because the novelty of a new child wears off, and they simply get tired of playing the role of parent? Whatever the reason, the child is often the victim of the parent's frustrations.

One nineteen-year-old, blond, blue-eyed boy is the type of teenage son many parents would like to have had: attractive, sensitive, intelligent. Abandoned by his natural mother as an infant, he was adopted by a couple from a small Texas town. He says that things "went okay" until his adoptive dad died, but his adoptive mother felt such resentment at being left with all the responsibility, "she turned into the Wicked Witch of the West."

She didn't seem to care about me after my dad died, so I just tried to stay out of her way. She started going out bowling and drinking and left me at home alone. She remarried three times, and all three of her husbands never acted like a father to me. They just thought I was in the way. They all beat up on me a little, and I guess my mother was afraid to interfere, so she just sat there and let it happen. Sometimes she would throw things at me or hit me, too, after that. I never could figure out what I did wrong. I guess she just didn't want me around anymore.

One day when I was just about fifteen, it was about twenty degrees outside and there was ice everywhere. My current dad got mad at something and started hitting me. He was really hurting me this time, and I knew I had to get out of there. All I had on was a pair of jeans; no shoes, no socks, no shirt or anything. I ran outside and down the street, but I didn't know where to go, and I was freezing. When it got dark, I curled up inside a phone booth, but I had no idea what was going to happen to me.

He moved to a large city, and managed to support himself and complete high school. But often the physical scars of child abuse heal much quicker than the emotional scars do. "I've had to go to a psychiatrist because I was getting ulcers. The doctor put me on tranquilizers because he said my ulcers were being caused by nerves," he says.

"I keep having nightmares about my mom. I wake up in a cold sweat, shaking, and I'm scared to go back to sleep. I usually dream that she is trying to kill me, so I guess I'm really scared of her."

Then there is another kind of abuse that is even more pathological in nature. An upper-middle-class mother of two children openly confessed how she had solved what she considered a rather sticky problem. When her children were preschoolers, she liked to sleep late in the morning, but the kids had other ideas. The two little "demons" would scramble out of bed at about seven o'clock each morning, climb into bed with Mama, cry, make noise, and get into mischief. The mother got around this by tying her youngsters, spread-eagle, to their beds, shutting off the sounds of their crying with a series of closed doors. She would release them several hours later when she had gotten enough sleep. She proudly stated that after they'd gotten the idea, the *fear* that she would do just that was enough to keep them in line.

She was a nice young woman who loved her children and found her role as wife and mother quite fulfilling. She measured up pretty well to at least one or two aspects of what constituted a good disciplinarian: She didn't make threats, and she was consistent. She merely demonstrated to the children what she would do if they didn't do as they were told, and then followed through until they thoroughly understood and behaved accordingly.

Another mother, according to an article on child battering in *Family Health* magazine, was a pretty, composed, young suburban housewife with three children. One of her children was a beautiful four-year-old girl who was "the image of her mother." This little girl was hospitalized after her mother pushed her down a flight of stairs, one of a string of similar incidents. Her mother was terrified of what she would do when her child was sent home. Hard as it may be to understand, she loved her child and wanted her safe from harm. This mother recognized that she represented a threat to her child's safety. Why did this nice middle-class woman beat her little girl?

The dynamic operating here was that she herself had been a battered child and she was a battering mother who abused the only one of her three children who bore a physical resemblance to her. It is not, according to the experts who deal with abuse, all that unusual for a parent who was battered to have such a low sense of self-worth that he or she projects that sense of worthlessness onto the child who most resembles him or her.

An eighteen-year-old boy told me he had been both emotionally neglected and physically abused as a child. The one thing that struck me was that this was one of the most physically beautiful human beings I had ever encountered. Everyone who knew him agreed that it was a sheer pleasure just to look at him. And everyone agreed that he was most charismatic, that he was the sort of person you just wanted to touch, wanted to hug. He bore no resemblance to his father, mother, two sisters, or three brothers.

When I commented on the lack of family resemblance, he told me he looked just like his grandmother. In passing, he added that his mother hated his grandmother.

A case that makes the point that abuse often moves from generation to generation and is a pattern that repeats itself is that of Mrs. K., described in an article by Dr. Vincent Fontana in *Medical Insight*. Mrs. K. said that she was appalled to discover that she "had spells of unprovoked viciousness toward" her child: "With the craftiness of a sick mind I hid all evidence of scars or bruises, or lied to explain them away. But something rational still operated enough to insist that my behavior was highly abnormal, and that I needed help. The horrible thing was that I did not know where to go for help, and even when I finally forced myself to the offices of various social agencies, I was so afraid of having the child taken away and my behavior thus exposed to friends and relatives that I could hardly speak of the problem. Even when I could, I found that social workers could not really help me. . . .

"Finally I moved up through the bureaus and agencies to a psychiatrist. Here I obtained help, but I might add that many people could not afford this."

This mother went on to say that she herself had been battered by her stepfather.

In a study of sixty families with battered children, University of Colorado psychiatrists Brand F. Steele and Carl B. Pollock (quoted in *Helping the Battered Child and His Family*, ed. C. Henry Kempe, Lippincott, 1972) discovered only one characteristic all these parents had in common: As children they had been battered themselves, either physically or emotionally. "All had experienced a sense of intense, pervasive, continuous demands from their parents. A sense of constant criticism. No matter what the patient as a child tried to do, it was not enough, it was not right, it was at the wrong time, it bothered the parents, it would disgrace the parents in the eyes of the world."

A number of astonishing factors that can influence the way we parent our children have surfaced in recent years. According to one person I spoke with at Parents Anonymous, the mother who is a hard-core child batterer nearly always was sexually abused (in addition to or instead of being battered) as a child. Furthermore, the mother who will allow her husband to brutalize a child was often a victim of sexual abuse herself. She is what social workers call a "passive abuser"; she allows a spouse or boyfriend to, essentially, do it for her. In most cases, the cycle of child abuse that began with a first sexual abuse encounter was initiated by a father, stepfather, uncle, brother, or a close family male acquaintance; this knocks the hell out of the idea that, all by themselves, mothers are responsible for the damage done to their children. My source at Parents Anonymous told me that it is estimated that one out of every three females will be sexually assaulted before she reaches the age of eighteen. And what is truly astonishing to me is that, according to Jeffrey Moussaieff Masson, a psychiatrist and the author of *The Assault on Truth* (Viking, 1984), the fundamental problem these females suffer is that, without therapy, many have no memory at all of the incidents that may well cause them to have serious neuroses, the least serious consequence of which might be that they will brutalize their own children.

As we look back on our own childhoods, how many of us can say with certainty that the relationship we had with our parents did not leave a great deal to be desired? How many of us can say we were "imprinted with that highly important and essential ability to mother a small child?" Even if we can look back on what we may think are storybook lives as children, remember that all of us, if we are parents, are capable of abusing our children.

I once asked Sharroll Blakely, the former director of the Office of Child Abuse for the State of California, what could be done to stem the epidemic of abuse. "The prevention of child abuse," she told me, "begins with family planning." She went on to explain that she meant *real* family planning that goes beyond just deciding when and how many, planning that involves honestly determining if you are cut out for the parental role.

# Chapter 9

# WREST AND WRECKREATION

About three weeks after we brought Lisa home from the hospital, I was scurrying around getting through the routine of infant care when the phone rang. I recognized the friendly voice of my obstetrician, who said he just called to see how we were getting along. We chatted for a bit, and then he asked, "Have you and Cal gotten out for an evening, or you for a day, since the baby was born?" When I told him no on both counts, he said, "I want you to get a sitter, go out with your husband for an evening, get away from the house and the baby, and that's an order!" He went on to say that all new mothers should have time to themselves, away from the house, diapers, baby, and formula, or they'll start feeling depressed and tired. I couldn't imagine leaving my tiny baby with a total stranger and going out to have a good time. But my doctor, seconded by my husband, finally persuaded me that it would be good both for me and the baby to get away from each other. Put in that light, I agreed—if it's good for the *baby,* then I'll go.

I called a local baby-sitting agency and stressed that I must have a registered nurse to come in and sit for one evening. Then I grilled the person on the other end of the line about the nurse they were sending.

Satisfied that the agency could provide us with someone qualified to care for our child, I made the arrangements, and the appointed evening for my maiden voyage arrived. For the first time, I was going to leave my child in the care of another person.

After the nurse arrived, I spent about thirty minutes giving her a rundown of the routine, although there were several sheets of handwritten instructions prepared in advance of the great moment. Finally, quite reluctantly, I left the house with my husband, bound for dinner and a movie. We were about three blocks from the house when I finally blurted it out: "She looks like she drinks. A *lot*."

We made it over that hurdle with my husband assuring me that the agency wouldn't send a drunk to our house to baby-sit, and he pointed out, rather irrelevantly, that she was wearing a nurse's uniform, so she must be a nurse. We went to the restaurant, had cocktails and dinner, and talked about the baby for more than an hour. Before leaving the restaurant, I excused myself to go to the powder room; I went immediately to a pay telephone and called to see if everything was all right (really to see if the nurse's speech might be slurred from raiding our liquor cabinet). At the movies, I felt as if we were 3,000 miles from home. During intermission I excused myself and called home again to see if the nurse was bombed out of her mind.

At the end of the evening I was tremendously relieved to get home and find that the nurse wasn't staggering around, and that my sweet little baby was just fine—Lisa probably didn't even know we were gone. But what an ordeal. An evening out should be relaxing, but how could I relax when I was worrying about my child and feeling like a selfish hedonist who'd neglected a baby to go out and paint the town red?

The next time it was a bit easier. And fairly soon we found some lovely, trustworthy, grandmotherly sitters, so at least we (or I should really say I) didn't worry too much. By the time Adam was born, I was more than ready to take off for an occasional evening, or day, but with that readiness to take off, a new paradox of motherhood surfaced.

Even though I had the security of knowing that the children were well cared for and that they even liked these nice ladies, I was far from content. I could be saying to myself that if I didn't get away for a few hours, I'd go completely daffy, while having the sinking feeling that I was a terrible mother for wanting to leave my two precious children. That I could admit even to myself that being with them all the time wasn't the ultimate paradise made me feel guilty. To make matters worse, there were those few times that the kids cried at our leaving. Here we'd be on the way out to a movie for the first time in three months, and one or both of our babies would be in tears. It is hard to enjoy yourself when you've just walked out on your crying baby, leaving him or her unhappy while sloughing off your maternal responsibilities.

A father of two told me that his wife's logic was beyond his grasp. He said she'd been complaining that the kids were driving her crazy, so he suggested that she farm them out for a couple of days to a friend who really enjoyed taking them occasionally. She snapped back with, "What? And be away from my babies? Never!" There may be no logic here, but it's true that while we're *dying* to be away from our kids, we feel guilty about wanting to. And curiously, we *do* actually miss them when they aren't hanging around.

Probably the worst trauma, after that first day or evening out, is the first time a mother is away from her child overnight. One mother confessed that when she went to the hospital to have her second child she felt terrible about leaving her two-year-old. She felt certain that her poor daughter was totally bewildered by her absence, and she worried about her constantly.

When a mother leaves her children overnight because she *wants* to, it is, of course, much worse. One young mother, an avid skier, had been counting the days until she and her husband could enjoy a vacation alone in Aspen. After they got back, she recounted that they were having a wonderful time, the skiing was great, and they were rediscovering each other when she spotted a little girl about the same age as her oldest daughter. That did it.

She couldn't wait to get home. Suddenly she was missing the kids and feeling unutterably guilty about having left them, even though they were being cared for by a grandmother whom they adored.

Another mother of two can well afford to go out every night, on weekend trips, and on long vacations with her husband. They don't, of course. It's not that she doesn't like to go out—she loves it. She loves traveling, too. Her lively youngsters frequently drive her nuts, and she admits that she'd love to get away from the routine and the pandemonium. But she can never bring herself to take advantage of all that her affluence allows. She says flatly, "Why, I couldn't *live* with myself if I were always running around and leaving my kids with sitters." The fact is, she rarely goes out and virtually never travels without the kids, and enjoying even her occaisonal respites leaves her with a sense of guilt. This not atypical mother feels guilty about wanting to be away when she's at home and guilty when she is away. Dr. Annye Rothenberg, who runs a parenting class for the Children's Health Council in Palo Alto, told me that one of the biggest problems her new moms have is giving themselves permission to be away from their children. Underlying this, she told me, is a conviction that even wanting to be away is evidence that they are terrible mothers.

I've never asked a mother how she enjoyed a child-free vacation without getting an answer that was qualified with "I missed the kids" or "I would have enjoyed it more if I hadn't been worried about Freddie and Julie most of the time."

One friend summed up the feelings of many:

> My husband and I have never enjoyed a vacation away from the kids, but about three years ago we both went to New York on business for nine days. I'd never been to New York City, so it was pretty exciting. Until we got to the airport. I wasn't even out of California—not even on the airplane— when it happened: that dull weight sitting on my chest that told me I didn't want to go. My husband managed to get me on the plane, embarrassed by my tears, and we winged our

way to Fun City. It was the most horrible nine days of my life, and I practically kissed the ground when we landed back in San Francisco.

Before we left for New York, my children, then two and six years old, were really getting on my nerves—and I was dying to get away. But I called home at least twice a day to make sure they were still alive and to reassure them with my voice on the telephone that I was still alive. And every time I heard their little voices there was a knife in my heart—I missed them so.

I felt incredibly guilty about leaving the kids. What kind of a mother goes off for nine days and leaves her little baby children at home? A bad mother, that's what. But probably the most irrational thought I had during the trip had to do with my being a white-knuckles flyer. I have no faith that a plane can stay up in the air; then there's the danger of midair collision, to say nothing of planes being hijacked. In the good old days I just used to worry about dying. But once I became a mother I worried about turning my children into *orphans!* Can you imagine how the poor little things would feel? They're robbed of their parents, and they wouldn't even understand that their mom and dad didn't leave them intentionally. I picture them emotionally crippled for life by being permanently rejected at a tender age by their parents. Rest in *peace?* Not possible.

Most parents I know, however, do not go on joint business trips or on vacations without their children. Once the kids arrive, for most of us, vacations become a family affair.

This is the way a mother of four describes her annual vacation:

My husband likes to fish, and we can't afford to do much else, so every year we go camping for about two weeks. I wash, iron, fold, and pack just about every summer garment owned by every member of this family. Then I dig out the camping cutlery and dishes, thermos bottles, and, of course, the chemical toilet. My husband sees to the tent, sleeping bags, and, of course, the fishing gear. We finally load up the station wagon, drive for about five hours, and after three dozen stops along the way, we reach our destination.

The first day or so is actually nice. *Any* change of scenery for me is refreshing. But after about a week of cooking over an open fire, boiling water to do dishes, enjoying the privacy and convenience of our chemical toilet, bathing in the icy water of a nearby stream, and washing clothes on the rocks, I yearn for the dull routine of our suburban house with its indoor plumbing, dishwasher, washing machine, dryer, *hot* water, television set, and telephone.

At least at home when I can't take the confusion, I can escape by turning on the TV or calling a friend. Here there's no escape. The kids flit through the woods and swim in the stream, my husband relaxes with his fishing pole, and I wash diapers on the rocks; the vacation's hardly a treat for me.

One father of four told me, "If you have never gone on a vacation camping trip with another couple and a total of eight children under the age of ten, you have not yet had the ultimate experience. You have yet to know how much you really do appreciate staying home."

And a couple who used to send us all kinds of postcards from places such as Yellowstone, the Grand Canyon, or Yosemite explained that the vacations had been strictly for the kids and once the kids were grown they were relieved to be free of the ordeal. What had appeared to be pleasant vacations from their postcards were, as they said, "endurance contests."

The closest we ever got to camping when our children were young was the annual company picnic, where activities included swimming, sack races, baseball, and a good old-fashioned barbecue. Other activities included lost children, bee stings, crying children, fighting children, cut knees, bumped heads, and an occasional domestic quarrel on the way home. The last time we went, Lisa got lost, Adam threw a tantrum, one father got so exasperated with his children that they left early, and three kids got stung by bees. By the end of that day, all the parents looked utterly exhausted, while all the young childless couples were making plans for the evening. The contrast between parents and non-parents was so striking at those functions that I marveled that those who hadn't started families yet didn't pick up on it. I wanted to say to them, "Here it is; take a good look. Do you want to look like a raving maniac? Okay, go ahead and keep making plans for your storybook lives, but you have a perfect opportunity today to see what it's like."

Thinking I was the only uptight mother, I stole glances at the others to see if they were enjoying themselves. I derived some kind of comfort from noting that all the other mothers seemed to be just as miserable. Everywhere, I saw mothers looking for lost children, yelling at kids, taking kids to the bathroom, changing diapers on the picnic tables, getting someone something to eat, or just sitting tensely waiting for something else to go wrong.

Knowing that this day was for the children—that my sole function was to be one of supervising my kids while they were having a good time—kept me from being frustrated while I was trying to talk to someone or swim or even eat. I just went along as an attendant, and the greatest reward the day could bring for me was that Lisa and Adam didn't get more than their share of insect bites, didn't get sick from too much soda pop, didn't slug it out with each other, and did have a nice time.

The company picnic was a lot like family get-togethers in the summer. My parents had a swimming pool, and they used to enjoy having the children and grandchildren come over on the weekends—at least I thought they enjoyed it. My mother always fixed plenty of food, and when we were ready to eat, my dad barbecued hamburgers and hot dogs. The kids would swim and play ball, trample Grandpa's prize begonias, and put garbage in the swimming pool. When the children were very young, there was the ever-present concern that they'd get into the pool while my back was turned and quietly drown while their hedonistic mother was laughing at the punch line of a good story. It's difficult to socialize while you're watching children, and besides, they wanted to be in the pool constantly, so that's where you'd find Mommy. As my nephew's wife, who was herself at the time a young mommy, told me, "You just never relax once you have kids, do you?" And then she ran off to keep her daughter from toppling into the deep end of the pool.

A mother of a nine-month-old described outings with a baby: "First there's the question of packing—even for a day—diaper bag, plenty of diapers, bottles, seven changes of clothes, blankets, playpen, a suitcase stuffed with baby toys. Taking the baby *any-where* for a visit is a very complicated process. Once I get there, I spend most of my time following my crawler around to make sure he doesn't destroy himself, pull over any lamps, or get into mischief; the rest of my time is spent changing diapers, cleaning up spills, and finally packing it all up to return home after an exhausting day of relaxation."

It's hard to believe that one tiny human being needs so much junk, even for a short visit to a friend's house, a picnic, or an outing in the park. Sometimes the advance planning is enough to make you think twice about even going. After Adam was born, whenever we went out, I'd pack a very large suitcase with enough diapers and clothes for two kids, take a sheet for the crib, blankets, toys, bottles, and of course the portable crib. My husband and I would each make a couple of trips to the car to load up for a fun day, pick up our kids, and be exhausted before we even got started. Then we'd go off for a day of diapering, feeding, supervising, and cleaning up at someone else's house, and if it was a really good day or evening, some snatches of conversation would get sandwiched into the routine of child care. If anyone wonders why the station wagon is popular even with small families, there's the answer: You don't get big cars to seat lots of people—you get them because you need a van for all the gear.

"By and large," however, one friend said, "the run-of-the-mill friends don't ask you over all that much after you have kids, because those very people who spent a lot of time questioning you about when you were going to start your family don't invite you over for fear you might bring the kids along—and they're too gracious to tell you to leave them home." Not everyone, I learned, is that gracious. I recall with a certain amount of amusement some people we know who had a child a year before we had our first. While they *always* brought their child to our house when they came to visit, when they invited us to their house they specified that the evening was for adults only. These were people who were eager that we follow their example and become parents, which tells me something about the level of sensitivity and graciousness of pressure bearers.

As our kids got older, and as we could afford it, we took the usual trips to Disneyland, Lake Tahoe, and other points of interest. Generally, because neither of us likes to drive long distances, we flew. But even under the best of circumstances, whenever we would arrive at our destination and my husband would register us, I noticed that his hand shook when he filled out the form. And the disadvantage of not driving is that when one of the kids would act up in a restaurant, there was no car for one parent to take the kid out to—a common practice, recognizable to any parent who has ever dined out with more than one child.

While I seem to have blocked out much of what took place and generally look back with fond memories on these vacations, I do recall that the last one we took was terrible enough that my husband nearly took Adam and flew home two days early. As I write these words, I realize that we have not had a vacation in six years, and I'm wondering if it was really true that, as we agreed, we weren't able to afford it.

By the time the kids moved into the teenage years, we could, however, afford to travel light—that is, just the two of us without the kids. We even reached a point where, having invested so much of our time, money, and energy into raising two children, we could do so without feeling guilty. But we found that while fifteen- and sixteen-year-olds are too old for sitters, only the most naïve parents would ever dream of going off for a vacation or a weekend leaving them alone. You don't even leave them at other people's houses.

We received nick-of-time enlightenment in this regard when we agreed to let the fifteen-year-old daughter of a couple we know stay with us while they vacationed in Mexico. She was a perfect angel the entire time she was with us. Naturally, she and our kids went out on Friday and Saturday nights, but they were always in on time. It wasn't until the parents came home that we learned that on a number of occasions, when they went "out," they went to *her* house and partied with dozens of other kids. The parents came home from a dream vacation in Mexico to a nightmare: The house was a complete shambles. After that, not only did we stop entertaining any notion of getting away for a couple of days, but whenever we went out, until just recently, we imposed a ten o'clock curfew on ourselves. If you've seen the movie *Risky Business,* you've got the idea. As one father of two teenage boys told us, "I've been grounded."

For a lot of people, having friends in is a lot easier than going out. But not that easy. One mother who used to entertain a lot and still likes to have people over, told me, "Most of the time when we would plan an evening with good friends, I would wind up vowing to my husband that I'd never try it again. Once it was a snap to put together a luscious dinner, lay a beautiful table, get the house whipped into shape, and have time to spare; with kids, I was lucky if I got anything cooked in advance and managed to be dressed on time." One thing every mother learns quickly is that you can't just plan a dinner or a party, you must plan for such interruptions as cut knees, temper tantrums, sudden fevers, requests for glasses of juice, or a mad desire on the part of the children to eat all the nuts.

We used to entertain a lot. But as our kids turned into teenagers, we found that we rarely asked anyone over for dinner. It only recently occurred to me that most of the people we know went through a similar phase, and I found myself wondering why. One very candid mother may just have come up with the answer for all of us: "When my son was in his teens, I was afraid to have people in for dinner because I was afraid he'd come home and embarrass me in some way. Or I worried that I'd get a call from the police, or from some other parent telling me to come and pick up my intoxicated kid." For the record, this "kid" is now a respectable twenty-eight-year-old stockbroker with a lovely wife and family.

When our children were young and we still hired sitters and went out, evenings out proved most revealing. In the middle of one pleasant party, one mother was saying to another, her voice quivering, "What do you do when you come home and find your baby-sitter doing the laundry at one end of the house, and your ten-year-old drunk at the other? I really shouldn't be here—I feel rotten. I'm so worried about him, and somehow I just feel that if I were a better mother, he wouldn't be so difficult to handle. What worries me is that this kid is smart; and he's curious—there's no end to what he might try." They wouldn't have come to the party, she explained, if it hadn't been a very special occasion; they would leave early; she felt guilty for even being here. "Oh, I made sure he's in good hands, of course, but I don't know—this thing is just weighing too heavily on me now."

At the same party, I found another mother unable to relax and enjoy herself. "I'm so depressed and worried over our daughter, I can hardly think straight, let alone enjoy myself," she said. "I had a meeting with her teacher last week, and I can't get it off my mind. I just know that there is something very wrong."

Then I caught this exchange between a husband and wife: "Where are you going?" "To find the telephone." "What for?" "I have to call home to see if everything's okay. The baby looked sort of funny this afternoon, and I probably shouldn't have left the house."

• • •

There's another kind of relaxation—that of just spending some quiet time alone with your husband. Those moments do exist; they can be caught or snatched. And yet so much of the spontaneity is gone—and not merely the spontaneity of picking up on a moment's notice to go off to the movies. So much of the ease of just being together is lost when children are lurking.

And then, of course, there's the last kind of relaxation. The kind that falls most naturally to non-parents and many fathers at the end of a weary day. I'm speaking now of simply relaxing in the evening—watching television, reading a book, or simply sitting and *being*. Few mothers ever know this pleasure, for most mothers are on call twenty-four hours a day. When two parents are sitting and reading after the children have gone off to bed, if a child cries or needs something, it's almost always the female adult who heeds the call. Sometimes the other adult doesn't even look up from the newspaper, and most often the child calls for his or her mother.

The mother of three children, ages three, six, and nine, described a typical evening at her house:

> After getting dinner, the dishes, and the kids' baths out of the way, feeling that I'd somehow miraculously survived this particular chaotic day, I sank tiredly into the sofa in the living room, and for a moment forgot my exhaustion and tension. I just sat enjoying the record my husband had put on. As I was finally starting to relax and feel human, the mood was shattered by a very loud and, as always, insistent "Mommy!" coming from the vicinity of the back hall.
>
> Feeling a perhaps unwarranted amount of self-pity, I got up and trudged off, along the way cursing every expert on motherhood who positively and pompously declares that all mothers should take time out for themselves—that to pursue interests, have time alone with their husbands, and time to relax is not only good for mommies, but for the little ones, too. Along with being annoyed at being disturbed and inter-

rupted yet again, I felt ashamed of myself for having such self-ish thoughts.

If this kind of thing happened once a day, I wouldn't have thought anything about it; ten or twelve times—many more times even—wouldn't have made me feel as if I were being attacked or punished even when I hadn't done anything to deserve disciplinary action. But the threshold had been reached somehow, and I'd gone past my normal tolerance level for routine interruptions. And those moments for myself while I was enjoying eight bars of music were well deserved and well earned. Stripping it away just then was like stripping me away personally. Pointing out to me that I don't really count, that time for me isn't even secondary to the needs, wishes, and whims of my family, are these instances—instances where I have every reason to believe that I can relax, only to have it demonstrated to me clearly that it isn't so. I resent this and I feel guilty over my resentment.

One mother told me that on most days she would respond immediately with concern when a child interrupted her to tend a cut knee or soothe a bumped head, yet at other times she was shocked to realize that she felt annoyed. She felt incredibly guilty. "What kind of a mother," she asked, "could feel annoyed when her child is hurt?" She wasn't even doing anything terribly important when she reacted this way.

So many women have expressed annoyance at being interrupted, prefacing their statements with some variation of "No sooner do you just sit down, when . . ." or "I'd just sat down to watch TV . . ." or "I just got comfortable sitting in the yard . . ."

Clearly we are annoyed because, first, nothing ever prepares us for the very real fact of being on call at all times, and second, when this fact is driven home by the reality of constant interruptions, it takes away our illusions that we still have some control over our lives and our destinies.

The mother of small children watches many of her freedoms go as her children grow and create a new array of demands. The big freedoms go all at once, but most parents are prepared to be tied down—even an idiot knows you can't just walk out of the house anytime you feel like it. And restrictions on the budget are relatively easy to understand and accept. Yet it comes as something of a surprise that it's difficult to pursue simple hobbies like sewing and painting, because doing these things requires your full attention, and because some of the tools are dangerous to have within the reach of young children.

The loss of privacy begins when your first child starts walking, and the loss grows. Some people dream of going to Hawaii to get away from it all. I just hope that someday I'll have privacy in the bathroom. Yes, even now. To this day, when there are any "children" in this house, my advancing toward the bathroom seems to trip a cosmic switch that triggers an uncontrollable desire on the part of one of them to communicate with me through the bathroom door.

Being able to simply sit and listen to music without interruption disappears, as does the chance to read a book when you want to—sometimes even finishing a short article becomes difficult. (How many of us have started to read an article, gotten interrupted, and by the time we got back to it found that the magazine had been thrown in the garbage, or that particular article had magically disappeared from the page, leaving only a gaping hole behind?) Obviously, no job allows a person to do whatever he wants whenever he wants to do it. But few jobs outside of motherhood include as part of their job description the stipulation that there is *no time off*—or, at best, that there is very little time off, but at the full discretion of the employer, and with no advance notice. As one friend put it, "It's not that I can't do what I want—I *can* read a book, I *can* listen to a record. It's just that I can never do it when I want to."

# Chapter 10

# THEY ARE WORTH
# THEIR WEIGHT
# IN GOLD

According to a study prepared by Lawrence Olson while he was with Data Resources, Inc., in 1980 it cost the typical American family $226,000 to rear a son and $247,000 for a daughter. In his book, *Costs of Children,* based on that study and published in July 1982, Olson calculated the costs of raising a child from birth through age twenty-two, basing his calculations on the historic spending patterns of the average American family. The reason why it costs more to raise a daughter is that transportation, recreation, and entertainment for a girl proved to be higher on the average than for a boy.

While it may well be debatable that girls cost more than boys, what isn't debatable is that the baby-sell that comes *after* you've been sold on the idea of having a baby is a fine example of clever merchandising. It closely resembles a tactic admittedly used by philanthropic fund-raisers: "The only way you can get money out of people is to shame them into contributing." And no cause can compete with a person's own child.

Parents have the usual amount of human guilt in varying degrees, frequently heightened by feelings of uncertainty and inadequacy about their capability as parents. And so they make excellent targets for this technique. The guilt, reinforced by the sincere desire of most parents to give their children the very best, results in a dream for professional merchandisers.

Look through a magazine or watch TV and count the ads telling you that baby's future will be more secure if you take out a policy with a certain insurance company. Notice those that talk about how Dad was disabled for life, but because he had insurance, his family will be taken care of. Or the ones that so helpfully inform new parents how to provide for that necessary college education for their two-week-old offspring. Anything, from cookies to air-conditioning units, is sold with the underlying message: "You're a bad parent if you don't buy it. Your children will be less happy if you pass it up."

The real baby-product sell starts taking hold when a woman becomes pregnant. Before the baby arrives, the expectant parents are buying cribs, cradles, bassinets, strollers, baby carriages, diapers, nighties, bottles, and sterilizers. After the baby is born, new parents discover they "need" many more things. While Dad is running to the store to pick up the forgotten cotton swabs or some extra diapers, the homestead is being bombarded. Three days after the birth announcement appears in the newspaper, your mailbox is stuffed with free samples of formula, baby food, baby powder, and douche powder; and letters and cards from insurance salesmen, baby furniture companies, baby clothing stores, photography studios, and the publishers of sex manuals (I was surprised at that one, too), with the accompanying promise of a free gift for purchasing an item or for agreeing to meet with a company representative. Then there are the phone calls. Shortly after I arrived home from the hospital with my first child, I logged eleven phone calls in one day from people peddling all of the above, plus items like subscriptions to women's magazines and books on child care.

One call came from a baby furniture company representative who told me that she had a free gift for our baby and a film strip to show, at our convenience, on child care and safety. Being very interested in anything free and extremely eager to be excellent parents, we thought it was terrific.

The appointed evening arrived and at seven-thirty we opened the door to a charming woman carrying an audiovisual rig. She set up her gear and started the film on "safety." The first frame showed a stroller with sturdier wire wheels than you'd find on a sports car. A well-modulated male voice talked to us from the speaker about the stroller's durability, explaining that it wouldn't collapse and break every bone in the baby's body. The next frame showed the same thing, only it was much taller. The voice explained that the stroller became a cradle. I see. Suddenly a baby carriage appeared on the screen and we were told that with the simple addition of a few components, the stroller-cradle became a baby carriage. The announcer described the excellent brakes—no matter what its function at any given time we could be comforted to know that the stroller-cradle-carriage would not roll down a hill. The guarantee covered so long a period of time that I wondered if after sixteen years it might turn into your offspring's first car.

But the last frame was the best. Suddenly, the "baby carriage" was stripped of handle and hood, a floor-length, ruffled, synthetic organdy skirt appeared, and—*voilà!*—a fancy bassinet. I stole a glance at my husband, and I saw it coming. He really tried to refrain, but he laughed in spite of himself. Then I started. Finally, our poor representative started laughing, too, and when we all quieted down a bit, she said, "I guess it *is* pretty silly." Then, looking meaningfully around the room at the eight-year accumulation of books, antiques, junk, art, and furniture, she said, "I should have realized—you're not exactly naïve kids." As we laughingly showed her and her equipment to the door, I asked her, as an aside, what that thing cost. She responded reflexively, "Only $499.95, and you can put it on a time-payment contract."

What had seemed so amusing that night was enough to outrage me the next evening. My husband came home and reported that two of the men he worked with had bought these things. The men were very young, and they were working on entry-level salaries. They could no more afford that baby carriage than we could afford a Rolls-Royce. And yet they had each spent $500.00 on something they hadn't needed because a master of merchandising had been able to convince them that to do otherwise would be to deny their babies the very best and safest equipment.

Fisher-Price, the leading toy manufacturer, has now branched out with a line of products, called Parent Helpers, that includes a door alarm that alerts parents when a toddler goes outside, a musical light dimmer, and a nursery monitoring system. Paul Valentine, a toy analyst with Standard and Poor's Corporation, offers this jaded view of companies that develop such products in an AP story by Cotten Timberlake (April 6, 1986) titled "How Do You Spell Guilt?". "They are trying to capitalize on the better parenting phenomenon where parents feel they are not fully doing their job unless they have the latest in safety and child development products. . . . Obviously, they are also trying to capitalize on the guilt factor. . . . you will see more of that."

Fear of physical harm to one's child is not the only fear waiting to be tapped.

A friend of mine, whose circumstances could best be described as impoverished, felt very guilty when her kids were about four and six years old. She kept getting hit by the encyclopedia salesmen. One time, while she was fretting over some dental bills, a saleswoman peddling the *Book of Knowledge* happened upon the threshold, and after my friend said, "No, we can't afford it," the woman cast her eyes downward and made gentle, sad noises about how deprived the kids were going to be. My friend wondered for a moment if, in fact, books weren't more important than teeth—only for a fleeting moment—and then she justifiably slammed the door. She, of course, never even began to wonder if something for herself or for her husband might be more important.

I remember once explaining to a salesperson (who, incidentally, had fraudulently gained entrance by saying she wanted to discuss the community's educational programs) that we could not afford a $400.00 children's encyclopedia set. She was eyeing our living room, and I found myself stupidly telling her that we didn't really have any extra money, and that our house was once a commune for students, and "it has termites" and "it was such a wreck that we got it for a song."

Keeping up with the Joneses frequently means keeping your baby up with the Joneses' baby. A wild one-upmanship arises. Babies don't seem to care particularly if they're dressed in terry cloth from Sears or organdy from I. Magnin, but mothers frequently do.

When my children were little, I spent a lot of time with other mothers and, naturally, we all compared notes on child care, giving one another tips and advice on what products were good and what methods worked well, and we tried to outdo one another at mothering. We started thinking about the development of our babies' little minds, which led to discussions of books to read, nursery schools, and toys. Toys were discussed very seriously because they are, it is felt, learning tools. A whole new world of peer pressure, competition, and high prices opened up.

There's a line called Creative Playthings, whose catalog is incredible—it pictures the most prestigious toys right along with some very prestigious prices. Creative Playthings toys are discussed in reverent tones, touted as splendid teaching aids for the very young and, by implication, for only the very elite. Somehow unreached, I courageously set the catalog aside and, much to the disdain of our friends, went to a discount store to buy my kids their blocks and other little-kid toys. But the catalog was nothing compared to the store that sold these CP goodies. The place was exquisitely appointed, with thick shag carpets, lots of natural wood, and elegant light fixtures. The saleswomen seemed to convey politely that they would grace you with assistance if they deemed you, the customer, an intellectual and social equal—an impression confirmed by a number of my more candid friends. The message was clear that kids who had these toys would have some sort of educational and social head start over those whose toys came from Sears.

Many people who drive inexpensive compact cars, watch the

food budget judiciously, and join baby-sitting co-ops to save money, spend three or four times as much on a simple set of building blocks or a puzzle labeled as having superior educational merit than they would on an ordinary similar plaything.

I've seen young parents spend money on an extravagant toy while they were worrying about paying the rent. But even those couples who can well afford it shouldn't be coerced into purchasing things children can't possibly appreciate.

Our children were not deprived of Creative Playthings or other exciting and sophisticated imports. Chic friends always selected these things as birthday and Christmas presents, not wanting us to feel that they'd give our children the low-status stuff. But the children, unimpressed by alleged educational qualities, superb design, and affirmations of good taste, have, as every child I've ever known, managed to break those toys just as fast as the Woolworth variety.

A friend of mine reported that the last time she got sucked in by the better-toy gimmick was when she bought her son the most beautiful set of boxes in boxes. They were imported from Germany, made of fine wood, put together in a tongue-and-groove fashion, and were beautifully varnished. Overlaid on the lovely finish of each one was a scene depicting a different fairy tale, and there were enough boxes to account for all of the classical tales. The last time she saw one of the boxes, her child was using it for a watering can while tending a weed he had planted.

Even the kids must get the message that something is wrong if they're not keeping up with the Joneses' kids: "I got a shiny new bike for Christmas, seven wooden soldiers, and a telescope; you only got a *used* bike."

While a number of studies, including the Olson study cited earlier, have been conducted on the high cost of bringing up baby, the one thing that is wrong with most of them is that studies conducted safely away from the physical reality of family life seldom, if ever, reveal some of the *hidden* costs of having children. Besides the possible costs of psychiatrists for a mom driven bonkers by her kids, or the cost of marriage counselors needed to patch up a marriage strained by the presence of children, there is the high financial (and emotional) drain caused by child-generated destruction.

A child doesn't really get expensive until he's been around for a couple of years, assuming, of course, that you have full medical coverage for the delivery, resist buying silly furniture, expensive clothing, and "in" educational toys, and if you discount the fact that an addition of one or two to the family may require a larger living space and may mean the loss of the mother's income.

The real increase starts when the kids are about three or four years old, big enough and imaginative enough to make very short work of a very large sofa, dismantle appliances, pull out newly planted trees and shrubs, and devastate their own and their parents' clothing.

While there is no way that any material object can possibly mean more to a human being with a heart than his or her own offspring, the discussion about the high cost of raising children would be incomplete without making note of these hidden costs. And any book devoted to exposing the realities of parenthood would be dishonest and incomplete without some mention of the way parents feel when they see the wanton destruction of their possessions, often either luxuries or necessities that were purchased as a result of hard work. Like most human beings, my husband and I have experienced unhappiness when we watched, over the years, our possessions vanish at a rate resembling a geometric progression.

Surely I was only human in feeling resentful that my little boy took an antique cameo ring given to me by my ninety-year-old grandmother. It is (wherever it might be) a thing of real beauty, and certainly I was sentimentally attached to it. He did admit to taking it (at least he was honest), but he couldn't remember just which kid it was he traded it with for a toy car. I canvassed the neighborhood in the vain hope of recovering the last of Grandma's treasures, all the while recalling that she gave it to me because she knew I'd cherish it. Maybe a few mothers value a million rings or a million dollars more than their children. I'm not one, but I still do value lovely things, so I can hardly feel bland about this loss.

When our children were young, my husband had few hobbies. He didn't play golf (too expensive), we couldn't afford to go out much, either separately or together, and he didn't have the time he once had. But he loved (still does) photography and music. It took us years to buy, piece by piece, the components for his sound system, and I hardly think he was a hedonist for feeling that this was one of his two most cherished material possessions. Imagine, then, how he must have felt when our young son completely destroyed his turntable, and then one year later destroyed its replacement. Loving Adam was quite separate from the justified distress that made my husband say, "Jesus Christ, Shirl, can't I have *anything?* Don't I count at all?" (That happened right after his camera was destroyed by the simple quick touch of a child's probing hand.) The point is scarcely that a camera or a turntable means more than a child. But we are all human, and we all tend to feel frustrated when our possessions, for which we have worked hard, are destroyed.

Is it too difficult to understand the frustration of having to spend a hundred dollars or more to replace a plate-glass window the same week the budget has revealed that it's time to tighten up? And that the reason it's time to be careful is that there was a fifty-dollar plumbing bill caused by some little innocent tossing wooden blocks in the toilet; and two weeks earlier the toaster toasting marshmallows met an irreparable end and had to be replaced; and just before the toaster was broken, the electric range had to be repaired because someone cooked plastic blocks in plastic pots while Mommy was showering and getting dressed.

A friend of mine had this to say: "I love them, but I get absolutely livid, struggling with a diminishing budget and imagining that our entire home will be just a memory soon. When our dishwasher was completely deactivated because our son tossed some plastic toys in while it was running, we'd been saving to buy a new tape recorder—a new one to replace the one that had been destroyed by a child's curiosity. We replaced the dishwasher and did without the tape recorder for a while longer, and the next thing to go was the TV set."

It's important to realize that we're talking about the destruction of the major sources of recreation for many couples. Because of the expense of rearing young children, and because the earning capacity may well have been reduced if the mother is home all day instead of working, they can rarely afford baby-sitters, movies, and dinner out.

Another mother made this comment: "I *know* Grandma didn't have a stereo or a TV set, but I'm not Grandma. Maybe we *are* materialistic today and maybe it's wrong. But we don't stop being materialistic just by giving birth. I feel I lose a little of myself every time something of mine is destroyed. I remember when my sewing machine—my friendly mechanical companion for many years, the one material possession that had saved me literally thousands of dollars and given me thousands of hours of pleasure—met its end. The thing *looks* fine, but it's been rendered inoperable by four tiny, curious, exploring hands. The solution is: Buy a new sewing machine. My considered answer is: We can't afford it."

I once believed that this sort of destruction lasted for only a short time—say about five or six years per kid. However, experience and observation have caused me to feel that, though there may be lulls, for many families it can continue well into the teenage years and beyond. If you get a thrill out of seeing all those cars demolished in those TV chase scenes, just wait until you give your teenager the keys to your car. And just wait until you see your insurance premiums triple or quadruple when the kids start driving.

Feminist purists like to believe that there exist few differences between males and females. I have a son and a daughter, and beyond the obvious physical differences, I noticed a striking difference between them from the moment Adam came into the world. Lisa, while a bit feisty and certainly not one to let people trample all over her, is far more docile. Adam has always been aggressive.

As he grew, he was the one who ran through the house like a tornado. He was the one who was more apt to wrestle with his friends. In fact, over the years, this house has been filled to overflowing with kids of all sizes and shapes, and always, always, always, it is the boys who wrestle, make the most noise and biggest messes, and tend to be destructive and determined to get what they want. And wreak the most havoc on the family possessions. For this reason, I challenge the contention that girls are more expensive to raise than boys.

I can count on the fingers of one hand the things that Lisa has destroyed since she was a young child. With Adam, I run out of fingers and toes. I have lost track of what he (and his friends) have reduced to garbage. I am on my third tape recorder, and I have resolved that if I move to number four (because the one I have is in bad shape as a result of his having "borrowed" it without my permission), he will never know about it. Even when he is thirty years old, I will never allow him anywhere near another tape recorder of mine. With no effort, I can recall just the tip of the iceberg:

Bicycles: He has taken apart no less than six of them
Radios: God only knows
Typewriters: Two
Windows: An easy dozen
Pool sweeps: One (broken twice)
Telephones: God only knows
Turntables: Two
Motorcycles: One (not his)
Television sets: Two
Alarm clocks: God only knows
Antique Victorian beds: one (broken three times)

An explanation of the last item is in order—especially for the uninitiated. When our daughter was about twelve years old, I foolishly allowed myself once again to buy into the idea that life can indeed imitate (media) art and proceeded to create teenage bed-rooms that would turn a TV commercial set director green with envy. Lisa's bedroom was decorated around one of those won-derful antique Victorian beds, complete with headboard, foot-board, and sideboards; it was something I'd bought long ago and hauled around for years. I refinished it, then papered the walls in a wonderful Victorian pattern and covered the floor with nine-teenth-century hotel carpeting. Louvered shutters were put on the windows, an antique frame (picked up for a song) was filled with a mirror. This room was a wonderful sight to behold—it was the room I had craved for myself all of my life. Picture it: nine-and-one-half-foot ceilings, beautiful Victorian wallpaper, great floor coverings, a dressing table, and a beautiful Victorian bed that sat very high off the floor. Now, it could be said that Adam was jeal-ous of her room were it not for the fact that he, too, had a won-derful room, designed and executed by loving maternal hands—a masculine room with full trappings, with plenty of space for him to do his soldering and other mysterious electronic and mechanical things. In truth, it was simply that Lisa's room was the one where the friends gathered. And, for some reason I cannot to this day fathom, Adam and his rowdy buddies made it a daily practice to jump on her bed. I would sit in my study typing away and I would hear it, or Lisa would call, "Mom, please come." After they broke the bed for the third time, I simply dismantled it and stored it in the garage. To this day, it remains in storage and in serious need of repair.

In any case, the list of items that have been destroyed or have completely disappeared goes on and on: scissors, hammers, house keys, pliers, staplers, can openers, desk drawers. Recently, Adam "needed" a transformer, so he cut one off of my electric tooth-brush. Since that device was prescribed by my dentist for special gum problems I have, I, of course, went insane. Shortly after that, he "borrowed" my computer cable and lent it to a friend because, as he later explained, "Dave needed it to interface his guitar with his amp." I spent hours looking for it, convinced that I had become demented, disconnected it, and misplaced it. After having confessed to taking the cable, Adam then had the utter gall to ask if he could "borrow" my microprocessor. Well, at least he asked.

There are boys and there are girls. And then there is a certain type of boy, and it seems that boys of this type find each other and form fast friendships. Not only are these kids generally more aggressive than females, they are also generally more of everything else: curious, boisterous, energetic, determined. I have talked to scores of parents who have at least one of them in the family and they all say the same thing: The only way you can keep them from turning the house and everything in it into garbage is to be constantly vigilant. But no parent who has responsibilities beyond that one child can watch him every single minute.

I was once roundly criticized for mentioning in public that my son had destroyed a number of things. The Perfect Parent who criticized me told me that I "should teach my child to respect the property of others." Well, I do. And he does respect the property of others. The problem is that occasionally that respect evolves into love for that property and a passion to do something with it. I truly felt like putting Adam on a plane and sending him to that judgmental mother. My guess is that she'd break in less than a month.

Plagued with guilt and feelings of inadequacy at my failure to get the message across that he must *leave things alone* (my husband has no success here either), I have talked to other parents with similar problems. A father of five told me that, experienced as he is at parenting, he's at a loss as to how to deal with the one of his three sons whose desire to take something apart overwhelms his better judgment. At the time, the boy had just turned sixteen and was still at it. I say that those parents who are always able to imbue the proper respect for other people's property in all of their children are no better than I; they just didn't draw one of these kids. I have no idea what the odds are of drawing one of them, but anyone who does had better be long on patience and either live a fairly spartan existence or have a lot of cash.

Much more than the dollar count, although that has to be considered, is the feeling that there are forces out to deprive you of any fulfillment or pleasure you seek as a person. You may begin to wonder if the next thing you reach for will simply vanish before your eyes.

Adults who are stripped of their accumulated and worked-for possessions can feel as if their very essence as individuals is being methodically taken from them. They can become quite paranoid about each new disaster, large or small. One woman with enough money to replace every object destroyed by her children put it this way: "You can be determined to remain a self, to have productive interests or interests that just provide simple leisure pleasure, and at each turn you become more apprehensive that something else has disappeared or has been destroyed."

How does a parent who works at a job that he or she hates feel when the fruit of tedious labor goes up in smoke? I may be the only mother who has experienced resentment that missed appointments with the orthodontist have cost me what it requires me two hours to earn—and that added to that particular insult has been the insult of having the orthodontist first tell me that keeping the appointments is the child's responsibility and then tell me I am a "bad mother" because the child did not keep his appointments. (Of course, if I were truly a "bad mother," I wouldn't even bother—I'd just let the kid go through life with teeth that resembled a Japanese fan.) But that heavy trip is beside the point.

The point is that when my labor pays for nothing at all, the implication is that my time, and hence my very essence, is unimportant.

Items that are neither very expensive nor apparently vital to the perpetuation of self can become incredibly important when heedlessly ruined. A very loving parent can feel resentment over something as trivial as the disappearance of a twenty-nine-cent comb, possibly because it's one more indicator the parent is not important as a person. The source of rage and hurt can be as simple as a thirty-three-cent snapshot—if it just happens to be the only picture you have of a deceased friend or relative.

Once, it was my last corn pad. I was frustrated; I was absolutely furious. The last corn pad can mean a great deal to someone about to put on a pair of closed-toed shoes, but nothing to someone guilty of using it in place of Scotch tape to keep a piece of paper attached to the wall.

"We couldn't keep Band-Aids in the house," said the mother of three grade-schoolers. "When my daughter was seven years old, she put them on imaginary cuts, and she put them on her dolls. I'd discover that we'd run out when I needed one to put on a bleeding knee or elbow."

It's amazing how the disappearance of the Scotch-tape dispenser, the stapler, pens, pencils, paper clips, or a ruler can cause total exasperation to the point of near rage. A frustrated adult can waste hours in a determined search for something as trivial (but vital) as a pair of scissors or a tube of glue. With resignation, I used to cut my manuscripts apart with a kitchen knife and rearrange their parts using straight pins. One father of four firmly (and oddly enough, proudly) announced that there would be no TV watching in his home until the scissors were returned to their proper place. He said he was sick and tired of never being able to lay his hands on something he needed because someone who really didn't need the thing had not only taken it, but had failed to bring it back. One of my better moments was when I took my scissors, among other things, to the city to set up a booth at a fair. That evening when Adam asked me where "the" scissors were, I smiled broadly and said, "I left *my* scissors in San Francisco."

Whatever the object, it's not so much its loss that drives you mad as the fact that nearly every elementary endeavor becomes a monumental task because you can no longer lay your hands on the simple tools you need to carry out simple jobs.

Of course, there are solutions. Scissors can be attached to chains. Can openers can be put on the top shelves of cabinets. Turntables can be put behind locked doors. (One mother I know kept her toolbox in the oven so her son couldn't find it. She got tired of never having a hammer or screwdriver when she needed it.) Yet even the most organized households suffer raids by the children. And none of the solutions seem to offer the advantage of living in a way one might wish to live. It is, after all, a bother to trek to the top shelf of the hall closet to get your makeup each morning. How much more convenient it is to keep it in the bathroom or on the dresser.

And how do you teach children respect for other people's property when you convey with a series of locks that you don't trust them? And what happens when the phone rings in the middle of locking something up and the forbidden object becomes available and tempting?

When our children were very young and I had completely child-proofed our house, my morning routine looked like this: To take my thyroid pill, I stood on a chair so I could reach the top shelf of my closet to get the pill out of a locked case. Then I unlocked the bathroom door, having first unlocked the linen closet to get a towel, remembering to lock it afterward. Then I took my two-minute shower, hastily dried myself, and threw my clothes on. After that, I got my makeup down from the top shelf of the closet, and proceeded to put on my face. During the entire ritual, of course, I had to return everything to its proper place, put chairs back in order, and make sure everything was once again locked up. A year or so of that is not so bad—maybe. But five years of it doesn't make for relaxed living.

To solve the problem of property damage (you can't put the sofa on the top shelf of a closet), one couple outfitted their home in furniture the Salvation Army would turn up its nose at; all of it sat on concrete floors that could be hosed down. They both said, almost in unison, "We have a great house. We plan to decorate it tastefully after the kids are grown and gone." True, there's nothing for a kid to wreck. Also true, there's nothing for the parents to enjoy.

Another couple went to the other extreme. Their son is allowed only in his bedroom, the hall bathroom, the family room, and the kitchen of their beautifully furnished home. The boy, so clean and cowed, seems less than happy. Two couples with kids solved this dilemma in the same way: They both have split-level homes. The upper level is adult territory, the lower level is for the kids, or, as one of the mothers put it, "Civilization is up here, the cave is down there."

The feeling of embarrassment when your child destroys a friend's possession perhaps can be dismissed as vanity. Concern over the destruction of material goods, however vital to the pleasure of the individual parent or the total family, perhaps can be disregarded as crass materialism. But I must note here for the record that those who are quick to suggest that modern parents are materialistic are usually the same hypocrites who put capitalism, free enterprise, and a growing GNP right up there with God, the flag, motherhood, and apple pie. The feeling that one's self is being stripped away with each new depredation or disappearance perhaps can be shrugged off as a neurotic attachment to objects. It could be said, quite validly, that a destructive dog could do as much harm. Yet all of the above feelings exist and are caused not by dogs but by children. What can hurt the most is the sense of defeat that comes to parents who wonder, as they watch their possessions disappear, if their children can possibly be growing up with a regard for other people's property.

# Chapter 11

# IN THE BEST
# OF FAMILIES

*During the years before we had children, the one thing we heard over and over again—I guess you'd say, as the ultimate persuasion for us to have them—was, "Yes, children are a huge responsibility, but it's all worth it when you know the rewards of having raised healthy, happy, successful children to adulthood." No mention was ever made of how you might feel if it didn't turn out that way.*

—A California mother

There is, for some parents, a pause that refreshes, so to speak. For me it came just after Adam's eighth birthday and continued on until Lisa became an adolescent. Roughly four years of relative calm. I say "relative" because those years were by no means stress-free. Rather, Lisa had entered into a very sweet stage and Adam was no longer bouncing off the walls every five minutes.

Adam being Adam, of course, meant some continuation of such things as riding his bike off ramps in imitation of Evel Knievel, going to the city dump to pet the rats, riding his bike down the train tracks (and being reported to Mother by a concerned neighbor), taking apart Mother's tape recorder, and occasionally breaking ironclad rules. This book, for example, would not be complete without my report of the time when he was ten years old and had been reminded repeatedly to lock his bike up so that it wouldn't get stolen. Well, of course, he "forgot" as he dashed into the thrift store in search of old motors, and, of course, his bike got ripped off. I learned this when the friend who'd gone with him came hurrying back to the house to tell me that not only had Adam's bike been stolen, but some "nice people" had come along and Adam had gotten into the car with them to chase the thief. "Never, never, never, under any circumstances, should you get into a car with strangers!" I must have said that at least a thousand times. My hand shook so hard that dialing 911 became a major feat.

"We'll get an APB out right away. Description, Mrs. Radl. Any identifying marks?"

"He's beautiful. Beautiful big blue eyes . . . white hair . . . I've told him a thousand times . . ."

Fourteen squad cars were dispatched. When, some time later, the car I was in returned me to my home, I saw his bike in the driveway. I did not consciously know until that moment that I never expected to see him alive again. I became so hysterical that the kind police officer held me in his arms to calm me down. And then he quietly asked, "Which way to his room?" A nice man, he took my son to task first for "doing such a terrible thing to your mother," then for placing himself in very real danger. The good news was the bad news. The people who had picked him up were nice people. They not only didn't harm a precious hair on my son's head, they got his bike back for him. So he never really learned a lesson. With very mixed feelings, I once again had to thank God.

But, all in all, those rather magic years were less eventful than earlier ones. Another thing that contributed, I think, was that during that brief period Lisa and Adam had the nicest teachers they would ever have.

Looking back, I now see that relative serenity as necessary to giving us—especially me—an opportunity to recharge the batteries, providing emotional strength we'd need to get us through

the adolescent and teenage years. When Lisa turned twelve, she
did so with a vengeance. That darling little girl I'd known in the
years before vanished without a trace. Where once she was quite
sensible, she became irrational. Friends became the center of her
universe, and the conviction that she had no friends at all became
unshakable despite evidence to the contrary. If, for one day, she
didn't have at least one friend around, she became convinced that
no one in the world liked her.

I recall a day when Lisa told me, "Mom, you're the most understanding mother in the world. I'm so lucky. None of my friends
have understanding moms like you," only to turn around fifteen
minutes later and tell me, "I hate you, bitch!"

Doing the "right" things for Lisa resulted in my suffering
nearly constant abuse and mental anguish. She blamed me for her
crooked teeth and then accused me of torturing her and "ruining
her life" when we spent several thousand dollars and several hundred hours carting her around, conferring with specialists, and sitting in the outer offices of orthodontists, oral surgeons, and speech
therapists.

Meanwhile things were going splendidly with Adam. His
twelfth birthday did not mark any noticeable change. When he
started junior high school, I waited for the other shoe to drop. But
it didn't. When I asked him about school, he said he loved it and
he was doing well. While I was getting sucked into wild arguments
with Lisa on an almost daily basis, and while all the other mothers
around me were going through the same thing, Adam was as docile as a lamb. It was the quiet before his nervous breakdown, which
was triggered by junior high school. To describe this in any detail
would require another book—and one that I do not think I would
ever be up to writing because, even though we survived them,
those were the most painful years I have ever experienced.

To rule out the possibility that Adam's problems may have
had an organic cause, his therapist sent us to the hospital for tests.
I recall sitting in the very hospital where he had been born, the
place where I'd counted his fingers and toes and thanked God for

a perfect, healthy child. I recall, on that day, so many years later, as I awaited the results of his tests, praying that they would show he was brain-damaged. At least it would have been an answer. But his brain was fine—he was having an ordinary, garden-variety adolescent disturbance. That many boys go through this when they hit adolescence is another one of the many things people forget to mention when they describe how much fun parenthood can be.

Every day was filled with stress, pain, and a sense that the family, along with the mother, was disintegrating. Yet, when I look around at all of the families we have "grown up" with over the past years, I thank God every day that there was (and I knock on wood with one hand as I write these words with the other) no lasting damage.

A mother wrote to me—understandably anonymously—to tell me about her experiences with a teenager: "Although my son drove me crazy all through high school, and although the only terrible thing that happened was that he drank too much beer a couple of times, it was after graduation that the sky fell in. He started running around with a group of young men who were dealing in dope. Fairly soon, he was smuggling it in from Mexico. I lived in terror that he'd be caught and sent to prison. Also, it was great fun when we went to the country club and listened as parents talked about their kids being accepted to Harvard or Yale. What were we to say when we were asked how Bill was doing? 'Oh, just great. He grossed forty grand last year.' "

This mother went on to say that, even though they had always been devoted to their son and attentive in the matter of teaching values, she and her husband felt they were to blame. Why not? I'm sure that virtually everyone who hasn't had a similar experience would hold that view as well. Usually you hear, "Well, they gave him everything but love." How can anyone who doesn't live with them know that for sure?

While some parents can afford to give their children more material things than others in an attempt to make their lives as carefree as possible, I can't believe that most parents would *substi-*

*tute* material things for parental concern. That's the stuff of which movies and sociological theories are made. It also gives young people an excuse to not accept responsibility for their own actions. Ah, suffering parents make such good scapegoats.

Sometimes the things that drive the parents of teenagers up the wall are laughable, especially when you aren't the parent of a particular teenager. Back in the late sixties, one mother I knew became overwrought about the long hair on her two teenage sons. She didn't know what to do. She didn't really understand why she felt so upset, because it didn't bother her when other boys let their hair grow down to their shoulders. She sought refuge by pointing to them, rolling her eyes, and hastily saying, "I can't talk about it." When her eldest son dropped out of college, she became depressed and again didn't know what to do. She feared that if she urged him to return, he would become more determined to stay out; but then she feared that if she didn't encourage him, she'd miss an opportunity to reason with him, to show him why this was a mistake. By this time, he was twenty-one years old and legally an adult. Should she throw him out of the house? He was, after all, an adult. But then he was her son. The question remained unresolved for her, and another cropped up. Would her sixteen-year-old follow in the same path? She had "failed" one of her children. Would she "fail" the other? Would she "fail" completely in the one thing that had been her life's work—motherhood?

Having a teenager drop out of school may traumatize some parents, but for others, that's the least of it. One mother, for example, seemed terribly distraught just because her nineteen-year-old son had dropped out of college. Finally, she said, "If that were all there was to it, I'd be grateful. He didn't really drop out voluntarily. We brought him home. He's sick. He started smoking a little grass a few months ago and then became interested in hallucinogens. Apparently, he and several of his friends started experimenting with mescaline. We had no idea until we received a call from one of his roommates telling us he'd been hospitalized. From what we're told by both our son and the hospital officials, he took an LSD trip, and it was a bad one—or, as the kids say, a bummer. He seems so strange now. I fear he is damaged for life. And I keep wondering where I went wrong."

Another mother who wonders where she went wrong, even though she and her husband gave the boy everything, has now bailed him out of jail at least six times. At this writing, he is in jail for a street robbery that netted him sixteen dollars.

One mother I know had ambitious plans for her eighteen-year-old son: Stanford University, a law career, a credit to the family, himself, and his parents. Now she says, "He's running wild, and there is nothing we can do. He dropped out of high school, and legally that's his right. He goes off with his friends and doesn't come back for days at a time. Sometimes he seems normal, other times I can tell that he's 'on' something. All our plans—down the drain. His father has washed his hands of him completely."

An excellent example of the expectations we have when we *plan* to have children is that of a couple who adopted a baby. The mother of this boy went so far as to get a job at Stanford University when she would have preferred to work elsewhere. Why? Because then her son would be able to attend Stanford at a reduced tuition rate. From the time this boy entered high school, he cut classes, smoked dope, and got in trouble with the law. He dropped out of high school at sixteen, and the very day he turned eighteeen his profoundly disappointed and burned-out parents threw him out of the house.

The mother of two teenage girls had this to say:

Nowadays, it's harder to deal with teenagers. Sometimes I think I'm too strict, and I know that I'm not "with it" about sex and drugs, but honestly, I don't want my daughters to wind up dope fiends or pregnant. Right now, one of the girls is "in love" with a bum. I don't let her go out with him, but how do I know she won't sneak around to see him because she has such a crush on him? How do I know that he won't talk her

into something? Sure she has values, but I remember what
"first love" was like, and it can be a pretty strong influence on
a young girl.

Sometimes I panic. The same things that work with one
of my daughters doesn't work with the other. And you can
only hope the years of trying to mold their values has some
effect. But if they fall in with the wrong kids, it doesn't seem
to matter whether you've done a good job. Sometimes I fear
that my strictness will cause a reaction, and yet I fear that if
I'm permissive, it will be less than nothing. It's damned if you
do, and damned if you don't.

"Nowadays, it's harder to deal with teenagers." Anyone contemplating parenthood ought to burn those words into their
brains. When Lisa and Adam were babies in the late sixties, the
drug culture was just making its way onto the college campuses.
Never in my wildest dreams did I think that a situation in which
college students used grass and LSD would become one in which
all dangerous illicit drugs were readily available to elementary-
school kids. Thus, it should come as no surprise that I think that
however bad things are today, they will be far worse in the future.

In any case, I have a five-inch-thick file folder bursting with
dozens of letters from a tormented mother of three girls. Over the
years, these letters have allowed me to chart the development of
each of the girls along with the progressive agony of their mother.
Almost on schedule, as each girl passed her sixteenth birthday, she
became involved with drugs, resorting to theft to buy them. Each
girl was arrested several times for drug possession and for theft,
and each was placed in a drug rehabilitation program. The once
stable marriage of the parents collapsed under the monumental
stress of the situation.

A father laments, "You get them through it. You finally get
them through the mumps, measles, elementary school, homework,
Scouts, high school, the fights over staying out late, using the car,
drinking beer, experimenting with pot. He's a good clean kid,

after all, thank God. And then he goes out and smashes himself up
on a motorcycle. He'll live, but you should see what he did to what
was once his face."

In another family, an eighteen-year-old son had a fight with
his girlfriend and immediately got drunk, jumped into his car, and
rammed it into a cement wall. Fortunately, he was unsuccessful in
his drunken suicide attempt. Unfortunately, he cannot walk, use
his hands, or speak. He had been an honor student.

One of Adam's best friends was killed instantly in a motorcycle accident, and Adam himself was seriously injured in a motorcycle wreck. We learned that even if you forbid your son to own
or ride such a monstrosity, there's no way to guarantee that he
won't ever get on one and head out into the path of an oncoming
car.

There is no guarantee our kids are safe even if they *do* try to
do what we have taught them. I know of an eighteen-year-old
honor student who was killed after he refused to ride with a friend
who had been drinking. He rode with another friend. Then the
party of the first car rammed his car into the party of the second
car, killing the boy instantly and sending the driver to the intensive
care unit.

On a recent evening, while I was working on this book, I
called a friend of mine to make a lunch date. Usually a cheerful, happy, and outgoing woman, she was on this night a whim-
pering, wounded soul. Her twenty-five-year-old son, a schizophrenic who had been wandering the streets, had come home. He
was encrusted with dirt, his clothes were shredded, his fly was
open. She said, "It's truly amazing that he wasn't arrested for in-
decent exposure." The agony of that moment could not possibly
be conveyed to someone who has not had the experience. How
horribly painful life must have been for her and her family since
her son suffered his first schizophrenic break some six years earlier.

I know no fewer than five families who have experienced the
trauma of having a teenager suffer a schizophrenic break. This is

not terribly surprising in view of the fact that at least forty million families around the world have at least one member who suffers from schizophrenia. Despite the large body of evidence that this disorder may be inherited or caused by a chemical imbalance, the parents of schizophrenic offspring are often held responsible by many health-care professionals and by society in general. According to Maryellen Walsh, the author of *Schizophrenia: Straight Talk for Family and Friends,* even when there may be as many as three perfectly healthy children in the same family, the parents are viewed as being responsible for illness in the one child so affected. The blame fixing comes in the form of "Well, they probably treated this one child differently from the others." Rarely is it suggested that the child so afflicted may be constitutionally different. About this blame fixing, Walsh makes an observation that could apply to all parents when she states, "As a parent of four I can only say that I wish I had the influence on my children that these researchers imagine. It's almost comic that they view parents as so powerful. One wonders if they ever asked a teenager to clean up his room."

When I met my friend—the mother of the schizophrenic son—for lunch, she was her usual chipper self. Less sensitive people would assume that the reason for her good cheer was that her son had magically recovered. The reason, however, was that she had finally gotten him signed into a mental institution. Need any more be said about how really terrible the situation had been for a mother to be happy about her child's commitment to an asylum?

The evening after my friend and I had lunched, I was cooking dinner when a young man came by to see us. He had just gotten out of rehab. He was (is) truly on the road back, but he had a drug problem that nearly destroyed him.

The only families I know who appear to have escaped trauma during the stormy teen years are the ones who send out printed mimeographed letters at Christmas time to inform the reader that young Claude has been accepted into Harvard, Nancy's piano teacher thinks the girl will one day be ready for Lincoln Center, and Fred has so many swimming medals the family is considering adding a room to house them.

Nearly every other letter I receive from a parent of a teenager (and I receive many of them) contains the sort of news that only a satirist would include in a Christmas letter. And then, of course, there are the families I personally know. Only a few seem to have escaped serious problems with their teenagers.

Some parents manage to hang in there, and for some of them the outcome is positive, while for others, it seems, no amount of loving, attempts at problem solving, or just plain haranguing can bring about positive change. Then, there are the parents who have simply burned out from it all. Many seem to have experienced one shock of reality after another, in part because their expectations were based on fantasies and not hard facts. I know parents who, a dozen years ago, were shocked at my candor in the first edition of this book about the parental role and who, ten years later, threw their kids out on the street when, at sixteen, they became too much to handle. I know parents who said "It will be different with me" when they watched someone struggling with an errant seventeen-year-old and who proved that it indeed was when they couldn't take it any longer and simply locked their doors on their own kids.

"Good people" are shocked when their middle-class neighbors cannot cope and turn their backs on their own children. There is an assumption that it is rare for parents to be so indifferent, so frustrated, so disappointed, or so angry at their children that they, in essence, desert them. But it isn't all that rare, and a fact that must be faced is that some people don't even *like* their own kids.

In an article in *Parade* magazine, Dotson Rader notes that over a million children, with a median age of fifteen, live on the street in this country. Many turn to prostitution to survive, and many die of untreated diseases or brutality, and some just disappear. The vast majority of these young people come from white upper- and middle-class families. According to June Bucy, executive director of the National Network of Runaway and Youth Services, "A small proportion are kids who leave because of school troubles or drugs or other problems. The rest are throwaways, kids kicked out of home." Rader reports that the majority of runaways are never reported missing by their parents.

Even when parents do like their own children, there exists a limit to how much individual parents can handle emotionally. If some people fall apart when their sons grow their hair long or pierce their ears, or their daughters wear too much makeup and tattered jeans at the wrong time, imagine the emotional state of parents whose children repeatedly run away, use dope, get drunk, steal from them, or get into trouble with the law.

Parent burnout is a real and widespread phenomenon that, according to Dr. Joseph Procaccini, affects "as many as fifty percent of parents." Dr. Procaccini defines this state as one of "physical, emotional and sometimes spiritual exhaustion resulting from chronic high stress and perceived enormous responsibility." He says it is caused by the enormous pressures our culture puts on parents to be perfect and provide children with all sorts of activities, and leads to intense feelings of anger, stress, and "responsibility without control." "The saddest thing about burnout," he says, "is that it happens mostly to highly motivated parents who embrace their child-rearing responsibilities most enthusiastically. . . . Unconcerned parents don't suffer this condition. To burn out, you have to be 'on fire,' dedicated, concerned."

Parents behave in various ways when they say they are burned out. One mother I know just became indifferent. As long as her daughter didn't destroy the family home, she ceased to care that the girl stayed out half the night, constantly cut school, came home drunk, and was on a self-destructive course. It was as if this woman, who once ran over to the school to try to solve problems at the drop of a note from a teacher, was just marking time until her daughter got older and left home. One couple had to endure much of the same, but their daughter was also sexually promiscuous (and flaunted it), and ran away constantly because she said her parents were "too strict." The seventh time she ran away, they changed the locks.

And then, of course, burnout drives some parents to ask their kids to simply pack up and leave. One couple I know moved out of the house and into an apartment, leaving their three teenagers behind. Rumor has it they didn't give the kids their new address or phone number.

Not every parent who throws a son or daughter out of the house has reached the burnout stage. Some have reached what I call the "energized stage of desperation," in which, "By God, we're going to solve this problem once and for all." Some of these parents follow the Toughlove plan, which, briefly, calls for setting "a bottom line" of behavior that will be tolerated and then following through with the consequences when the rules (against doping, stealing, drinking, raging, etc.) are violated. "Following through" can mean anything from locking an incorrigible teenager out of the house to having one arrested for stealing to support a drug habit—or just for doing drugs.

With or without the Toughlove organization (which has chapters across the country), scores of devoted middle-class parents practice the methods. This should tell us that there are scores of very troubled teenagers from good homes in this land of ours— and an equal number of desperate parents. Just looking at the parents I know personally, I see an easy dozen Toughlove practitioners, including a university professor, a psychiatrist, a family therapist, and an entrepreneur, all of whom have either thrown a teenager out of the house, or had one arrested, or both.

This is a good place to underscore the fact that mental-health-care professionals are no more exempt than any other parents. The Toughlove organization was founded by the psychologists Phyllis and David York, who were motivated to put together such a program because of their own incorrigible and drug-abusing children, one of whom had been arrested for armed robbery. I have about a half-dozen friends who are psychologists and all but one of them has been down this path with at least one of their children. One friend told me that not only was her daughter a sexually promiscuous drug abuser, but with or without drugs her behavior was off the wall. Once she slipped an LSD tab into her mother's drink, for example. She also taught her three-year-old brother to smoke dope. She was fourteen years old at the time.

The mother of two adopted children—a boy and a girl—told me that her daughter has never once gotten into trouble and is a straight-A student. The boy, on the other hand, began his "life of crime" when he was nine years old. "He burned down a goddamn school!" she told me. "He has been to dozens of psychiatrists, had every test in the book. He steals, lies, cheats, gets drunk. The least offensive behavior is that he always cut school and finally dropped out. I have bailed him out of jail at least ten times." She went on to say that the last time he called her after having been arrested for stealing a car, she decided she'd just leave him there. "I don't get upset anymore," she told me. "I'm numb."

Another friend of mine is a psychology professor. His son has done the full range of things, beginning with sucking laughing gas out of an inner tube while walking down the corridor to his next class—he was just a freshman in high school at the time—to trying every illicit drug except heroin. Oddly, the boy never cut school and maintained a high enough grade-point average (GPA) to get into one of the nation's finest universities. Which was where he was attending one day when he went to his father's office and told him he had something "heavy" to talk about:

> He stood before me, his hair nearly to his waist, a long rhinestone-studded earring dangling from one ear. He was wearing black satin pants, a lace shirt, and sneakers he had painted with black enamel, and had black polish on his long fingernails. Suddenly a wave of nausea swept over me and I told him to wait a minute, left, went to the restroom, and vomited. After I'd regained as much composure as could be mustered, I returned, sat down at my desk, and calmly asked him what was on his mind. He said, "Dad, I want to transfer

to another school." I almost fainted from sheer relief. I had been sure he was going to tell me he was a transvestite.

One of the saddest stories I know is that of a family that, from all outward appearances, was the ultimate, living manifestation of the perfect American family: handsome father, beautiful mother, devoted to each other, three absolutely beautiful and accomplished children—even two cats and one dog. Going into their wonderful home, the first thing to catch your eye was a large bulletin board on which were affixed ribbons, medals, and certificates that told the story of scholastic and athletic accomplishments. The next items you'd see were the framed pictures of family members, together and separate: a portrait here, a picture of a laughing, lovely family at Yellowstone, Disneyland, or the beach there; someone proudly holding a fish; someone else proudly holding a trophy; a joyful Christmas scene.

The mother was a great cook, and the family sat down to dinner together every night. Both parents attended every school function and participated fully in the lives of their children. They really did all the things most of us are led to believe that we ought to do: They had high moral standards, they gave each child responsibility for chores, they taught them to be independent and self-reliant, they attempted to imbue high self-esteem through accomplishment and good appearance. They even threw the best birthday parties ever.

A dark cloud appeared on the horizon when their handsome athletic son was about fifteen. He had some sort of breakdown, which, quite possibly, was drug-related, though no one knew for sure. He did become suicidal, which, for obvious reasons, threw the parents into a state of panic and the family into therapy. But the boy would say nothing, so the therapy was not all that helpful. Finally, the parents took the boy out of public school and put him in a small private school. He improved dramatically; in fact, he was in such great shape that he was able to return to public high school the following year. He then deteriorated dramatically:

He drank, he drugged, he raged at his parents, he stole.

As a consequence of years of stress, the once-devoted parents became estranged. (In case you don't know it, parents of troubled children fight with each other almost constantly.) They put their lovely home up for sale and made plans to go their separate ways. And then the son seemed to straighten out. He graduated from high school, was accepted by a fine university, and went away to school.

Enter a well-deserved happy ending: The parents decided to try again. A new town, a new house. A new beginning, a second chance. All was right with the world again.

Enter fickle fate: The next child in line, a daughter, started on the drug trail. She advanced rather quickly through pot and mushrooms and made her way up to cocaine, purchased from the dealers who hung around her school. To support her habit, she forged checks. Well, these parents had been down that path and this time they would get tough. Like others before them, they were going to have her arrested. She would learn the consequences of her acts, and she would get into a rehabilitation program.

As the story went, on the way home to this fateful confrontation, the girl smashed the car she was driving into a tree. The original account that came to me was that when she was admitted to the hospital, she was already brain-dead, and two days later the plug was pulled and she died. The next account was that she was so distraught over what awaited her at home that she lost control of the car. This reasonable speculation was replaced with an account that held that, as she was driving, she thought about what awaited her and decided to kill herself, slamming the car into a tree. How anyone could possibly know what might have been going on in the mind of a girl who was reported to be alone in a car is beyond me. It was also beyond others, which led to another rumor—that there had been no accident, but that the girl hanged herself and her parents had manufactured the accident story for the sake of appearances. One year after this tragic event, the last of the rumors was confirmed when our local newspaper did an in-depth piece on the pressures that lead to drug abuse and teenage suicide, and cited this girl as an example. She had indeed hanged herself. The parents were found guilty by virtually everyone I talked to who had read the piece.

I was not surprised at the verdict since I know one thing is for sure: If there is a way to blame parents for the terrible things that happen to their children, it will be found. The desire to do this completely overwhelms facts and is indifferent to the very real agony of parents who have experienced tragedies of such magnitude that they will never fully recover. It doesn't seem to matter at all that drug abuse, alcohol abuse, criminal behavior, and mental illness all occur randomly in the best of families. The need to blame parents, spawned by the psychological revolution just after World War II, has become so pervasive that even a child can do it. For example, a Gallup poll published December 13, 1984, revealed that *teenagers* blamed parents for everything from drug abuse to unemployment. The young people who were surveyed indicted their parents for lack of discipline, child neglect, poor parental example, delegation of too little responsibility to children, lack of understanding, and children having too much money.

A sad footnote to the beautiful family's story is that six months after their daughter's tragic death, their son was arrested for drunk driving and attempted to hang himself in his jail cell. Fortunately, a guard caught him in the act. The boy was, at some point, transferred to a mental institution.

Inevitably, I will be asked by some readers, "Don't you know any kids who weren't troubled?" Of course I know many kids who did not have problems with drug abuse, mental illness, or sexual promiscuity, or did not have encounters with the law. (I even have one.) And the one thing I've learned by knowing all of these kids is that whether or not children experience serious problems in their teenage years is owing more to luck than any other factor. Some parents are good, some are bad, and some fall somewhere in the middle. But loving parents of children who escape catastrophe are no better than loving parents of those who don't—they are simply luckier.

There is, in fact, a growing body of evidence that strongly suggests that, unless parents are *extreme* in their dealings with children, how a child turns out depends largely on such things as inborn traits, school experiences, physical problems, and the peer group. You need to know in advance, however, that should you be so lucky as to have a child who turns out to be a paragon, you will receive no credit. If, however, you have one that winds up in Joliet or San Quentin, that sought-after credit—called blame—will be your reward.

It happens—all of it—in the "best of families." Rich and poor, famous and obscure. I recall one rather transient feeling I had when I watched Geraldine Ferraro accept her party's nomination for vice president of the United States. As the TV camera panned her perfect family, mixed in with my euphoria that a woman had been nominated for the second highest office in the land was a tinge of envy that this woman, just two days younger than I, probably never experienced the problems I had experienced with our son. *Her* children, I told myself, probably never gave her a moment's genuine grief. I wondered what it must be like to have it all, to *be* all—to come from the common folk but not experience what the more "inadequate" among us have experienced. And then, on February 22, 1986, I opened up my newspaper and read a brief account that John A. Zaccaro, Jr., a senior at Middlebury College, had been arrested for selling cocaine. Normally those who sell do so to support habits, and habits don't develop overnight. On the same day, the same newspaper carried an account of the arrest of a seventeen-year-old son of a Filippino news executive, Oscar Salvatierra. The son, Arnel, and his eighteen-year-old girlfriend were arrested on suspicion of murdering the boy's father. And, same day, same paper, there was a report of the son of a county sheriff who was being sought on charges that he and four others gunned down two Modesto men to avenge a burglary. The "People" section of the paper, which usually runs cheery pieces on physical fitness and other trendy subjects, devoted itself entirely to teen suicide. In the town of Redding, California, it seems that people were worrying that an epidemic was under way. In the body of the article, notice was made of other cities and towns—most quiet and affluent—wherein there was concern that suicide was epidemic. After accidental death, it should be noted, suicide is the leading killer of teenagers.

It happens in the best of families—all of it: drug abuse, teenage pregnancy, mental illness, suicide, murder.

# Chapter 12

# MARITAL BLISS AND CHILDREN

*There are two marriages in every marital union, his and hers, and his is better than hers.*

—Jessie Bernard, *The Future of Marriage*

*Mind you, I love my boys more than anything else in the world. After all, they're all I have left of a disastrous marriage. I knew years ago that my husband and I could've made it work if it weren't for the boys. Sounds crazy, I know. But nevertheless, it's true. The patience of that man! With the kids, that is. I'm afraid he couldn't tolerate my impatience. Nor could he understand my need to be a person in my own right. I hated being just "his wife, their mother." I envy these women who can be completely fulfilled that way. I can't.*

*I think the kids have adjusted to "our" divorce. Not that they no longer miss their daddy. They do. What's worse is that I do, too. I mean, I never loved a man quite like I loved him. But we cannot live together as a family. Two of the biggest reasons for that are the kids.*

—A Minnesota mom

When I was five months pregnant with my first child, my husband and I celebrated our eighth wedding anniversary. He gave me an exquisite bracelet, made of hundreds of tiny seed pearls. It was elegant, feminine, and provocative—everything he believed me to be.

Six years later, I was picking up the pearls with my vacuum cleaner and by hand whenever I spotted one on the floor. That torn and twisted bracelet is a sad symbol of the effect two children have had on a once beautiful relationship. My young and very beloved son destroyed that token of my husband's devotion, and, to some extent, the affection and devotion itself slipped away in the complicated and demanding process of caring for small children.

I didn't have to read most of the popular ladies' magazines to know that children add a new dimension to marriage. I found it out by becoming a mother, and I also learned that the dimension added is not quite what, back in the late sixties and early seventies, those magazines made it out to be. The pervasive theme was that babies enhanced good marriages, and saved bad ones from the divorce courts. And, of course, it was a theme that was heavily orchestrated on daytime television. While much of that sort of nonsense has disappeared from the print media, the song remains pretty much the same in TV Land. And there are still pressure-bearing people around who put out the message that no marriage is complete unless there are children. Furthermore, what still seems to be hidden from general view is the fact that often a child is, to borrow a phrase from Richard V. Austin, Jr., "the straw that breaks the back of the marriage."

Studies to substantiate this sad fact of life have been around for a long time. In 1957 Dr. E. E. LeMasters reported in an article in *Marriage and Family Living* that extensive or severe home crisis situations occurred following the birth of a child in eighty-three percent of the cases he studied. Arthur P. Jacoby reported that eighty-seven percent of new parents were disturbed rather than pleased with the changed family situation. Dr. Harold Feldman, a professor in the Department of Human Development and Family Studies at Cornell University, did a study of 852 middle- and upper-class urban couples and reported that "those with children had a significantly lower level of marital satisfaction than those without children. When a couple become parents the marital satisfaction declines."

In *The Case Against Having Children* (1971)—a book whose title must have killed it in this dewey-eyed society—Anna and Arnold Silverman postulated: "The reasons for the decline in marital satisfaction are largely the same as those which caused the initial adjustment crises following the birth of their first child. We can assume then that the psychologically, physically, and socially unsatisfactory conditions of early parenthood did not disappear as adjustment took place but rather that they became an integral part of the family relationship."

On second thought, perhaps it wasn't the title that killed it. What the authors meant, in plain English, is that when baby makes three, adjustment can be so difficult that it reaches the dimensions of a crisis. From that point on, each adjustment to each new revealed reality of parenthood is fraught with tension, misunderstanding, and downright hostility.

The seeds of discord between a married couple with children, according to Dr. LeMasters, are sown just shortly after the birth of a child. There are studies that can pinpoint dissatisfaction or stress down to night feedings, loss of sleep, dirty diapers, loss of freedom, financial worries, or a combination of them all. There are studies enough to make you fall asleep from dry statistics and tedious psychology, dealing, for example, with the loss of sleep of new parents, so why belabor the obvious? No one really likes to be awakened in the middle of the night by a crying baby or relishes changing dirty diapers.

It is common for ill-prepared new parents to be not quite so pleased as they had anticipated about the whole scene. And if a little innocent baby who hasn't even learned how to run the television set full blast yet can be a cause for "severe home crises," it ought not to be too difficult to accept that a growing child can wreak havoc in a marriage. For a lot of parents, coping with real children doing real things is more disturbing than the upheaval a baby causes by simply getting born.

For those who have not experienced, first hand, the realities of rearing children and trying to make a marriage work, these statistics and conclusions may come as a revelation. However, those of us who have experienced it can skip the professional journals and reach the same conclusions without ever leaving our kitchen.

One evening my husband and I had a blockbuster over shredded potatoes. It was nearly divorce after that episode. My hostility level was unbelievable. Until I became a mother of two screaming toddlers, I was known for my great patience. My husband, normally a quiet, sensitive man, displayed sheer hatred. Another time, I (Shirley the Pacifist) threw an egg across the kitchen in the middle of a discussion that had nothing to do with our personal lives. When the smoke cleared, we were astonished to find out that we had not even been in disagreement.

Just before both of these idiotic demonstrations, a variation on the following theme was taking place: I was preparing dinner, the TV set was blaring, the kids were wrestling on the floor, screaming at the top of their lungs, one of them had kicked over a glass of milk (which one of them had put on the floor), and my husband had just walked wearily into the kitchen, stepping on raisins and Rice Krispies along the way.

In a similar setting, a friend of mine who rarely raises her voice threw a hamburger at her husband; he stalked out of the house, leaving one of his business cards on her pillow. Another generally nonviolent woman cleared the drainboard off in fifteen seconds flat—onto the floor—when her husband commented on the messy kitchen at just the wrong moment.

Disproportionate rage is common in homes where young children generate almost constant confusion, noise, and messes. The fuse can get very short very fast, and a trivial incident can trigger an ugly, and sometimes a dangerous, dispute. Women aren't exactly eager to admit to this sort of behavior, and yet most of the women I have spoken to or heard from over the years have had more than a taste or two of it.

It is interesting to look at marriages, totally successful for many years, that have undergone radical changes since the children were born.

Two people we know well, whom I'll call Helen and Jack,

were married for seven years before they had children. We spent many weekends with them (we were childless for a bit longer than they), and it was so obvious that they had a magnificent relationship. One rarely sees a couple who are lovers and friends, and who even possess the ability to work well together. But these two worked side by side for years and seemed to enjoy every minute of it. After Helen became pregnant with their first and only child, she did everything right. Went to Lamaze, subsequently delivered naturally, had rooming in, and breast-fed her child for eight months. She is, to this day, one of the most loving, tender mothers imaginable.

The first hint that something was wrong in Helen's marriage came one day many years ago when I was pregnant with my first child, and her son was about two years old. Everything was fine, she told me, except that she didn't know if Jack was coming home for dinner; she went on to tell me that she never knew anymore when he might be home any night before midnight. In my prenatal naïveté, I found it difficult to believe that their unity was not even further cemented now that they had this wonderful child.

However, after seven beautiful years, the joy of motherhood was not a bonus to Helen's already quite lovely life. A very nice marriage was the price she paid for her motherhood. Jack tried hard, in his own way, to be a good husband and father, but he had difficulty accepting the fact that he had to share his wife or, worse yet, take a backseat. The child's noise and crying bothered him, and as the boy got older, the messes he made drove his father nearly mad. Helen became quite defensive about everything that Jack found objectionable. He would be firm with their son, and she would think him unreasonable and tell him as much. She would be loving and kind to the boy, and Jack would feel shut out. Eventually, friends and acquaintances became witnesses to their snide remarks to and about each other, their outright battles and tears of agony as time went on. Two discreet people who had shown the utmost respect for each other turned into people who were fighting in public!

Helen's situation doesn't really have much to do with a wife becoming a mother and therefore becoming dowdy, dull, or sexless. It more realistically underscores the responsibilities and agonies of parenthood. Helen's story is not unique. It is like many others that reflect a change in a basically good relationship after the children come on the scene—changes that occur when hitherto unknown qualities of both parties emerge because of parenthood and when a life-style has been radically and irreversibly changed.

Another couple were married for fifteen years before they had their first child. They appeared to have an idyllic marriage: Like Helen and Jack once were, they were friends and lovers. The one acknowledged "flaw" in their marriage was that they had no children. She was grateful to learn that surgery could correct her infertility. The operation was successful, and they had two children, a boy and a girl. They were absolutely delighted—for a while. After their little boy passed the magic age of three, and their little girl started making noises like a real child, it didn't take long for this mother to discover that the joy of parenthood wasn't quite what she had expected it to be. And she was in for a few surprises about her husband.

Where for years she had thought he was the finest man she knew, she discovered that he had some unpalatable ideas about raising a son. He liked to hunt. He was disappointed when he learned that his six-year-old son could not bear to see an animal killed. He tried to "make a man of him," and succeeded in turning him into a nervous child. He had his own methods of dealing with the boy's timidity, too, and all the while she got more frantic.

While his behavior can hardly be condoned, had this couple never had children this unreasonable trait would not have shown itself. And the marriage would not have been turned into a shambles.

Both of these couples' experiences illustrate one of the most important causes of child-related disharmony in a marriage: a basic difference of opinion regarding the way in which children should be treated and brought up, a difference of value systems. It reminds me that perhaps parents are wise to want their children to marry people with backgrounds similar to their own. Many parents object to interfaith marriage because they fear that conflicts regarding the children's religious upbringing may occur. In truth, such concerns would be more complete if they included not just social status, ethnicity, and religion, but also how each party feels about discipline, punishment, affection, and what constitutes "a real boy" or "a real girl."

What happens when a father is very punitive and a mother empathetic and tender? Does he not see her as "indulgent" when she should be firm, while she may see him as some sort of a monster? While it is true that some mothers defer to their husbands as "head of the household" and the ones to mete out the punishment, or serve as the "heavy," there are other mothers who are gentle as lambs but who turn into ferocious mother tigers when they feel that their young are being attacked. It required monumental control, for example, for me not to interfere when my husband took disciplinary action. And on those occasions when I did not manage to control myself, the ensuing battle went from the difference of opinion over how children should be dealt with on to the questioning of my undermining my husband's authority. Carried to a rather absurd extreme—there are mothers who believe that they can be punitive, but if their husbands behave in the same manner in an identical situation, that ferocious mother tiger is unleashed. For example, the mother of a thirteen-year-old boy, whose incessant arguing and back talk one evening drove her to grab the child by the throat, told me that if her husband hit that child one more time, she would pack her bags and leave.

That kids can cause specific disputes is just one more burden on a relationship that may be strained by many of the factors already discussed. And children do indeed cause parents to argue with each other. Sometimes it is innocent and unintentional. But sometimes the kids quite intentionally pit one parent against the other in order to gain attention, to get permission to do something or go somewhere, or just to see if they can bring it off. As one teacher put it, "Kids have real ESP; they know exactly what's going on. They're more clever than we believe."

The most obvious and commonly staged battle occurs when a child wants something. He or she will ask one parent for whatever it is, and if that parent says no, then, after a calculated interval, he or she will ask the other. Until my husband and I became more experienced, one of us would fall into this trap, and then we'd have the usual arguments about undermining each other's authority. And usually—at least when the children were young—the entire episode was over nothing more important than a cookie.

The parents of a little boy I'll call Timmy have a basic difference of opinion over how to handle their child. When Timmy's father disciplines him, he almost always runs sobbing to his mother for comfort. Sometimes, not knowing what's happened, she innocently comforts him. Sometimes she does know what's transpired and disagrees with her husband's actions and ends up simultaneously comforting her son and scolding her husband. The child has gotten the idea that Mom will probably come to the rescue, and he takes full advantage of it. According to Dr. Spock, letting a child cause this sort of dissension can be psychologically damaging *to the child.* But parents find it difficult to always present a unified front, especially when they privately disagree. Timmy, through this ploy, has managed to drive a wedge between his parents, an accomplishment, Dr. Spock adds ironically, that can cause a kind of guilt in young children with which they're not equipped to cope. An interesting paradox. We must not let the children affect a marriage adversely because it is upsetting to the children.

With all of the staged battles, the actual blowups, the differences of opinion regarding the kids, the undercurrent of negative feelings each partner may have about his or her respective responsibilities and role, the confusion, work, worry, and chaos, a once happily married couple can become so sensitized that even trivial irritations or imagined slights can take on exaggerated proportions.

Maybe a wife "hasn't had time" to talk to her husband about something or other because she has been busy with the children or dinner preparations. Then the phone rings; it's the friend not heard from in a while, and suddenly she has time to chat for a few minutes. Then the kids start acting up while she's talking (they always do when the phone rings) and she calls in to him to "do something," perhaps with a note of irritation in her voice—returning to the call on a brisk cheery note. Somehow she can always be nice to *other* people, he thinks. Or she doesn't have time to sew a button on his shirt, but he comes home and finds her playing Scrabble with one of the kids. Or they have just spent part of the evening in stony silence and friends drop in unexpectedly, and she's suddenly the life of the party. Or, he is. Or, he's in the middle of paying the bills, and he's trying to trace an error in the checkbook; she's in the kitchen, clearing up the dishes, the kids are acting up, and it's time for their baths, and she interrupts him at a crucial moment of accounting, imploring him to "at least assume part of your responsibility" and help with the kids.

We are told by many experts that husbands often feel left out after their wives have babies. The love of his life no longer showers him with the attention he has become accustomed to receiving. And his once beautiful lover turns into someone's rather unglamorous mother—this can be most disappointing.

It is at this point, we are warned, that he might start looking longingly at the young women in the office or at his friends' better-kempt wives and make some unflattering comparisons. He may even be thinking that, in addition to his wife becoming dowdy, she's becoming a bit of a bore. So maybe he starts thinking about doing a little more than just looking, now that the old girl is no longer the bright, witty, leggy life of the party. As one man put it, "I love my wife, or rather, I used to before we had kids and she changed."

Why did she change? How does she feel? Some women just

feel bad—they get hurt when they learn that the man they love can be so superficial and that the woman who's tried to make him happy can't offer him nearly as much as the pretty secretary who has just joined the firm.

Some women begin not to care if their husbands start looking around. As one woman said, "I wish to God he *would* get a girl-friend, then maybe he'd leave me alone. I simply can't stand him anymore."

And there's another side of the coin. "There's a type of man," said a friend, "who, after he's made his wife pregnant and turned her into a domestic slave, has the gall to blame her because the marriage is no longer *exciting*. Speaking to such a man, I'd say this: 'Don't forget—the iceman cometh, and *his* wife may be even uglier.' "

Even today, the double standard prevails. A man may assert that it is perfectly all right for him to look elsewhere for exciting feminine companionship because his wife is uninterested in him or she "hasn't kept herself up," and he has therefore lost interest in her. But that same man would find it wholly unacceptable for his wife to do the same thing. Many men don't recognize that women have needs, and many don't realize that when they neglect their wives, they make them vulnerable. Don't her feelings and disappointments count for anything? On top of everything else is the fact that the greatest cause of marital strife, even among couples who have no children, is money. And, as I've noted, raising children is one of the most expensive enterprises anyone can undertake. And, there is an endless number of purchases over which to do battle.

While young children can create much dissension in a marriage, there is absolutely no match for the havoc that adolescents and teenagers can wreak. I speak from the vantage point of one who has gone through every stage and who knows dozens of battle-scarred parents of teenagers. Where once the difference of opinion was over whether Becky could or could not have a cookie or a dollar, at twelve or thirteen that difference of opinion has to do with whether or not she can go to school dances and what kind of clothes she should wear or whether or not she is too young for makeup. At fourteen those problems have been settled—with no small amount of disagreement—and parents argue over whether Becky is too young to date. The debates then go on to her choices of friends and boyfriends, how late she can stay out, and reflect fears over premature sexual activity. And then, of course, Becky has developed a *mouth* that seems to become progressively more motorized with every passing birthday. And there is Steven and his developing love affair with motorcycles and cars.

With both, the arguments center around developing a sense of responsibility, their grades in school, the cutting of classes, their choice of friends, their general behavior in the house, whether the friends can come to the house, how much recreational eating will be allowed, and the ever present *mouth.*

Under the very best of circumstances—that is, when parents are not plagued with "sex, drugs, and rock and roll"—there are tremendous conflicts. Each parent brings to each conflict his or her personal experience and private agenda, to say nothing of his or her hopes for a child's future. And, it is at this point that the expectations really are on trial. When things aren't going according to the master plan, then it is somebody's fault: "She cuts school because you . . ." "He smokes cigarettes because you . . ." "He got drunk last Friday night because you . . ." "She smokes pot because you . . ." Often the accusations are verbalized. Just as often they are just tucked away in the resentment file to build up to some future blowout.

Long before the actual different values about child guidance may have surfaced, quite likely a complicated undercurrent has been operating, a pervasive resentment that, even without conflicting values or whopping battles, can turn a happy marriage into a shambles once children arrive on the scene. It starts with the division of the work of maintaining a family. It moves along when a husband is the provider and a mother is the homemaker and he has no idea whatever what her role at home may entail. Complicating matters is that we stand at a sociological crossroads of sorts in that some mothers are full-time wives and mothers in the home, while some hold down jobs outside the home.

Despite the fact that over half of all mothers work outside the home, our culture still operates under the "traditional" concept that holds that having children is an integral part of a happy marriage and that the motherhood/homemaking role is a fulfilling one. But for many women who are functioning in that role, the traditional values fall flat—far short of their fantasies and the image the media projects. Women in such "traditional" roles, quite simply, may not like the job they've been handed.

While I do believe that the stresses of caring for children— the awesome and often unexpected responsibility, the noise, the messes, the loss of sleep, the general fatigue, the financial problems, the loss of freedom—contribute significantly to the deterioration of a marriage, I have come to feel truly and deeply that what underlies the vast majority of serious disputes between otherwise nice and stable husbands and wives boils down to an ongoing general absence of understanding of just what it is a mother has to do.

People in unpleasant jobs are not happy people, and frequently they find themselves resenting their employers. A wife who sees herself stuck with all the crappy jobs may resent her husband for making her a mother. Most women who, when childless, never really minded too much that their husbands read the newspaper while they took care of the "wifely" chores become resentful, if not downright angry, when the duties of correcting young children, cleaning up their spills, and soothing their hurts is added. While the Lord of the Manor, seemingly removed from the situation, is sipping a cocktail, listening to Bach and reading the Dow-Jones averages, or watching Monday Night Football, a seething resentment builds that can lead to a dispute he in no way expects. "What's all this confusion got to do with *me?*" he says. Sometimes, of course, a mother/wife just tucks this new irritation away in her "hostility compartment" as part of a growing collection.

What changes once gentle tolerance or mild annoyance toward a husband who does little more than sit around into outright hostility? Usually, it is children. It is the children who put the woman on twenty-four-hour call, who make her job harder. It is the children who cause the woman to gravitate to the role that ties her to the home, and who snap the trap shut. And no amount of liberating rhetoric can change the deep feelings of most mothers.

Several things add to the resentment that many women feel about holding down a job they don't like and against their husbands for forcing them into that job. Just as it is still the responsibility of the woman to care for home and children, whenever anyone talks about "making the marriage work," the onus for bringing off the operation is put on the female partner. Just pick up any woman's magazine (save for *Ms.*), leaf through, and learn how to put excitement into the marriage, how to communicate, how to get him to help with the housework or spend time with the children, etc. But pick up *Esquire* or *Playboy* and you will find those publications devoted to "manly" things, which do not include such trivia as how to become a more sensitive husband.

Besides the unfairness of the idea that one party of a marriage should be responsible for the success or failure of the relationship, and the attendant resentment that unfairness may engender, there is a small degree of blackmail involved that hardly causes warm feelings. If never explicitly stated, the message is: Keep him happy if you want to stay married. Blackmail can exist only if there is a need, and need, for most women, is caused by their children. Being a mother takes away for most women—for all practical and relatively unpainful purposes—the option of not being married. The unpleasant paradox is that children who contribute so much to the conflict between husband and wife are almost always the consideration that traps a woman into a marriage she might well wish to be out of. That divorce for many women is scarcely a welcome and viable option ("What will it do to the kids?") can make a woman all the more resentful. And what of the father who has bought the same bill of goods as the mother? True, he is not subject to the intense feelings of responsibility, guilt, and fear that his wife is, as evidenced by the number of fathers who take a walk and never look back. Yet why, he may justifiably wonder (because of prevailing myths), can't she make him a home and family the way it's supposed to be? It is a rare husband who doesn't feel cheated and indignant of his wife's resentment. It is a vicious circle, and in the middle of it sit the children.

A marriage that can withstand the trials of children—surviving in feeling as well as name—is a rare one. A woman who dislikes her role and responsibilities as a mother may be quite unhappy, and a happy marriage cannot exist when one of the partners is unhappy. As one woman very pointedly put it, "My husband is a very happily married man. I'm miserable. Our marriage is a dismal failure."

Marriage, for all its own and very special joys, is not without its problems. Two people who spend their lives together are bound to have differences and difficulties. Yet, in most marriages, after children come, the differences and difficulties multiply and most are directly or indirectly traceable to those children.

One mother whose situation pretty well sums up the dilemma many seem to share wrote me a long and cathartic letter. The following excerpt sounded a familiar refrain:

> Husbands are funny creatures. I've come to the conclusion that men just aren't as child-oriented as women. It's not that they are genuine creeps, they just don't think.
>
> One time a few months ago I told myself, "No, Marsha, this is the role you *chose*," but I also said, "Now wait a minute, if a man has a job and is unhappy, bored and fed up after seven years, he can quit. Not us mothers." I think that frightens me the most. I can't quit. I can't even change. Oh, to feel so trapped. I recently had a lump removed from my breast and was asking the surgeon if I shouldn't do certain things (hoping

he'd say complete bed rest!). He laughed, and said, "Usual
routine, dear." What? Surgery yesterday and the floors aren't
mopped? My husband had lots of sympathy, not much else,
but "Gee, they need me at work. Have dinner ready at six-
thirty. I want to work on the boat."

One woman said that a common battle she and her husband
had early in marriage resulted from her rather casual approach to
housework and his fastidiousness.

We were able to resolve this in the early days of marriage
because it's a lot easier to be an artful and careful homemaker
when you don't have kids. After the kids came, it became increasingly difficult. Not so much when they were very small;
but as they grew, it became a real contest to keep things in
good shape. We went from a well-maintained home, good
meals, order, and a pleasant, well-groomed wife to a real
shambles—with me trying to keep up the standards we, particularly my husband, had grown accustomed to.

Imagine for a moment the feelings of a forty-year-old
man who has become accustomed to a particularly pleasant
and desirable life-style. He enters his home each night, not to
the sights and sounds he has enjoyed for a number of years,
but instead to the sights of total disorder and the sounds of crisis (Johnny just fell out of the tree), a distraught, nervous wife,
dinner half started, perhaps half burned, food on the floor that
gets stuck to his shoes, house half cleaned, and the TV going
full blast.

What's noteworthy is her conclusion:

Imagine, also, my own frustration, when I've knocked
myself out all day trying to maintain a nice home and been
frustrated by my children and their playmates at every turn.
The kids vomiting, breaking things, crying, falling out of

trees, bumping heads, skinning knees, getting into mischief—
these things mess up the simplest plans. While I love the children dearly, I can't help resenting my husband's lack of understanding, and I wind up resenting everyone and everything
and, as usual, feeling incredibly guilty. It's hard to blame the
kids, but you really have to admit that if it weren't for them,
the reason for this tense situation wouldn't exist.

It's all too easy to argue that women shouldn't be so concerned with the state of their homes or with pleasing their husbands. Yet the reality exists and reality is what we are exploring.

Another young woman, shocked by the realities of parenthood but more capable of saying, "Oh, well, what the hell,"
noted that in the early days, she really did feel bad and guilty
when her husband came through the door expecting her to be all
pretty and the house to be looking lovely, only to find a stack
of unfolded diapers on the sofa and his wife looking like a
walking disaster. She said, "He didn't have to say a word. One
look at his face conveyed precisely his disappointment—the
acknowledgment that the honeymoon was indeed over."

There are more stories of women who have truly tried to be
first-rate homemakers and have been frustrated in the process because of the demands made by their young children. I could go on
at length about how they feel about their husbands, their children,
their marriages, and their self-worth. But it seems enough to say
that so many of us try so hard to bring off the world's greatest domestic scene, only to know failure. It hurts not to make the grade,
and then it hurts more to know we've knocked ourselves out and
no one really notices or seems to care. Husbands just see what
*needs* to be done, not what *has* been done during the course of the
day. And because housework can get *undone* by small children,
and the actual care of the children is not a tangible, the work of
many homemakers becomes invisible to their husbands. Why on
earth else would a husband ask his weary wife, "What have you
been doing all day?"

My husband feels that a well-ordered world is little to ask and that it should always be a fact of life. And I can't say that I totally blame him for feeling that way. He works hard all day. Although I have labored to educate him over the years, he still has little understanding of what is involved in the day-to-day routine. When the children were young, he seemed vaguely amazed that I had to do more than twitch my nose (like Samantha the Witch) to keep everything in apple-pie order. I used to be very frustrated because I couldn't quite win the gold star in homemaking—somehow the little kids not only got in the way of this dubious achievement while I was trying to get it all together during the day, but it continued well into the evening. Most of the time I was able to bring off the beautiful setting, but the ultimate goal of having everything in good shape by six o'clock and having that be the end of the matter, just wasn't a real one the way it was before we had children. It didn't take me long to realize that a woman can spend the entire day working and not be at all off the hook at day's end. For young children, there is giving them baths, reading stories, answering questions, getting them into pajamas, brushing their teeth, picking up toys, putting things away. And when they're older, teaching them how to do these things themselves, and after that, making sure they do it. There is also listening to prayers in many cases.

When my husband used to come home at night and tell me how tired he was, I would either openly express my annoyance or stick that comment where it added to the others to come out later and worse. Either attitude didn't do our relationship much good. So he's tired, is he? I'd think. Well, I'd still be hard at it, and as he would mix the drinks and then flake out on the sofa with the newspaper, I used to think rather angrily of the old proverb: "A man may work from sun to sun, but a woman's work is never done." Then I would get twice as mad because I am, after all, a twentieth-century woman.

I remember one time, after my husband told me how tired he was and settled in with his drink and newspaper, I joined him in

the living room for my usual ten minutes of maintaining the illusion of "you're home now, how nice to see you, let's make believe
nothing much has changed from the pre-kid days." Probably just
to make conversation, he said, "Gee, you've got spots on that nice
dress."

"*Spots!*" I spat. "Look at the *scars* on my arms and hands
from cooking! Cooking with little children underfoot. Let me tell
you how many times I've been so distracted and my mind so jum-
bled that I picked up a casserole dish without using pot holders.
And how about the time I nearly took off my index finger with an
electric knife? Spots? You'd have spots—yes, even you—if you
had to be a drudge. In fact, the spots won't even come out of this
dress, and that really makes me uptight, because I don't have
many dresses. By the way, that reminds me, I ironed today. Did
you know that you have twenty-seven shirts? Excuse me, I must
finish cooking dinner."

I was never proud of behavior like that. But this is the kind
of thinking—or nonthinking—that was behind such an outburst:
Here I'd been cooped up with the kids, the dog, the stove, and the
termite man all day, somehow had struggled through sufficiently
to have dinner well on its way and enough of the routine taken
care of as possible, and had put on the only decent clean dress—
spots and all—I had in an effort to look halfway presentable. Then
he walks through the door, and in five minutes he's telling me how
tired *he* is, followed by how much the kids get on *his* nerves, and
soon after that discussing the spots on my dress. Five minutes of
the kids and his precious nerves are shot! What in the hell did he
think mine must be like? That is, of course, if he ever thought
about my nerves.

One friend who echoed my thoughts about my husband's
level of concern told me, "I have the feeling that if I dropped dead
on the spot, my husband would be *annoyed.* Not grief-stricken, but
annoyed because he's tired and my demise would be just one more
inconvenience."

It is very difficult for many women to admit, even to them-

selves, that they resent their children and feel trapped because of
their motherhood. Their children, they feel, are innocent. Certainly not all mothers are this benevolent, but one twenty-eight-
year old woman speaks for many on this aspect of the effects
young children can have on a marriage:

> I was most reluctant to admit, even to myself, that my
> longed-for, planned, and terribly wonderful children could be
> resented even mildly—because, by God, they didn't ask to be
> born, and I owe it to them to give them every benefit of the
> best I have to offer as their mother. I did realize at some point,
> after considerable damage had been done to our marriage, that
> a lot of the anger I was directing toward my husband was quite
> misplaced. I was angry at the children because they were more
> troublesome than I ever imagined that children might be, but
> because it isn't "normal" to have these feelings about little be-
> loved innocents, the target for my wrath wound up being the
> male adult who turned me into a mother. To admit this is not
> in any way painless.

One woman I know has detested her husband since their son
was two years old. They have two children, and since the birth of
their second child two years after the first, their domestic situation
has deteriorated steadily. The woman is a very talented musician,
but she and her husband could never afford any household help or
even an occasional baby-sitter. Developing or even enjoying her
talent and years of training was a nearly insurmountable task while
the kids were little. Every scale and every note practiced was the
result of rigid and careful planning, eking out a half hour here and
there, often only to be interrupted by the needs of her small children. She became very bitter and showed her resentment of her
husband in many ways, the least destructive being her often-
uttered cliche, "If it weren't for him . . ."

While this woman was, and is, an excellent mother, her marriage has become a shambles. The things that kept her from ful-

filling herself as an individual, and thus led to her extreme hostility, had little to do with her husband, except that he couldn't afford to provide her with time to herself. Yet, if this couple hadn't had children, would she have any reasons for being bitter? Despite all the bitterness over the years, now that their kids are in college their relationship is improving.

Another woman had this to say: "I don't know him anymore. Before Tommy was born, I thought he was the kindest and most considerate man in the world. It's shocking to see how uninterested he is in our child and how little interest he has these days in my pursuits and problems. He had no understanding of the difficulties there are in raising a child, and yet when we had no children, he was always so very considerate of me. During those days, after I got off work, he was the one to say, 'Take it easy, honey, you've put in a hard day.' And now, he won't even watch the child willingly so that I can enjoy a minute off now and again."

The mother of four girls traces the root of her marital disharmony to the fact that her husband takes her for granted but never takes her anyplace. They no longer visit their friends without bringing the kids along because they have nowhere to leave them. Similarly, they no longer have their friends over for an evening's entertainment because "there are too many demands generated by the kids." Who is really preventing her from enjoying life as she would like? Her husband or her kids? In her view, her husband is the villain, but she rarely says anything to him about it. Telling another woman may give vent to some hostility, but it certainly doesn't make it disappear. It merely serves to reinforce her conviction that her husband keeps her from having a happy life and helps her to ignore the fact that they were quite happy before the kids came along. In fact, they were very much in love and enjoyed their life together before they had children, just as most of us do who get married in the first place. It certainly isn't mutual hatred that brings us together.

The feelings of so many mothers seem well put by one mother of three: "As soon as I hear the crunch of my husband's tires in our gravel driveway each evening, I'm automatically irritated."

It seems only fair to discuss the man's point of view. A man's happiness certainly has a good deal to do with the success of a marriage. It can't be comfortable to live with the financial responsibility for three or four other people, to be constantly concerned that the bed and board for his family is dependent upon him. Many men become locked into jobs they detest because they need the financial security—something they probably would not need as much if they were not fathers.

Yet it is hard for a mother to sympathize fully with her husband. To the mother who is trapped in the house with screaming children all day, her husband's life can look absolutely dazzling. I recall my own feelings when that was my situation. My husband did not have what one would call an "exciting" job, *but* he got up every morning, put on some clothes that someone else laundered for him, ate breakfast that someone else prepared for him, gave his children a fond pat on their little heads, kissed his wife, and left for the office. Left! He didn't even have to make arrangements for child care or leave instructions for a baby-sitter. He already had a *permanent* baby-sitter, working for a very low wage, and she was completely familiar with the children, their needs, and the household routine. He got into his car, and he drove to work. He entered the building and said a cheery hello to the pretty receptionist, proceeded to his office, and performed some tasks he enjoyed. Yes, he did enjoy his work. He could take a coffee break, a lunch hour, and he could go out with his friends for cocktails and lunch on occasion. On returning to the office, he did some more work, and then he drove home, maybe stopping along the way at a record store or a bookstore.

Once home, as he mixed a drink for himself, he might say, "Hey, did you know that Phil Futz and old Ethel are getting married?" "Let me tell you about a new artist—I went to this art show at the shopping center while I was picking up the bread." "How was your day?" "Oh, yes, very interesting about the termite man."

To say that I was jealous of his freedom is an understatement. A number of years back a survey indicated that when it came to wives being jealous of their husbands, the vast majority of the housewives interviewed said they most envied their husbands' freedom—their ability to more or less come and go at will. Before we had children, I had no such feelings, because I, too, could leave the house without taking my constant companions or making arrangements for their care. I also had a car, an interesting job, and my own money.

But the other side of the coin, as my husband explained it, was that he *had* to get up at a fixed time, *had* to get dressed, and *had* to leave the house and go to work while I, on the other hand, really could sleep late if I wanted to, not fix breakfast, not get dressed, and not leave the house every day. "You don't go to an office every day to bring home the money for the very food we all eat," he said. "And you don't worry about things like whether your life insurance would be sufficient to take care of the family, as you watch men my age dropping dead from heart attacks."

What this particular battle of the sexes really boils down to is the issue of housework. And underlying its dismissal as insignificant lies a broader view that whatever it is, if a woman does it, it's neither difficult nor important. Early in this century, for example, males predominated in the secretarial work force, and then the secretarial position was prestigious; similarly, nursing. As women moved into those professions, they dropped in prestige. Recently, I read a report in the newspaper that stated that as women are moving into the legal profession in greater numbers, that profession is becoming less prestigious. Now then, while housewifery is far from being given its due, please note that occasionally, when a man either shares fully or switches roles with his wife, he is applauded as no woman ever was. Furthermore, in all of the articles that report such activities, great attention is focused on the fact that parenting is very important, and that housework is very difficult, tedious, and boring. You can bet your Aunt Tillie's antimacassars that if all men were househusbands, and all women were breadwinners only, taking care of the home and the family would be viewed as the most important and difficult job on the face of the earth.

This cultural and male bias contributes to the myth that it is easy to be a mother and also hold down a full-time job. The resentment and downright anger a housewife may feel when her husband sits around while she runs herself ragged is nothing compared to the feelings that can build up when a woman works outside the home and still must do everything. Even when she does this willingly, because she wants to be all things to all people, eventually the human response to fatigue and unfairness takes over.

A friend of mine, a thirty-five-year old executive and the mother of two young children, has been brimming over with anger for years, but she says that she has so little time to herself that she wouldn't bother wasting one more minute trying to make her husband understand how she feels about being stuck with "all the crappy jobs." She told me that one Saturday she'd managed to farm out the kids and had gotten the house cleaned in record time. The clothes were washing and drying, the dinner was well on its way, and she was reading a book. Her husband came home from wherever he'd been and saw her relaxing in her clean house, sat down beside her, and said, "This is really nice, and we are alone." And after a bit of slipping his arm around her and nuzzling her, he finally said, "Let's make love," to which she replied, "Are you crazy? This is the first time I've been able to read peacefully in a year," and picked up her book and went into another room.

*Chapter 13*

# DOCTOR, LAWYER, INDIAN CHIEF . . . OR MOTHER?

---

*One of the most dangerous promises made by the decade is that as a woman you can now have it all. Not only should you be able to have a promising career and marriage and children and a love life that will provide you with the plots for at least two romance novels, but you should be able to have them all without ever being depressed, angry, tired, vulnerable, or guilty. . . . Today the smorgasbord of choices for women is tempting, but a wise woman knows she doesn't have to sample everything to the point where she is fit only to waddle away and take a nap.*

—Lee Morical, *Where's My Happy Ending?*

*The myth of "supermom" has come into being. The original intention of the women's movement was to expand the options available to women, to convey the message: Being a tax accountant is a legitimate role for women. Likewise, being a mother is okay, as is being a pilot, a nurse, an engineer, a housewife, or any combination of the above. Unfortunately, the optional emphasis of this message seems to have gotten lost. Instead, society's message seems to be: "You should be a loving wife, tender, compassionate mother, and successful career woman." The supermom expecta-*

*tion doesn't give new options to women—it simply adds more duties to the original job description.*

—Dr. Joseph Procaccini and Mark W. Kiefaber,
*Parent Burn-Out*

*It would be nice if Dad took his job of parent one half of the time. I'm so tired of reading Dad should do this and Dad should do that! Because what Dad will do and what Dad perhaps should do are two entirely different stories.*

—An Idaho mother

When Geraldine Ferraro received her party's nomination for vice president of the United States, I must admit I was moved. This single act conveyed to me, as no amount of rhetoric had been able to, the idea that a woman could indeed aspire to the highest office in the land. Her ascent to this point in her career reinforced the idea that a woman does not have to make a choice between being a wife and mother and having a career. Nevertheless, however implicit that message was, I by no means was left with the impression that *all* women, or even most of us, have the same choices that the majority of men take for granted.

As uplifting as it was to see a mother of three children rise to the heights of a stunning career—prosecuting attorney, congresswoman, vice presidential candidate—I never lost sight of the fact that we are all different as individuals. Though one woman has achieved these goals, we cannot assume that every woman can, just as we cannot assume that every American male has what it takes to be president. It is our own aggregate of characteristics and circumstances—our individual levels of aptitude, energy, and financial and emotional resources—that determines our ability to achieve an ideal.

Where one woman may have the inner resources to be a

shrewd, hard-working manager and at the same time deal with several children with apparent ease, another woman may barely be able to combine a part-time job with mothering one child. Consider the case of Karen Gunderson, a talented attorney who became a judge—the consummate example of a high achiever with a deep need to be perfect.

Ms. Gunderson was a "hard-working competitor and winner all her life." According to an account in the *San Francisco Examiner* (January 27, 1985), however, she "was tormented by fears that she had failed as a wife when her husband of twenty years left her for another woman." Moreover, she was convinced that she was not raising her two-year-old son, Tyler, properly.

Ironically, what caused her downfall, according to friends, were the high standards she set for herself. At forty years of age, Gunderson, an attractive and successful woman, attached a household vacuum-cleaner hose from the exhaust pipe of her car to the car window and ended her life. The note she left said, "Please tell Tyler I loved him, but I couldn't go on. . . . I cry all the time and can't raise him right."

While most of us have not bought the superwoman image to the extent that we cannot face life knowing we are less than perfect, many of us are influenced by the promises of success that may actually set us up for failure.

The headline of a 1975 newspaper article about working women asked, "Are Careers a Mistake?" Another headline in 1981 answered the question by informing us that "Pregnant Women Stay on the Job" because "Economic Considerations Keep 1.5 Million Working." A current article that focuses on Stanford MBA women is subtitled, "They Want It All—Career and Family." The same newspaper earlier in the year ran a three-part series on latchkey children, which detailed the expense and lack of quality child care and the problems of school-age children left to their own devices. And every day it seems we hear about day-care-center personnel suspected of abusing children.

Meanwhile, the media hype offers an image of the "now"

woman as bright, beautiful, energetic. Superwoman may not be able to leap tall buildings at a single bound, but she starts her day before the chickens rise, running four miles or Jazzercising at the gym, wearing a chic workout suit or leotard, after which she dresses her lithe, fit frame for success and bounces into the office to work for ten or twelve hours. If she has children, she has a nanny or a splendid day-care situation, the arrangements for which were made so easily they never became a visible part of the scenario. Because she *has* it all, she can *do* it all; cooking, cleaning, and taxiing kids to appointments and lessons are easily sandwiched into the routine. Of course, she manages to work in some "quality time" with the family, and everyone is better off because she is "refreshed" from her stimulating career.

In the other corner is the woman who has chosen the career of housewife and mother. She, according to recent accounts, feels that her role is diminished by the very existence of superwoman, and so she lashes out with allegations that career women are lousy and neglectful mothers. This "cold war," as the author Nancy Rubin calls it, between homemakers and career women reinforces the idea that all women have a choice in the matter.

In her book *Where's My Happy Ending?* Lee Morical zeroes in on the problems created by the myth of having it all. There is the feeling of defeat women experience when they truly believe they "should" be able to do absolutely everything, and when, with so many hyped-up options presented to them, they become increasingly confused about what they "should" do and unhappy about what they *are* doing.

The debate over whether a woman should be a mother or have a career is pointless for all but the privileged few who just happen to be independently wealthy or married to someone who is. Few people ever mention that for most mothers their "career" is not one of their choosing but rather one of economic necessity. Most working mothers are not in zingy executive positions; more often than not, they hold ordinary secretarial and clerical positions. One of the greatest ironies of this decade is that the very reason why some women (and people in general) still believe that a mother should stay home—because she has children—is the one factor most likely to guarantee that she cannot ... because she cannot afford to.

In an article entitled "No Kids" in the New York newspaper *Village Voice* (January 15, 1985), Ellen Cantarow explains: "Most people take for granted that women must work (as of last October, over two-thirds of women twenty-five to fifty-four were in the work force, and so were three out of five mothers with children, forty-six percent of whom had children under the age of six). But it also seems to be assumed that no woman is complete without a child. Witness the proliferation of news articles about the feats women perform to have children. . . .

"But even women of the elite ... have to perform heroics these days to raise children. Universal high-quality child care, a feminist demand in the early seventies, is a vanishing mirage ten years later. The appalling state of public education prompts many people to send their children to private schools sooner or later, which adds to the already crushing expense of raising children."

Thus, the question "Doctor, Lawyer, Indian Chief, or Mother?" is no longer a valid one for the vast majority of American women. A more relevant question for the eighties and nineties is: Do you want to be a working woman without children or do you want to be a working mother?

In reviewing the various figures on the high cost of bringing up baby that have surfaced in various studies, Ellen Teller, in the *Greenville Advocate* (November 18, 1981), concludes: "I guess the pessimist would say children are a real liability. The realist would say that child rearing is a heavy responsibility not to be undertaken lightly. The optimist would say 'We'll make it some way.' Most of us would agree, despite the cost and the occasional problems, our children are worth it."

I can think of no expenditure in the world as worthwhile as the money my husband and I have spent on our children. In fact, there is nothing else on the face of the earth that would have caused me to drop my writing career in midpage, with the possibility that I might not ever be able to return to it, to go to work at a job I despised. Had I been childless, of course, that predicament might not have confronted me. We could have managed through periods when my income was, to put it delicately, uneven. But, that is not to say that my children were not worth it. They were and are, and I am very lucky that such is the way I feel.

I am also very lucky that I stayed married to a man who remained employed and who did not force me and the children to leave our home to go live in a small cramped apartment, as many women I know have had to do. And I am lucky that I do not have to live out my days working at a job I hate just to pay the rent.

Not everyone is so fortunate. Even if a woman "marries well," there is only a fifty-percent chance that the marriage will last, and should it not, there is no guarantee that Papa will be good for child support. According to recent statistics, eighty percent of all not-so-dearly departed husbands do not willingly make their support payments. A woman on the threshold of making an informed decision about parenthood would do well to go a little further than optimistically saying, "We'll make it some way."

A young woman I know deliberately got pregnant, feeling that was a natural next step after getting married. When she was seven months along, she told me, "I just found out that it's going to cost eighteen hundred dollars just to have a baby." It seems that her young husband had recently changed jobs, so neither his old or new company plan would cover her. She had a difficult pregnancy and had to quit her job. They had saved not one cent. I bit my tongue to keep from saying to her, "That eighteen hundred dollars is nothing. It is only the beginning."

As I noted earlier, one study found that in 1980 it cost between $226,000 and $247,000 to raise a child, on the average, in this country. My own feeling is that most of the time it costs much more, especially when parents are forced to send their children to private schools. In any case, this young woman has apparently bought all of the hype about how great it will be to be a wife and mother. Tuning my crystal ball to a year after the birth of her child, I do not see a housewife who must defend having made such a choice as she happily sews chintz slipcovers. Instead, I see a housewife holding down a full-time job simply because, as she will find, raising a child is an expensive undertaking. Before she celebrates her twenty-first birthday, I predict, she will have joined the ranks of the ordinary—and even extraordinary—working mothers who exhaust themselves doing two jobs instead of one.

While the U.S Census Bureau projects that half of all children will live in single-parent homes before they grow up, futurists Marvin Cetron and Thomas O'Toole predict that by 1990 the average American will have been through divorce. If my young friend becomes one of these "average Americans," it is easy to prophesy that she and her child (or children) will live at the poverty level.

My seemingly pessimistic view is based on these facts of life: (1) Normally, mothers request and get custody of the children; (2) women are still not equitably compensated in the workplace; (3) the cost of living, especially housing, continues to rise; (4) child-support payments made by a former husband are not equal to his full support, if he makes those payments at all; (5) child-support payments generally do not increase as the cost of living climbs; (6) quality child care, when available, is rarely affordable.

Given the circumstances, it is no wonder that *National NOW Times* (February 1985) reported that twenty-two percent of all the nation's children live in poverty or that the Census Bureau projects that more than half of the women and children in single-parent situations today will in the near future live *below* the poverty level.

Guy Wright made some significant points in his column in the *San Francisco Examiner* (March 3, 1985):

> I make no brief for continuing a miserable marriage, but neither is the dissolution of a marriage something to celebrate, especially if there are children, and opinion makers who tell

mothers that life without father is the trendy way to go ought
to have their ears boxed.

A somewhat more honest approach was taken last month
in a state study titled, "The Feminization of Poverty." It acknowledged that the growth of single-parent families is a significant factor in poverty statistics.

Unfortunately, instead of seeking ways to end that
growth, it treated single parenthood as acceptable, or at least
inevitable, and then put the onus on "the failure of public policy to address the resulting economic problems."

It called for a medicine chest of Band-Aids, ranging from
higher welfare grants and child care subsidies to state paid
health insurance for single parents.

It continually baffles me that most observers, Wright included, fail to suggest *prevention* of poverty as a way to erase it.
The general assumption is that women *must* make babies, and then
their babies must be taken care of either by maintaining their
marriages or by maintaining a welfare state.

While I personally believe that all mothers and children
should have a decent quality of life, I am equally convinced that
poverty is not merely the result of social inequities. Rather,
women find themselves impoverished simply because they have
children. Thus, it seems sensible to me that society in general and
women in particular should rethink the largely male edict to "be
fruitful and multiply" and stop subscribing to the male myth that
there are only two things women are good for: sex and having
babies.

Though the impoverished second- and third-generation welfare mother is highly visible, in recent years thousands of sisters,
once middle-class, have begun to lurk in her shadow. Even those
observers who are aware of the "new poor" woman fail to suggest
that a very practical way to prevent this sort of poverty is to prevent conception in the first place.

"Oh, but that would deprive a woman of the joy of having

children" is the cliche that pops out of the mouths of the unthinking. Such a response is nothing more than a reflection of the simplistic and unrealistic view many people have of parenthood. In America, we *say* we love children, but our actions belie our words. For if we really did love them, none would be malnourished or physically or sexually abused as thousands are.

Which brings me to something else women should know before they choose motherhood as either a first or second career. The myth that our culture loves children is perpetuated by everyone who stands to gain economically by its existence—from baby-carriage manufacturers to those who print up bumper stickers that allow you to announce there is a "Baby on Board" to those who write and publish child-guidance manuals that never dwell deeply on the dark sides of the job. And it is a myth that hides from potential and new parents the fact that the world in general will not welcome your children with open arms. The working mother learns it very quickly when she finds that quality child care is available only for the lucky few. The young couple who cannot afford a down payment on a house or the entry fee into a suitable apartment learns it when they try to find shelter. Or, if they can afford the entry fee, they may learn it when they discover that, increasingly, new apartment developments do not allow children.

In smaller ways, young parents learn that all the world does not love children when they take their kids to restaurants not equipped to seat small people, or sit at a table adjacent to adults who cast disapproving glances when the children cry or make noise—as children often do. And, of course, noisy children are not especially appreciated by other passengers on trains, planes, and buses. Nor are they always welcome at social events, such as dinners and weddings, or at the theater. Children, novice parents soon learn, are largely viewed as objects that should be seen and not heard—and sometimes not even seen.

As children grow, it becomes evident that the communities in which young families may live do not revere children when one school-bond issue after another gets voted down despite the fact that the quality of education is steadily eroding. The sad truth is that people who have already raised their families and those who have no children simply aren't interested in supporting the educational system for other people's children.

The current mush we are being fed clearly hasn't caught up with the way we, as a nation, really do feel about children. Whether we are conscious of it or not, perhaps the lives of children have been cheapened because neither this world nor this nation needs any more people, because we have allowed them to become dangerously overpopulated. What we need is personal and social responsibility. If we don't accept it, as Marvin Cetron and Thomas O'Toole warn, one day we may not have a choice in the matter: "In part to crack down on welfare mothers and in part to ease the overpopulation burden, by the year 2000, there could be laws allowing a $1000 deduction for the first child, $500 for the second, none for the third, and a $500 penalty for a fourth child. Believe it. China already has a similar law on the books."

Meanwhile, back in the present perfect, the debates continue to center around whether a woman should choose between home and career and whether men should share in the housework and child care. *But these debates are purely academic for the thousands of women who have no husbands.* Considering that most husbands don't share in the responsibilities anyway, the basic difference between most single and married mothers who work is purely financial.

For the better part of a dozen years now, we have been told by optimistic and trendy reporters that husbands and fathers are becoming more nurturing and more likely to share in the domestic responsibilities. However, hard research shows that such husbands are rare. In May 1978, for example, *Redbook* reported the results of a survey that revealed that a majority of American husbands of working women shared the housework little or not at all; only a scant twelve percent shared equally. In 1981, the Worldwatch Institute reported that although almost half of all adult women in the world work outside the home, nearly all of them carry the entire housekeeping burden. A more recent study conducted by Lee Morical revealed that ninety-seven percent of all husbands of working women do little in the way of assuming any portion of the domestic responsibility.

Why?

One answer, according to Laraine Zappert of Stanford University, is that women set extremely high standards for themselves when it comes to homemaking. In a paper presented to the American Psychological Association meeting in June 1982 in Montreal, she said that women feel they must do more than men and be the best in all they do. They have, she asserts, internalized society's dictum, "It's okay if you go to work as long as you don't give up the other stuff."

But there are other reasons why fathers don't share and mothers keep knocking themselves out doing two jobs. There is one type of man, for example, that does nothing whatever in his home beyond sleeping there, changing his clothes, getting some sex, and grabbing an occasional meal with the family. There is no explanation for his behavior other than the simple fact that he is a swine. Paula's husband is a good example:

> Not only does my husband not do anything around the house when he happens to be in it, but he makes almost as much work for me as the children do. By the time I get home, after picking up the kids from the center, he has flung his coat on a chair, hung his tie on the nearest doorknob, and scattered the evening newspaper all over the place. Sometimes, if it's hot, he takes off his shirt and drops it somewhere, and takes off his socks and tosses them behind the sofa or someplace else. Naturally, it is expected that I will pick up everything.
>
> One night when I was reading an article in our local paper about this couple who share everything, and take turns doing the cooking and all, I became infuriated and showed him the article. After he read a few lines and looked at the picture of this couple doing the dishes together, you know what he

said? "That guy is obviously a fag." After that, I decided that the most help I could ever get from him would be to get him to stop contributing to the mess.

Happily, I believe that men like Paula's husband are in the minority and that the major reason why most husbands don't share is, as I stated in the previous chapter, that they have no real idea of what's involved in taking care of a home and family. They've never had to do it, and the media has conditioned them to think that it's a breeze.

If you were born before 1960, the odds are that you were conditioned to believe that women do housework and men do not. Regardless of any modern views you may have, watching television or reading popular magazines will show you that the same conditioning continues unabated. You just don't see many fathers having to decide between Spic and Span and Mop & Glo. (In fact, TV has changed so little in the past ten years that I sometimes wonder if the commercials that are being aired are ones that have been in the can for ten or fifteen years.)

Yes, in the world according to Madison Avenue, women— and usually they are mothers—do everything: They cook sausages at eight in the morning, dressed fit to kill, naturally, presumably so they will look nice while they clean their houses. They do the laundry, clean the bathrooms every day, shampoo carpets. They may not do windows, but they push the buttons on the cans of products that do. They shop for groceries, cook the dinners, hand-wash the dishes and look into the plates to see their reflections. Male participation is reduced to mowing lawns and to voice-overs that instruct simpleminded women in the fine art of contemporary home-making.

Is it any wonder that people still believe that this is the way it's supposed to be?

A mother of three school-age children told me, "I get up at six, I shower and dress, make breakfast for my children and make the beds. My husband gets up at seven-thirty, and he simply gets dressed and leaves. As early as I get up, I'm still late nearly every day simply because something comes up. We have to find some shoes, or a sweater, or I must write a note, or talk to someone about something or other."

A mother of two said, "My husband is really a very nice guy. But he has no concept of how much there is to do, otherwise how could he sit and read the newspaper every evening while I run around like a chicken with its head cut off? He does a few things: He empties the garbage, changes the light bulbs, and stuff like that. But I really do just about everything. While I do the major cleaning on Saturdays, he goes off and plays golf. Like most men, he thinks that after working all week, he deserves a little relaxation. What about me?" She went on to explain that her husband truly believes that, because of modern appliances, there's nothing more to housework than pushing a few buttons.

Not only is there a lot more to it than that, but according to a recent report out of Cornell University, modern appliances have not substantially reduced the amount of time spent on household chores: "Some changes have made it [housework] physically easier to do," say the researchers William H. Gauger and Kathryn E. Walker, "but many people mistake 'easier' for 'less time consuming.'" And, they emphasize, "Many labor-saving devices commonly used today lighten the work load, but they require time for service, maintenance, and repair."

And who takes care of this modern chore? One woman, a busy account executive, recalled, "One night when I was loading the dishwasher, the top rack fell. It's because it's old and worn. When my husband heard the crash, he ran into the kitchen. When he saw what had happened, he said, 'I told you at least a dozen times to have a new dishwasher installed.'

"I'm away from the house just as many hours a day as he is, so obviously it is no easier for me to take care of the problem than it would be for him to do it. Someone has to stay home and wait for the delivery and installation. But since the machine is supposed to make the job of doing the dishes easier, and since that job is delegated to me, getting the machine fixed or replaced becomes *my* problem."

This is just one of the many chores that may be invisible to husbands and observers. Another that is largely invisible to home-making mothers is the job of keeping up the wardrobe for the office, a chore that has Mother rinsing out her nylons and ironing a blouse after the family has gone to bed. Driving a child to the sitter gives a mother another "invisible" chore that keeps her away from the house for a longer total period of time each day than her husband. She has, obviously, more to do and less time to do it than he has. Nearly all of the working mothers of young children that I know say they are away from their houses every day at least one hour longer than their husbands.

One woman told me, "I was sitting in the waiting room at the orthodontist's office when it hit me. I had taken time off work to take my daughter in, a practice that had proven necessary because otherwise she'd 'forget' her appointments and we'd be billed for nothing. Her orthodontist came out to the waiting room and told me that he really needed my help: My daughter wasn't wearing her headgear for as many hours each day as she should, so instead of progressing, her teeth were regressing. What hit me at that moment was that the straightening of her teeth was *my* responsibility. Not hers, not her father's, but mine. I work just as many hours every day as my husband does, but since this relates to our child, it is *my* responsibility."

One mother of two elementary-school children said, "Everything that relates to the kids is my responsibility. I always take them to the doctor, to the dentist, to their lessons. And most of the time I go to the parent-teacher conferences, little plays during the day at school, parties, and Scout ceremonies—alone. Out of the thirty-odd parents that show up at these things, there will be only one or two fathers each time. It's because fathers work, I'm told. Well, I just happen to know that most of the other mothers I see at those functions work, too. In fact, the husband of one of the mothers I always see works the night shift and is home during the day. But he never comes with his wife to any of those school functions."

Several working mothers I have talked with said that their husbands have never even met their children's teachers or their doctor.

According to most women I have talked to over the years, it is the rare father indeed who stays home from work with a sick child. The psychologist Paula Englander-Golden, who studied the matter in 1982, reports that women are absent from work much more often than men, but not because they themselves are ill. Although her survey found that a common belief is that women take more sick time than men because of menstrual pains, she says that they stay home to take care of a sick child or take a child to a doctor or dental appointment, but they say they're sick so they can get sick pay.

Of course, it is Mother who gets the phone calls at her office from teachers and counselors, or from the children themselves, when there are problems. In *Parade* magazine (January 13, 1985), Sey Chassler explains that both he and his wife work outside the home while trying to raise three children. He says, "During the day, if the children needed help, they never called me. They called my wife. While I could and did ask them to call me, I had the choice of offering them that 'privilege.' My wife did not. Similarly, if I came home whipped by a day's work, I had the choice of taking a nap or going down to the basement, pretending to be the good husband who fixes things, but really relaxing, away from the busy household. My wife had no such choice."

In some cases, *any* mother will do. Once I took a few days' leave of absence from my office job to stay home to meet a writing deadline. The phone rang, and the caller identified herself as the nurse at the grammar school my children used to attend. For an instant, a familiar wave of fear passed through my body. Then I remembered that my children were in high school. The nurse explained, "Cindy [my neighbor's child] fell down and hurt her ankle. It could be broken. Her mother's not home. Can you come and get her?"

I dropped what I was doing and sped over to the school. As I was helping Cindy out to the car, reason overwhelmed my reflex-ive action. It occurred to me that I could not authorize medical treatment, so then I asked, "Were you able to reach her father?" The answer, swift and sure, was, "Oh, no. We didn't want to bother him at work."

In the final analysis, there is one very big reason why the situ-ation will never be a fully equitable one for the working mother: There simply isn't anything in it for men. The uncommon man who does share in the duties does so because his wife's conscious-ness has reached a positively vengeful level, or he simply does it out of a sense of decency.

Sey Chassler provides a sensitive analysis:

> Suddenly, unable to stand my complaints any longer, my wife threw something at me and said: "From now on, you do the shopping, plan the meals, take care of the house, every-thing. I'm through!"
>
> I was standing in the kitchen looking at the shelves, the sink, the refrigerator, the cleaning utensils. At my wife.
>
> I was terrified. Tears trickled down my face. No matter what, I knew I could not handle the burden she had flung at me. I could not do my job and be responsible for the entire household as well. . . . I had important things to do. Besides, how could I get through a day of dealing with personnel, bud-gets, manuscripts, management, profit-and-loss figures and, *at the same time,* plan dinner for that night and the next night and breakfasts and lunches . . . and shop for it all and make sure the house is in good shape and that the woman who cleans for us was there on time and the laundry done and the children taken care of?
>
> How could *anyone* do all that and stay sane? Natalie sim-ply watched me for a while. Finally she said, "Okay. Don't worry. I'll keep on doing it." She put on her coat and went to her hospital office—to manage dozens of people and more than 100 patients.

Despite her simple statement that she would go on taking care of our home and family, I stood awhile telling myself that *no one* could do all of that. Slowly I saw that *she* was doing it.

In this era of what *Boston Globe* columnist Beverly Stephen calls "pregnancy chic," it is out of fashion to discuss maternal guilt. However, this guilt is real, and it may cause a mother to irrationally believe that if she hadn't been working, her child may not have become ill, had an accident, or developed problems in school. A thirty-two-year-old mother of two remembers: "I was sitting at my desk when the sitter called. The minute I heard her voice, I felt a stab of fear. Sure enough, my six-year-old had fallen off the backyard swing and the sitter feared she'd broken her leg. I dashed home, picked up my daughter, and rushed her to the emergency room. Indeed, she had broken her leg. As the cast was being put on, the guilt settled in. If only I'd been home, this wouldn't have happened. It was only later that I realized that even if I *had* been home, I couldn't have prevented it unless I'd forbidden her to play on the swings. But even that realization didn't really make me feel less guilty."

These days, we have seen a new trend toward delaying parenthood, mostly to allow women to take advantage of their options before becoming ensconced in motherhood. Every trend has its buzzwords, the big one here being the "biological clock," which turns previously satisfied career women into mothers.

Beverly Stephen in "The Joy and Guilt of Over-30 Mothers" points out that delayed parenthood is no panacea. While many of these "older" mothers have a real sense of joy about their babies, she quotes one researcher, Judith Langer, as saying, "They feel guilty about so many things. Mothers feel guilty if they work. But there are also new reasons to feel guilty, such as staying home and not working outside the home. Increased options complicate life."

Ms. Stephen noted that "one of the most drastic changes the women found was that their time is no longer their own." These mothers found that they must juggle their work life and their personal life around their babies. One woman lamented, "I found I couldn't take my own days off anymore. My sick days are his sick days now. When I'm sick I go in."

Another woman said, "I have to take my son back and forth to my mother, who takes care of him while I work. I really don't have time for a social life. I spend a lot of time traveling, and as a single person I feel guilty about any time I don't spend with him."

So, the new news is the old news: Education level, career status, and maturity eliminate neither guilt feelings nor the difficulties posed by the fact that all working mothers are at war with time.

For years now, I have heard it said, especially with respect to career women, that it isn't the *quantity* of time spent with one's children, but the *quality*. I will not argue that certainly fifteen minutes worth of good conversation or a similar amount of time spent playing a game with a child has it all over several hours of irritation or indifference. But you can't have quality time unless there is some quantity of time from which to extract it. Many working moms simply do not see that there exists *any* free time. If they do find an extra minute or so, like one woman I know who stays up late to be alone, they naturally want it for themselves, if for no other reason than just to stay sane.

For a mother in a hurry to get to work, the moments she spends with a child can hardly be described as "quality time." As one rushed mother told me, "Before I returned to work, I used to patiently help my four-year-old dress himself. I would give him lessons in tying his shoes and buttoning his shirt or sweater, and then give him abundant praise for any progress he made. I would talk to him, kiss him, cuddle him. Now, I yank him into his clothes, and if I talk at all, it seems that I yell."

I remember one day after I had once again returned to the labor force, I managed to have a fight with every member of my family before I left the house. My husband got up ten minutes earlier than usual that morning and I accused him of deliberately interfering with my scheduled time in the bathroom. Then Adam kept talking to me about a bad dream he had the night before, and, where under normal circumstances I would have sat with him and listened and comforted him, I became noticeably irritated. Not only was he not comforted, his feelings were hurt, and he slammed out of the house. Finally, Lisa did or said something—I can't remember what—and I suddenly blurted out, "I feel like slapping your face!" My, everyone certainly got off to a good start *that* day! It was one of a number of mornings that this mother held back tears of remorse and regret on the way to work.

A working mother usually must throw dinner together after five or six o'clock, when hungry children—and a hungry husband—are lurking. The fuse grows short, and she may be less than sympathetic to the needs of her family as, for example, one woman who told me, "My little girl came running into the kitchen crying. She'd fallen down and hurt both her shins. The mother I once was would have kissed her shins and kissed away her tears. The mother I now am got mad at her. I was inconvenienced by what was an avoidable accident."

Some people feel that there are fewer problems if a mother waits until her children are teenagers before returning to work. Of course, not all mothers have that choice.

In my case, the first time I went to work full time in an office, Lisa was four and Adam was three. Even though I had splendid child-care arrangements, I suffered immense guilt feelings for the two years I remained on the job. When I went back home—to stay, I thought—I was glad to be there and I carved out a nice life as a writer and a mother. The next time I went out, Adam and Lisa were fourteen and fifteen, so finding just the right child-care situation for young, impressionable children was not one of the things I had to do. I was grateful for that because I learned that nowadays good child care isn't all that easy to come by. The trade-off was that we had to leave two teenagers to their own devices after school and during what seemed like dozens of holidays and vacation periods.

From the beginning, there were rules, the violation of which would result in being grounded or having their allowances suspended. It was not always easy to know if the rules had been broken, and enforcing the grounding was next to impossible when we weren't around. Thanks to a generous vacation policy where my husband works, however, he was able to take days off sporadically, so that Lisa and Adam were never sure that he wasn't going to pop in some time and catch them red-handed doing something wrong.

So as not to lead our children into temptation, we locked our liquor and beer supply in the trunk of my husband's car. As time went on, our parentless home became the hangout after school, and dozens of kids were eating us out of house and home. We took to storing food in the trunk as well. We were aware that our neighbors regarded us with raised eyebrows as we went out to the car to extract a soda, a beer, or a loaf of bread, but the savings were worth it.

We eventually abandoned the practice of grounding them for afternoons during the week since we couldn't enforce it anyway. We grounded instead on weekends. There is nothing, unless it's a friend you disapprove of, so treasured to a teenager as his weekend. Naturally, it is pure hell for the parents who have to suffer these large caged animals all weekend long, so sometimes when a minor infraction occurred, we just looked the other way. Weekends are treasured by working parents, too. So much for consistency.

The weekends of this working mother were normally reserved for such relaxing activities as doing laundry, shopping for groceries, paying bills, and fixing the things that broke during the week. Just when I reached the point where I felt that if just one more thing, no matter how trivial, came along I would crack, it would be time for the holidays.

Until I returned to work I actually enjoyed the Christmas holidays. Since the very first Christmas season that I worked outside the home, I have experienced a hideous sense of dread upon seeing the first decorations go up in the stores each year. For a mother working full time both inside and outside the home, Christmas becomes an enormous chore. In most cases, Mom is totally responsible for every aspect of Christmas: She must do the shopping, wrap and send the packages, send the cards, write the messages, plan the dinner, and spend the entire day cooking. I am intrigued that even some of the most avowed feminists I know write, produce, and send the obligatory mimeographed "Christmas letter."

It was being a working mother that made other events, such as birthdays and Halloween—times that are supposed to be fun— become wearisome, something to be endured. They require the time and energy of people who often simply have none free in their daily routines.

When I started working the second time around, there were lots of little tasks that I quit doing simply because I just didn't have the time or energy. Whereas I had once been diligent about folding the laundry and putting it away, my attitude changed—the clothes and towels would get used whether or not they were folded, and that was one chore that I could do without. Another was ironing a blouse that needed it. If something needed ironing, or if it needed a hem or a button, I simply didn't wear it anymore. I stopped shaving my legs ten years too late for it to be construed as a political statement.

The worst side effect of being a working mother of teenagers was that I got out of touch with them. If I didn't hear from them, I assumed that no news was good news. Not having time, I didn't look for problems, nor did I see them when they were there. So, when Adam fell apart at the seams for the second time, I was hit with a shock wave, and, of course, with the painful and time-consuming burden of helping him work through it. The paradox made me feel helpless: I needed to work to make the money to pay for Adam's therapy, but I felt that I shouldn't be working at all because I should be available for my troubled child.

I didn't have time for the good things either.

"Play a game of backgammon with me, Mom?"

"I don't have time, Adam."

"Did you read the book I got you from the library, Mom?"

"I haven't had time, Lisa."

It isn't clear whether that's a cut above or below what would pass for "interaction with my family" in the morning. "Mom, I need a note for sixth period."

"Why? Did you cut?"

"Mom, I went to the orthodontist! Jeez, you drove me."

"I wish you'd ask me for notes the night before. Not in the morning, when I'm so rushed."

"Mom, I dropped my contact lens."

"Oh, goddamnit, now I'll never get to work on time."

"Mom, I can't find it. I'm blind as a bat."

Women's magazines often feature articles on how a working mother can make most efficient use of her time. I have seen nothing that offers tips on how to "efficiently" get down on one's hands and knees to look for a contact lens, write a note, dig through the trash to look for a current-event clipping a child desperately needs for school, and deal with people who have the audacity to call at seven-thirty in the morning, all while trying to get to work on time.

"Mom, I've got to talk to you."

"I don't have time to talk now, Lisa. I'll be late for work. We'll talk later."

Late for precious work. Later we'll talk. When the hours, months, and years of the last part of your childhood have disappeared and you are grown and gone. Then I won't have to work at a job that eats up my time, destroys my soul, and turns me into a wretch. When the nest is at long last empty and the expenses no longer require me to work, then, darling, I'll have time.

Just as man cannot live by bread alone, neither can a woman. Because of the division of labor in the home, we will never know how much talent may have been lost to the world. We may never know the suffering of women who were counterparts to great male artists. In *Silences* (Delacorte, 1978), Tillie Olsen described her thoughts about having deferred her talents to work for twenty years as a secretary and raise a family:

> This was the time of festering and congestion. For a few months I was able to shield the writing with which I was so full, against the demands of jobs on which I had to be competent, through the joys and responsibilities and trial of family. For a few months. Always roused by the writing, always denied. I could not go to write it down. It convulsed and died in me. I will pay.
>
> My work died. What demanded to be written did not. It seethed, bubbled, clamoured, peopled me. At last moved into the hours meant for sleeping. . . .
>
> Drowning is not so pitiful as the attempt to rise, says Emily Dickinson. I do not agree, but I know whereof she speaks. For a long time I was that emaciated survivor trembling on the beach, unable to rise and walk.

Dreams. To be an author, an artist, or a musician requires not discipline, but time and privacy. In today's jargon, "space." A woman I have corresponded with for nearly ten years—her letters are works of art that cry out to this point—has gone nearly mad for being denied the opportunity to express herself creatively. I mean that quite literally, since she has gone to the psychiatrist's couch many times and has tried many new self-help disciplines to try to figure out what is wrong with her. I think that what is wrong with her could be cured by her having the opportunity to create. Creativity is like a demanding infant; when denied what it needs, it cries out even more desperately. Or, like the neglected infant, it dies from "failure to thrive." This woman can only write letters to me, as she does not have the time to organize her thoughts and polish her prose and make her work presentable to the critical eye of an editor. My instincts sense immense talent that will never be shared. Moreover, I truly fear that this woman—mother of three, secretary in an insurance company, wife of a man who simply goes to and from work and expects his dinner to be on the table as if dispensed from a machine—will descend into madness. Perhaps then, when she's locked up, she will have the time and the space to create.

It could be said that gifted men suffer similarly if they must hold down nine-to-five jobs to support the family. However, such men, while they may not have all the time they want, can do their writing early in the morning, immediately after dinner, or on weekends, shielded from domestic concerns by their supportive, well-programmed wives.

Virginia Woolf knew better. She had no children.

After reading my words here, mothers who work outside the home and feel defensive about doing so may make the false assumption that I think mothers *should* not work outside the home. Mothers who either must or choose to work outside the home have enough "shoulds" piled on their shoulders, and I would not dream of placing even a small one upon them. Maybe some women can really have it all. My hat is off to them if they can bring it off; they deserve applause for the juggling acts they do. Experience has taught me that I am not one of them. I am not a person who can divide herself up so many ways, nor am I one who can avoid the guilt and remorse that comes with missing parts of my children's lives.

And casual research has taught me that I'm far from alone. In addition to most of the mothers who work outside the home I've spoken with having experiences similar to my own, popular literature attests to the dilemma that most women become familiar with only after the fact of motherhood. I have before me a stack of articles that, because I stopped collecting such material, probably represents only the tip of the iceberg. From *Newsweek* (March 8, 1982) I clipped an article entitled, "Working Time and a Half," in which Christine Davidson writes, "There she is, the working mother of America, self-assured and jaunty with her briefcase swinging at her side. Her smile seems to say she 'has it all': husband, children, stimulating job, independence, fulfillment. It doesn't show guilt, frustration, weekend headaches or exhaustion. Well, I have 'had it all' since my kids were in diapers, and I have finally had it."

Another article, "Rise of the Too Pooped, Two-Pay-check Marriage" (*Chicago Tribune*, May 31, 1985), explains in detail the hidden underside that smolders beneath the surface of the dual-career families who seemingly have worked it all out. Another from *Savvy* asks, "Are You Flunking Quality Time?" *Working Mother* (December 1981) offers thoughts on the exhausting tasks of being a modern mother in "Something's Got to Give" (which rather says it all), and in the same issue of the same magazine, there is a piece, "Stop the Merry-go-Round, I Want to Get Off," which explains why some women who have been able to quit their jobs have done so. *Ladies' Home Journal* gives us a piece called "Do I Have It All, But No Time to Enjoy It?" in which just reading about the treadmill is exhausting in and of itself. And a March 1977 issue of *Redbook* carries a young mother's story called "What the Books Don't Tell Working Mothers," which charts the course of a mother who quit her job to stay home again for the obvious reasons. Along with this collection, of which I've given you just the briefest sampling, I have another collection of articles that spell out in grim detail the fact that quality child care is an elusive dream for most mothers who either must or choose to work outside the home. Given the weight of the dilemma in the print media, I have great difficulty understanding how it is that trendiness continues to overwhelm reality, leaving intact the naïve conviction that working and mothering is a snap.

Having been in their ranks, I know that working mothers are no less conscientious than any other mothers. I also know that motherhood—even under the best of circumstances—is never easy, and it is the most difficult when one must do two jobs instead of one.

Parenthood is a lifetime contract making you responsible for another human being. If you have yet to make that fateful, irreversible decision, know what you might be in for—a grueling, painful, formidable job that cannot take a backseat to any other career. It is a commitment that must never be taken lightly, for there is nothing that can compete with the importance of another life.

Think about it.

# Chapter 14

# THE NEVER-ENDING STORY

*When it hit me that I was a divorced mother of a six-year-old daughter and a three-year-old son and would therefore have to go it alone, I did some quick calculations. I very quickly added three years to the youngest getting to be six and in school most of the day and another twelve until he got out of high school. I said to myself, "I've got fifteen more years and then I can do what I want." Now he's twenty-three, he's still with me, still in and out of trouble. I, of course, am still not able to do what I want. Judging from his level of maturity, I figure it will be at least ten more years before I'll be free. I figure I'll be so old it won't matter anymore.*

—A Dallas mother

*We have three children, spaced about five years apart. As the youngest at eighteen years of age was getting ready to leave for college, our eldest, who was then twenty-eight, was coming back in. And she wasn't alone. She had with her our three-year-old grandbaby. I think they are here to stay.*

—A San Francisco mother

*Our children will be our children for the rest of our lives.*
*And sometimes that's not fair.*

—Bill Cosby, *Evening Magazine,* February 24, 1986

I have a theory about the "empty-nest syndrome," which, to the best of my knowledge, has never been suggested by those august souls who study such matters or coin such terms. The syndrome, as I understand it, is something that occurs when a woman is a housewife and the last child leaves home. As the argument runs, the housewife mother "loses her job" and thus loses her usefulness. She is no longer needed and hasn't all that much to do. The argument continues that had she developed some career interest along the way, she'd have something with which to fill the void when separation occurs.

This may be true. But what I believe is far truer is that mothers endure a situation in which they are so deprived of solitude and privacy for such a protracted period of time that should they ultimately find themselves with an abundance of either or both, they remain programmed for interruptions and demands upon their time and energy. They may well have developed, out of necessity, short attention spans and be unable to expand them when their circumstances change and make it possible for them to do so. Put in that light, the syndrome takes on new meaning for mothers who have deferred their own lives to be available to their families—provided, of course, that they wind up with truly empty nests.

Popular legend holds that this occurs when the last child reaches the magic age of eighteen, graduates from high school, and goes away to college or gets a job and a place to live and clears out once and for all. Well, life isn't always that cut and dried. For example, not all young adults who go to college leave home. Many in fact continue to live with their parents for however long they may stay in school. And those who work full time don't necessarily leave the nest either.

My own reality suggests such allowances. As of this writing,

Lisa and Adam are twenty-one and twenty years old, respectively. They continue to live under this roof, and there exist no concrete signs that they are planning to change their residence in the near future. Lisa is a part-time student at the community college, and she has a part-time job. Her days are filled, but her wallet is usually empty. Adam, who is a jack-of-all-trades, works in construction by day, works on his music by night, and repairs equipment and invents gadgets on the side. In addition, he is planning to return to school to study electronics.

Even if our children were emotionally ready to leave home, which they are not, they could hardly afford to live on their own and go to school at the same time—not everyone gets scholarships. And, as the process of raising them has cleaned us out, we cannot afford to subsidize their living away from home.

Neither the magic age of eighteen nor even twenty-one has bestowed upon our children the financial and emotional independence to be on their own. And they are far from alone. As a matter of fact, most of the kids they grew up with are still living at home. Most still need the security of their families (often single-parent families, I must add), and very few can afford to move out. Of those who can, most are subsidized by their parents or supported entirely as they continue their education.

Just for openers, in the Palo Alto area, rents for one-bedroom apartments in safe neighborhoods start at $600.00 a month. The biggest hurdle to overcome is that normally the first and last month's rent, plus a cleaning or security deposit (and good credit) constitute the entry fee. Even if two or more go in together, they still have utilities, food, telephone, automobile expenses, enormously expensive insurance, clothing, and recreation. Most simply cannot make it on their own. This should come as no surprise when one considers the growing number of young families—even when both people work—who live in motels because they can't get together the first and last month's rent, plus cleaning deposit.

As an aside, I wonder what goes on in the heads of young couples who start families without any clear picture of where they will bring up baby. I wonder what goes on in the heads of those who are settled into apartments or houses? If things are tough now, what will it be like for the children they bring into the world? I have visions of a future, some twenty years hence, of great numbers of people residing with their once middle-class parents in cramped apartments or living on the streets. I submit that little goes on in their heads—they are so overwhelmed with the baby-mania myths that never deal with the future that they just don't think.

Back to the present, while sociologists discuss the empty-nest syndrome, I am surrounded by people who fear they will never have the opportunity to suffer it. While it is true that many people just toss their birds out whether or not their wings are strong enough, conscientious, loving parents generally do not, nor do they pull in the "welcome" mat when the last one has left the nest.

"My daughter is thirty years old, intelligent, and well educated," one mother, who is also a writer, told me. "I love her dearly and enjoy her company. But she's moved home because she's going to graduate school at Stanford and my life has been turned upside down as a result. She gets depressed and it drags me down. I have trouble writing with another presence in the house. Let's face it, at fifty-five, I don't have the energy I once had, so it's difficult for me to stay focused. I truly believed that once my daughter was grown and on her own, my time would be my own. But she came back."

Another mother in a similar situation told me, "Sure. Some people can turn it off when their kids are grown but still needy. But no woman with a heart can turn her back on her children when they are in pain, no matter what their ages. Still, I hadn't expected to be living with my children once they were past twenty-one, let alone twenty-five. But they come and go, and with each trip home they each bring home a load of emotional baggage. They say to me, 'I know you're busy with your art, and I don't mean to interrupt, but I need to talk to you.' And even when they don't interrupt, the presence of one or the other of them in the house is terribly distracting. I recall with longing that brief period when my time was my own and my productivity was high."

One of the reasons I was overjoyed when a new book contract sent me back home from the office was that working at home makes it possible for me to set my own schedule and allows me to map out good chunks of time to spend with each child. However, I looked forward to Lisa's and Adam's finishing high school with a whole list of expectations of what it would be like to be a mother of adult children, even though the kids would still be living at home. I fully expected that I would have at least as much solitude as I had enjoyed when Lisa and Adam were in grammar school for six hours each day during the school year. In fact, I expected more. Wrong. Not only do they still live with us, but for a time, we had two of their friends in residence. Someone was always home— someone was either ill, had a day off work, was out of work, had a day off from school. Furthermore, it seemed that each had a set of friends who had days off, were out of work, out of school, and they dropped in and out just like they did in the good old days.

I fully expected that my husband and I would have far more discretionary income than ever before. After all, articles appear on a near daily basis in the business sections of the newspapers that discuss how people in our age group have so much more spending power now that the children are grown. Wrong. Both of our children remain to this day financially dependent upon us.

I expected that once the children were grown they would stop taking my things—my stapler, scissors, Scotch tape, pens, pencils, combs, etc. Wrong. It still takes me a couple of hours to wrap a package—115 minutes to find the paper and the tape, and five minutes to do the job.

Once the children are grown, I used to think, Adam and his friends would sit like normal adults and have adult conversations. Wrong. They still wrestle, bang on the table, and make so much noise that I have to reprimand them as I did when they were only eight years old.

For some idiotic reason, I fully expected that once Lisa and Adam reached adulthood, my worrying days would be over. Wrong. I still worry when they stay out late. I still worry even when they don't. Worry, like love, does not get turned off at a magic age.

When I really think about it, I cannot imagine why in the world I had such expectations. My own mother, a dear and loving soul with whom I enjoyed immense rapport, had often told me that she never stopped worrying about any of us. Even though my living sister and I have always been independent and generally capable of handling our lives, she worried when she didn't hear from us for a week or so. And, as for her ever having an empty nest or a quiet life in her golden years, her son lived at home and my late sister returned, with a child in tow. In fact, my mother took considerable responsibility for raising my nephew. She really was a mother four times in overlapping stages: first my sisters, who were slightly under a year apart; then me, seven years later; then my brother, nine years after me; and then my nephew, five years younger than my brother. And, after my nephew grew up, got married, and moved out, my troubled sister remained, alternately irritating and worrying my parents, and even causing trouble between them.

"At just that point," one mother of two grown daughters and a grown son told me, "that my husband and I began to feel that we'd finally have a life of our own, our eldest daughter—the first to leave—turned up on our doorstep. Mixed in with my sadness for her failed marriage was a true stab of dread." This mother went on to say that her daughter had taken the children and left because her husband refused to leave the house. Whether or not the daughter should have capitulated is not the issue; the issue is that she and her two young children had altered the anticipated peace of the grandparents.

Another mother of grown children told me that, at forty-eight, she felt young enough to pursue a life of her own. She had just enrolled in the community college when her son's wife up and left, leaving the young man devastated and overwhelmed by his two young children. While he didn't move in, this tenderhearted grandmother felt she had no choice but to help him with the care of the children. Her plans have been permanently deferred (her husband's life, it should be noted, remains unchanged by this turn of events).

Another explained that her son zigzagged back and forth between living at home and living on his own until he was twenty-eight and finally decided to marry. And another, and another, and another. . . . And always the lament: They lend not just their presence, but a load of problems. "It would be one thing," one mother remarked, "if the kids just lived with you. But they don't. All too often they need guidance and continue to make demands. And all too often, they lay their emotional trips on you. In my own case, I can be in a fine frame of mind and then whichever kid is living here at the moment can drag in his depression and just simply wipe me out. After dumping on me, he may go off happily to work or to a tennis game, but I'm still down. The greatest trip of all, of course, is to have one of your kids tell you that life isn't worth living. When my son pulled this on me, I found myself checking on him as he slept, just as I did when he was a baby."

Then there is this, from the divorced Dallas mother whose letter opened this chapter:

At long last. I had my house to myself. It was wonderful. My daughter had long since married and was very independent. My son and his new wife had moved in briefly to stay with me, but were finally gone. I was in hog's heaven. Little did I know. First crack out of the box was that I had to cosign so they could get a phone. Next thing I knew, I had to pay the phone bill because they couldn't. Then they needed help with the rent. In one month I shelled out over $1,200. And then he and his wife split up.

Because he was despairing over his loss, my son came home. I told him he could stay until he got a job and got on his feet. Month after month went by and he never got a job. Finally he did land one, but he quit after three days. Exasperated, I told him that I couldn't stand to have him living with me and told him he'd have to move out. By this time, he'd gotten a DUI [driving under the influence (of alcohol)] and had lost his driver's license. The bottom line is that when I told him he had to get out of my life, it hit him harder than when his wife told him she wanted a divorce. If I slam the door on him, it's the same as having a twenty-three-year retroactive abortion. He can't handle it. So, I guess I'm stuck with him forever.

At the same time, my life is over. If I find a man I would like to spend time with, I can't bring him home because I still have my son with me. Because I had kids to raise, I've been alone for a very long time. It looks like I will be alone for the rest of my life.

For many parents, their adult children's dependence involves great pain and stress. In the summer of 1985 I received a letter from a mother of now-grown children. Her story, with some variation, could be my own. It could also easily be the story of a dozen other middle-aged mothers I know:

Getting our two children through high school was no small feat. At different points, each had fallen so far behind that they were about to drop out. To make sure that didn't happen, we sent them to an expensive private school. When finally the last one graduated, I made the mistake of saying to my husband, "This is our time. Any extra money I make is for us."

I think that only tempted the fates. In the fall, after our daughter had been working part-time and going to college part-time, she managed to get herself pregnant. Marriage, for a number of reasons, was out of the question, so the only alternative was to terminate the pregnancy. Because of all of the terrorism, she was afraid to go to a clinic, so we sent her to our gynecologist, and the procedure was performed in the hospital—at a cost of $1,200.

At this point, the emotional cost far outweighed the dollar cost—her sense of loss, both of the baby and the young man, permeated the air. The good news is that she stayed in school and continued to work, which, of course, was the best therapy in the world. Sadly, however, in her stressed state, one day she rear-ended a truck at about 35 miles an hour and totaled my car. This devastated her. We went through three rental cars before I gave up. As no buses run to the school or to her work, I remain her taxi service.

At the same time that all of this was going on with our daughter, our twenty-two-year-old son started going through a second adolescence. He had had such a serious drug problem when he was seventeen that we sent him through rehab. Everything was great. He graduated from high school, went to college, got a part-time job, had a girlfriend. And then for reasons known only to him, he relapsed. He dropped out of school, lost his job, and finally got arrested on a DUI. Naturally, we bailed him out and hired a lawyer. He's off drugs now, but can't get a job. He's in a very fragile state, has the maturity level of a twelve-year-old, and is once again living with us.

I can just hear someone saying either that the parents are to blame because these adult children can't seem to get their lives in order or that the kids are no good and the parents should wash their hands of them. Such judgments, I have found, generally come from those ostriches who pay little attention to news reports that tell us that one million teenagers get pregnant every year and that drug and alcohol abuse have reached epidemic proportions. It has been my observation that such judgments seem to come from people who also hold the view that everyone should have children and that those who don't are selfish hedonists or mental defectives.

If I am touchy, it is because I, like just about everyone else I know, have been down the parental path to pathology and been surprised both by every sad step and by the fact that it is a never-ending story.

I named this book *Mother's Day Is Over* because of my sense that the trials of motherhood are such that Mother's Day, for many of us, turns out to be hardly a day to rejoice—and it was on Mother's Day in 1985 that my son forcefully drove that point home.

Adam was nineteen, had graduated from high school the year before, was working full time and making plans to go to school in the fall. All had been very quiet on this home front. And then on Mother's Day he drove a friend to Lodi. On the way home, he and the friend got lost in Modesto and got into an enormous fight. As he put it, she just "ragged and ragged" until he felt like belting her in the mouth. So he jumped out of the car. When she drove off and left him there, he panicked and decided he had to catch up with her. So, what does a young person who is a mechanical wizard do? Hot-wire a car, of course.

To make a very long story as short as possible, when he couldn't find the friend, he drove the "borrowed" vehicle home. The next morning he called both the Modesto Police and the Palo Alto Police, turned himself in, and was arrested on a charge of grand theft auto and taken to North County Jail.

To someone who hasn't been there, or someone who has been there so many times that she or he may be numb, it is nearly impossible to convey the sense of despair a mother can feel when she walks down that long corridor to bail a child out of jail. I had never before been to a jail. I had never before seen, let alone walked through, the electronically controlled door to the holding room where the criminals are contained. I had never before stood in such a place, nervously clutching a certified check that would be the passport to get this child of mine out of harm's way—the child who called and begged me to come as fast as I could lest he be gang-raped or driven mad. For all the love and fear I felt on that day after Mother's Day, I felt a sense of degradation I had never before experienced. And when Adam came through the door in the holding room, I felt as if I was looking at a total stranger. Just when he desperately needed to be cherished.

South County Jail is different. Because the jail is very crowded, processing prisoners takes much longer. This I learned a month later. This time he was riding in a car driven by an old friend who'd just been discharged from the Army. Honorably, I should add. Well, the friend was driving recklessly and when he heard a siren, he said, "I can't be pulled over," hit the gas pedal, and the car flew through the air, across the expressway, and hit a fence. When Adam, his friend, and another passenger in the car jumped out, they were looking down the barrels of guns being held by police officers, who said, "Freeze, or we'll blow your heads off."

My husband and I were watching television when the call came telling us first that our son was in the hospital, and next that he would be taken to South County Jail when it was determined that it was safe to do so. Then Adam called. He was hysterical. South County is different. He feared for his life. So, after a sleepless night spent arranging for bail (I'd already depleted our savings the last time around), I sat on a hard bench for several hours, waiting for him to walk up that long corridor to freedom, however temporary. This time when he finally appeared, he was shirtless—to this day, neither of us knows what happened to his shirt—and he looked utterly exhausted. But this time, I did not feel degraded. Only terribly sad and terribly afraid.

These two events seemed to trigger a whole rash of brushes with the law. Warrants for reckless driving, acts of vandalism, loud mufflers, bald tires, and all manner of seemingly petty offenses seemed to flood our mailbox. Because of his crowded "court calendar," Adam lost his job. From that point on, he deteriorated emotionally and physically, and felt that life wasn't worth living.

In the space of less than two months, our son had gone from being a happy, healthy, hard-working young person with dreams and plans to a physical and emotional wreck with a dismal view of life.

His father and I went to his first two court dates with him.

Then, as is generally true, his father's life returned to normal and Adam's problems became my problems, and I became consumed with getting his fines paid and maintaining our "court calendar," much of which had us traveling back and forth between Palo Alto and Modesto. Somewhere along the line, I became seriously ill for the first time in my life—I am certain that only five percent of the cause was physical.

By some miracle, I recovered in time for the final court date in Modesto, when Adam would be sentenced. By this time, one grand-theft-auto charge had been dropped on the basis of his having been an innocent bystander and an innocent passenger in a stolen vehicle. On that day, the other charge was reduced to a misdemeanor and Adam received a suspended sentence. Thus, instead of kissing my son good-bye, I kissed him and took him home.

Why did I take it on? Why did I become Adam's sole defender and loyal friend to the end? Why, some people asked me, did I take out loans to bail him out of jail and retain an expensive attorney? How could I, devotees of the Toughlove approach asked, stand by his side every step of the way?

Well, for openers, there's the fact that Adam's first "crime" was more one of bad judgment than of deliberate larceny. And, despite the fact that it seemed to set the stage for a whole string of incidents, I believe to this day that Adam is a decent human being. Then there was my concern that were he to go to jail, he would not survive the experience. That being the case, I struggled to keep him free because that's what a mother does.

Underlying everything, however, is that I entered into a contract of unconditional love with each of our children when I learned that each was scheduled to come into our lives. The fine print on my heart reads, "For better or worse and in sickness and health." In the end, and in my son's early adulthood, I remained his protector and his faithful friend because that is, for life, what a mother is.

# BIBLIOGRAPHY

Austin, Richard B., Jr. *How to Make It With Another Person: Getting Close, Staying Close.* New York: Macmillan, 1976.

Bernard, Jessie. *The Future of Marriage.* New York: World Publishing, 1972.

——.*The Future of Motherhood.* New York: Dial Press, 1974.

Bird, Joseph, and Lois Bird. *Power to the Parents.* New York: Doubleday, 1972.

Brazelton, T. Berry, M.D. *Infants and Mothers.* New York: Delacorte, 1983.

Caine, Lynn. *What Did I Do Wrong? Mothers, Children, Guilt.* New York: Arbor House, 1985.

Cantorow, Ellen. "No Kids," *Village Voice,* January 15, 1985.

Carroll, Jerry. "Housecleaning: It's Still Women's Work," *San Francisco Chronicle,* March 25, 1986.

Cetron, Marvin, and Thomas O'Toole. *Encounters with the Future: A Forecast of Life into the 21st Century.* McGraw-Hill, 1983.

Curtis, Diane. "Teen Suicide," *San Francisco Chronicle,* February 22, 1986.

Chassler, Sey. "I Need To Know You," *Parade,* January 13, 1985.

Cohen, Sharon. "The Mother-Child Illusion," *San Francisco Chronicle,* January 20, 1986.

Donovan, Jennifer. "Is Preschool Really Worthwhile?", *San Francisco Chronicle,* December 20, 1984.

Dorman, Marsha, and Diane Klein. *How to Stay Two When Baby Makes Three.* Buffalo, N.Y.: Prometheus Books, 1984.

Feldman, Harold. "Changes and Parenthood: A Methodological Design," an unpublished study, Cornell University, Ithaca, N.Y.

Fogarty, John. "1 Million Teenagers a Year Get Pregnant, Report Says," *San Francisco Chronicle,* February 10, 1986.

Fontana, Vincent J. "Which Parents Abuse Children?", *Medical Insight,* October 1971.

———. *Somewhere a Child Is Crying.* New York: Macmillan, 1973.

Friedan, Betty. *The Feminine Mystique.* New York: Dell, 1977.

Gallup, George, Jr. "Where Parents Go Wrong," Associated Press, December 13, 1984.

Gill, David. *Violence Against Children.* Cambridge, Mass.: Harvard University Press, 1971.

Ginott, Haim. *Between Parent and Child.* London: Stapes Press, 1969.

Gottschalk, Mary. "Sexism Still (Soft) Sells," *San Jose Mercury News,* March 12, 1986.

Heffner, Elaine. *Mothering.* New York: Doubleday, 1978.

Helfer, Ray E., and C. Henry Kempe. *The Battered Child,* 3rd rev. ed. Chicago: University of Chicago Press, 1980.

Herrnstein, Richard J., and James Q. Wilson. "Are Criminals Made or Born?", *This World,* November 10, 1985.

Holt, John. *Freedom and Beyond.* New York: Dutton, 1972.

Irwin, Victoria. "Pregnant Women Stay on the Job," *The Christian Science Monitor,* December 15, 1981.

Jacoby, Arthur, P. "Transition to Parenthood: a Reassessment," *Journal of Marriage and the Family,* Vol. 26, November 1964.

Kempe, C. Henry, and Roy E. Helfer, editors. *Helping the Battered Child and his Family.* Philadelphia: Lippincott, 1972.

Kenniston, Kenneth, and the Carnegie Council on Children. *All Our Children.* New York: Harcourt, Brace, Jovanovich, 1977.

Kozol, Jonathan. *Illiterate America.* New York: Anchor Press/Doubleday, 1985.

LeMasters, E. E. "Parenthood as Crises," *Marriage and Family Living,* vol. 19, no. 4, November 1957.

LeShan, Eda. *How to Survive Parenthood.* New York: Random House, 1965.

McBride, Angela B. *The Growth and Development of Mothers.* New York: Harper & Row, 1973.

———. *A Married Feminist.* New York: Harper & Row, 1975.

Masson, Jeffrey Moussaieff. *The Assault on Truth: Freud's Suppression of the Seduction Theory.* New York: Penguin Books, 1985.

Miner, Robert. *Mother's Day.* New York: Richard Mark, 1978.

Morical, Lee. *Where's My Happy Ending? Women and the Myth of Having It All.* Reading, Mass.: Addison-Wesley, 1984.

"Mormons Seek to Tackle Child-Abuse Problem," Associated Press, June 27, 1982.

Newton, Niles. *The Family Book of Child Care.* New York: Harper Brothers, 1957.

Nocera, Joseph. "A Father-to-be Learns How to Hate Lamaze," *San Francisco Chronicle,* August 9, 1984.

Olsen, Tillie. *Silences.* New York: Delta/Seymour Lawrence, 1978.

Olson, Lawrence. *Costs of Children.* San Diego: Lexington Book Co., 1983.

"Parent Burnout: Latest Sign of Today's Stresses," *U.S. News & World Report,* March 7, 1983.

Paulson, Tim. "Our Unnatural Childbirth," *Parents,* September 1979.

Pollock, Jack H. "Why Marriages Break Up After Forty," *Family Health,* July 1972.

Procaccini, Dr. Joseph, and Mark W. Kiefaber. *Parent Burn-Out.* New York: Doubleday, 1983.

Rader, Dotson. "Who Will Help the Children?" *Parade,* September 5, 1982.

Radl, Shirley Rogers. *New Mother's Survival Guide.* New York: Western Publishing, 1984.

———. *The Invisible Woman: Target of the Religious New Right.* New York: Delacorte, 1983.

Read, Grantly Dick. *Natural Childbirth.* New York: Harper Brothers, 1944.

Rubin, Nancy. "Women vs. Women," *Ladies' Home Journal,* March 1982.

Salter, Stephanie. "Teacher Burnout," *San Francisco Examiner,* July 12, 1982.

Schneider, Carol, Carl Pollock, and Ray E. Helfer. "Interviewing the Parents," Chapter 4 of *Helping the Battered Child and His Family,* edited by C. Henry Kempe and Roy E. Helfer. Philadelphia: Lippincott, 1972.

Shulman, Alix Kates. *Memories of an Ex-Prom Queen.* New York: Knopf, 1972.

Silverman, Anna, and Arnold Silverman. *The Case Against Having Children.* New York: David McKay, 1971.

Spock, Benjamin. *Baby and Child Care.* New York: Pocket Books, 1968.

Steele, B. F. and C. B. Pollock, "A Psychiatric Study of Parents Who Abuse Infants and Small Children," in *The Battered Child,* edited by Ray E. Helfer and C. Henry Kempe. Chicago: University of Chicago Press, 1973.

Stephen, Beverly. "The Joy and Guilt of Over-30 Mothers," *Tribune Company Syndicate,* July 18, 1983.

Teller, Ellen. "Child-Rearing Costs," *Greenville Advocate* (Ohio), November 18, 1981.

Timberlake, Cotten. "How Do You Spell Guilt?," *San Jose Mercury News,* April 6, 1986.

Traub, James. "Goodbye, Dr. Spock," *Harper's,* March 1986.

"$247,000 To Raise A Daughter," Associated Press and United Press International, July 9, 1982.

Walsh, Maryellen. *Schizophrenia: Straight Talk for Family and Friends.* New York: William Morrow, 1985.